T0214517

Lecture Notes in Computer Science   10986

Commenced Publication in 1973
Founding and Former Series Editors:
Gerhard Goos, Juris Hartmanis, and Jan van Leeuwen

Editorial Board Members

David Hutchison
  Lancaster University, Lancaster, UK
Takeo Kanade
  Carnegie Mellon University, Pittsburgh, PA, USA
Josef Kittler
  University of Surrey, Guildford, UK
Jon M. Kleinberg
  Cornell University, Ithaca, NY, USA
Friedemann Mattern
  ETH Zurich, Zurich, Switzerland
John C. Mitchell
  Stanford University, Stanford, CA, USA
Moni Naor
  Weizmann Institute of Science, Rehovot, Israel
C. Pandu Rangan
  Indian Institute of Technology Madras, Chennai, India
Bernhard Steffen
  TU Dortmund University, Dortmund, Germany
Demetri Terzopoulos
  University of California, Los Angeles, CA, USA
Doug Tygar
  University of California, Berkeley, CA, USA

More information about this series at http://www.springer.com/series/7412

Reneta P. Barneva · Valentin E. Brimkov ·
Piotr Kulczycki · João Manuel R. S. Tavares (Eds.)

Computational Modeling of Objects Presented in Images

Fundamentals, Methods, and Applications

6th International Conference, CompIMAGE 2018
Cracow, Poland, July 2–5, 2018
Revised Selected Papers

Springer

Editors
Reneta P. Barneva
State University of New York at Fredonia
Fredonia, NY, USA

Valentin E. Brimkov
SUNY Buffalo State College
Buffalo, NY, USA

Piotr Kulczycki
AGH University of Science and Technology
Cracow, Poland

Institute of Mathematics and Informatics
Bulgarian Academy of Sciences
Sofia, Bulgaria

João Manuel R. S. Tavares ⓘ
University of Porto
Porto, Portugal

ISSN 0302-9743   ISSN 1611-3349   (electronic)
Lecture Notes in Computer Science
ISBN 978-3-030-20804-2   ISBN 978-3-030-20805-9   (eBook)
https://doi.org/10.1007/978-3-030-20805-9

LNCS Sublibrary: SL6 – Image Processing, Computer Vision, Pattern Recognition, and Graphics

© Springer Nature Switzerland AG 2019
This work is subject to copyright. All rights are reserved by the Publisher, whether the whole or part of the material is concerned, specifically the rights of translation, reprinting, reuse of illustrations, recitation, broadcasting, reproduction on microfilms or in any other physical way, and transmission or information storage and retrieval, electronic adaptation, computer software, or by similar or dissimilar methodology now known or hereafter developed.
The use of general descriptive names, registered names, trademarks, service marks, etc. in this publication does not imply, even in the absence of a specific statement, that such names are exempt from the relevant protective laws and regulations and therefore free for general use.
The publisher, the authors and the editors are safe to assume that the advice and information in this book are believed to be true and accurate at the date of publication. Neither the publisher nor the authors or the editors give a warranty, expressed or implied, with respect to the material contained herein or for any errors or omissions that may have been made. The publisher remains neutral with regard to jurisdictional claims in published maps and institutional affiliations.

This Springer imprint is published by the registered company Springer Nature Switzerland AG
The registered company address is: Gewerbestrasse 11, 6330 Cham, Switzerland

Preface

It is our great pleasure to welcome you to the proceedings of the 6th International Symposium on Computational Modeling of Objects Represented in Images. Fundamentals, Methods and Applications (CompIMAGE 2018). It was held during July 2–5 at the University of Cracow, Poland. The previous editions took place in Coimbra (Portugal, 2006), Buffalo, NY (USA, 2010), Rome (Italy, 2012), Pittsburg, PA (USA, 2014), and Niagara Falls, NY (USA, 2016).

The purpose of the symposium was to provide a common forum for researchers, scientists, engineers, and practitioners around the world to present their latest research findings, ideas, developments, and implementations in the area of computational modeling of objects presented in images. CompIMAGE 2018 attracted researchers who use various approaches for solving problems that appear in a wide range of areas – as diverse as medicine, robotics, defense, security, material science, and manufacturing. CompIMAGE symposia have always been truly international, and this one continued the tradition: Symposium participants came from eight different countries from Europe and Asia.

In response to the call for papers, we received full-length articles as well as short communications presenting work in progress. This volume contains the full-length papers that were accepted. The authors of the accepted short communications had the possibility to present them at the symposium and receive feedback for their ongoing work.

All submissions underwent a rigorous double-blind review process by members of the international Program Committee. The most important selection criterion for acceptance or rejection of a paper was the overall score received. Other criteria were: relevance to the symposium topics, correctness, originality, mathematical depth, clarity, and presentation quality.

As a result, 16 contributed papers were selected for publication in this volume. Some of these advanced the theory while others presented new methods and applications in various areas of human practice. We hope that all these works will be of interest to a broad audience.

A co-event—ITSRCP 2018, the Third Conference on Information Technology, Systems Research and Computational Physics—was held at the same time and in close proximity. Participants of CompIMAGE 2018 could take part in ITSRCP 2018 and vice versa. The proceedings of ITSRCP 2018 will appear in Springer's *Advances in Intelligent Systems and Computing* series.

We would like to thank all those who contributed to the success of the symposium. First, we would like to express our gratitude to all authors who submitted their works to CompIMAGE 2018. Thanks to their contributions, we succeeded in having a technical program of high scientific quality. Our most sincere thanks go to the Program Committee members whose cooperation in carrying out a rigorous and objective review process was essential in establishing a strong symposium program and high-quality publications. We express our sincere gratitude to the invited speakers Leila De Floriani (University of Maryland at College Park, USA), Hanan Samet (Distinguished Professor at the University of Maryland at College Park, USA), Janusz Kacprzyk (Polish Academy of Sciences), Ioannis Pitas (Aristotle University of Thessaloniki, Greece), and Andrzej Skowron (University of Warsaw and Polish Academy of Sciences), for their remarkable presentations and overall contribution to the symposium. We appreciate the hard work of the local Organizing Committee providing excellent symposium organization and conditions. Finally, we wish to thank Springer for the pleasant cooperation in the production of this volume.

March 2019

Reneta P. Barneva
Valentin E. Brimkov
Piotr Kulczycki
João Manuel R. S. Tavares

Organization

The 6th International Symposium on Computational Modeling of Objects Represented in Images: Fundamentals, Methods, and Applications, CompIMAGE 2018, was held in Cracow, Poland, July 2–5, 2018.

Honorary Chair

Janusz Kacprzyk

Systems Research Institute, Polish Academy of Sciences, Poland

Conference Chairs

Reneta P. Barneva (Scientific Chair)

SUNY Fredonia, USA

Valentin E. Brimkov

SUNY Buffalo State, USA

Piotr Kulczycki (General Chair)

AGH University of Science and Technology, Poland

João Manuel R. S. Tavares

Universidade do Porto, Portugal

Steering Committee

João Manuel R. S. Tavares (Founding Chair)

Universidade do Porto, Portugal

Renato M. Natal Jorge (Founding Chair)

Universidade do Porto, Portugal

Reneta P. Barneva

SUNY Fredonia, USA

Valentin E. Brimkov

SUNY Buffalo State, USA

Local Committee

Małgorzata Charytanowicz

Systems Research Institute, Polish Academy of Sciences, Poland

Piotr A. Kowalski

AGH University of Science and Technology, Poland

Szymon Łukasik

AGH University of Science and Technology, Poland

Organizing Committee

Grzegorz Gołaszewski

AGH University of Science and Technology, Poland

Tomasz Rybotycki

Systems Research Institute, Polish Academy of Sciences, Poland

Joanna Świebocka-Więk

AGH University of Science and Technology, Poland

Keynote Speakers

Janusz Kacprzyk	Systems Research Institute, Polish Academy of Sciences, Poland
Leila De Floriani	University of Maryland at College Park, USA
Ioannis Pitas	Aristotle University of Thessaloniki, Greece
Hanan Samet	University of Maryland at College Park, USA
Andrzej Skowron	University of Warsaw and Polish Academy of Sciences, Systems Research Institute, Poland

International Program Committee

Fernao Vistulo de Abreu	Universidade de Aveiro, Portugal
Enrique Alegre Gutiérrez	University of León, Spain
Fernando Alonso-Fernandez	Halmstad University, Sweden
Luís Amaral	Polytechnic Institute of Coimbra, Portugal
Jorge M. G. Barbosa	Universidade do Porto, Portugal
Reneta P. Barneva	SUNY Fredonia, USA
Jorge Manuel Batista	Universidade de Coimbra, Portugal
Valentin Brimkov	SUNY Buffalo State, USA
Nathan Cahill	Rochester Institute of Technology, USA
Robert Cierniak	Czestochowa University of Technology, Poland
Miguel Velhote Correia	Universidade do Porto, Portugal
Alexandre Cunha	California Institute of Technology, USA
Jorge Manuel Dias	Universidade de Coimbra, Portugal
Mahmoud El-Sakka	The University of Western Ontario, Canada
José Augusto Mendes Ferreira	Universidade de Coimbra, Portugal
Jose M. García Aznar	University of Zaragoza, Spain
Bernard Gosselin	Faculté Polytechnique de Mons, Belgium
Ewa Grabska	Jagiellonian University, Poland
Gerhard A. Holzapfel	Graz University of Technology, Austria
Patrick Hung	University of Ontario Institute of Technology, Canada
Daniela Iacoviello	Sapienza University of Rome, Italy
Krassimira Ivanova	Institute of Mathematics and Informatics – BAS, Bulgaria
Kamen Kanev	Shizuoka University, Japan
Bill Kapralos	University of Ontario Institute of Technology, Canada
Constantine Kotropoulos	Aristotle University of Thessaloniki, Greece
Slimane Larabi	University of Science and Technology Houari Boumediene, Algeria
Rainald Lohner	George Mason University, USA
Andre R. S. Marcal	Universidade do Porto, Portugal
Ana Maria Mendonça	Universidade do Porto, Portugal
Lionel Moisan	Université Paris Descartes, France

Antonio Luis Pereira Do Amaral	Instituto Superior de Engenharia de Coimbra, Portugal
Alvaro Quevedo	University of Ontario Institute of Technology, Canada
Petia Radeva	Autonomous University of Barcelona, Spain
Luís Paulo Reis	Universidade do Porto, Portugal
David Ress	Baylor College of Medicine, USA
Angel D. Sappa	ESPOL Polytechnic University, Ecuador and Computer Vision Center, Spain
André Vital Saúde	University of Lavras, Brazil
Dinggang Shen	The University of North Carolina at Chapel Hill, USA
Miguel Tavares da Silva	Universidade de Lisboa, Portugal
K. G. Subramanian	Madras Christian College, India
Petra Wiederhold	CINVESTAV-IPN, Mexico
Jinhui Xu	University at Buffalo, USA
Yongjie (Jessica) Zhang	Carnegie Mellon University, USA

Additional Reviewers

| Mingchen Gao | University at Buffalo, USA |
| Di Wang | University at Buffalo, USA |

Contents

Theoretical Foundations of Computer Imaging

Endpoint-Based Thinning
with Designating Safe Skeletal Points

Kálmán Palágyi$^{(\boxtimes)}$ and Gábor Németh

Department of Image Processing and Computer Graphics,
University of Szeged, Szeged, Hungary
{palagyi,gnemeth}@inf.u-szeged.hu

Abstract. Thinning is an iterative object reduction: border points that
satisfy some topological and geometric constraints are deleted until stability is reached. If a border point is not deleted in an iteration, conventional implementations take it into consideration again in the next step.
With the help of the concepts of a 2D-simplifier point and a weak-3D-
simplifier point, rechecking of some 'survival' points is not needed. In
this work an implementation scheme is reported for sequential thinning
algorithms, and it is shown that the proposed method can be twice as
fast as the conventional approach in the 2D case.

Keywords: Digital geometry · Shape modeling · Skeletonization ·
Thinning

1 Introduction

A *binary picture* [6] on a grid is a mapping that assigns a color of *black* or *white*
to each grid element that is called a *point*. A regular partitioning of the 2D
Euclidean space is formed by a tessellation of regular polygons (i.e., polygons
having equal angles, and sides are all of the same length). There are exactly three
polygons that can form such regular tessellations [10], these being the equilateral
triangle, the square, and the regular hexagon. Although 2D digital pictures sampled on the square grid are generally assumed, triangular and hexagonal grids
have also attracted significant interest [6,10]. In the 3D case, the attention is
generally focused on the *cubic grid*, where the points are unit cubes [6].

A *reduction* [3] transforms a binary picture only by changing some black
points to white ones, which is referred to as *deletion*. *Parallel reductions* can
delete a set of black points simultaneously, while *sequential reductions* traverse
the black points of a picture, and focus on the actually visited point for possible
deletion at a time [3]. Two reductions are said to be *equivalent* if they produce
the same result for each input picture [14]. One of the authors gave a sufficient
condition for *equivalent deletion rules* that provide pairs of equivalent sequential
and parallel reductions [14].

Thinning [3,8,16] is a frequently used method for approximating *skeleton-
like features* in a topology–preserving way [6]: border points of a binary object

© Springer Nature Switzerland AG 2019
R. P. Barneva et al. (Eds.): CompIMAGE 2018, LNCS 10986, pp. 3–15, 2019.
https://doi.org/10.1007/978-3-030-20805-9_1

that satisfy certain topological and geometric constraints are deleted in iteration steps. The entire process is then repeated until no points are deleted. Most of existing thinning algorithms do not delete *endpoints* (i.e., terminating points of thin curves). Those algorithms are said to be *endpoint-based*. Note that Bertrand and Couprie proposed an alternative approach by accumulating curve/surface interior points that are called *isthmuses* [1]. Sequential and parallel thinning algorithms are composed of sequential and parallel reductions, respectively.

One of the authors introduced the notion of a *2D-simplifier point* for pictures sampled on the (2D) square grid [15]. In this paper that concept is extended to the pictures on the remaining two regular planar grids and the (3D) cubic grid. An advanced scheme is also reported for implementing endpoint-based sequential thinning algorithms and endpoint-based parallel thinning algorithms with equivalent deletion rules [14]. In the 2D case, it is shown that the proposed implementation scheme can be twice as fast as the conventional approach.

2   Basic Notions and Results

Here, we apply the fundamental concepts of digital topology as reviewed by Kong and Rosenfeld [6]. Despite the fact that there are other approaches based on cellular/cubical complexes [7], here we shall consider the 'conventional paradigm' of digital topology.

Let us denote the triangular, the square, and the hexagonal grids by $\mathcal{T}$, $\mathbb{Z}^2$, and $\mathcal{H}$, respectively, and throughout this article, if we will use the notation $\mathcal{V}$, we will mean that $\mathcal{V}$ belongs to $\{\mathcal{T}, \mathbb{Z}^2, \mathcal{H}\}$. The elements of the given grids (i.e., regular polygons) are called *points*. Two points are *1-adjacent* if they share an edge and they are *2-adjacent* if they share an edge or a vertex (see Fig. 1a–c). Note that both relations are reflexive and symmetric. Let us denote the set of points being j-adjacent to a point p in the grid $\mathcal{V}$ by $N_j^{\mathcal{V}}(p)$, and let $N_j^{*\mathcal{V}}(p) = N_j^{\mathcal{V}}(p) \setminus \{p\}$ $(j = 1, 2)$. It is obvious that $N_1^{\mathcal{T}}(p) \subset N_2^{\mathcal{T}}(p)$, $N_1^{\mathbb{Z}^2}(p) \subset N_2^{\mathbb{Z}^2}(p)$, and $N_1^{\mathcal{H}}(p) = N_2^{\mathcal{H}}(p)$.

A sequence of distinct points $\langle p_0, p_1, \ldots, p_m \rangle$ is called a *j-path* from p_0 to p_m in a non-empty set of points $X \subseteq \mathcal{V}$ if each point of the sequence is in X and p_i is j-adjacent to p_{i-1} for each $i = 1, 2, \ldots, m$. Two points are said to be *j-connected* in a set X if there is a j-path in X between them. A set of points X is *j-connected* in the set of points $Y \supseteq X$ if any two points in X are j-connected in Y. A *j-component* of a set of points X is a maximal (with respect to inclusion) j-connected subset of X.

Let $(k, \bar{k})$ be an ordered pair of adjacency relations. Throughout this paper, it is assumed that $(k, \bar{k})$ belongs to $\{(1, 2), (2, 1)\}$. A $(k, \bar{k})$ *(binary digital) picture* on $\mathcal{V}$ is a quadruple $(\mathcal{V}, k, \bar{k}, B)$ [6], where $B \subseteq \mathcal{V}$ denotes the set of *black points*, and each point in $\mathcal{V} \setminus B$ is said to be a *white point*. A *black component* or an *object* is a k-component of B, while a *white component* is a $\bar{k}$-component of $\mathcal{V} \setminus B$.

A black point p is an *interior point* if all points in $N_k^{*\mathcal{V}}(p)$ are black. A black point is said to be a *border point* if it is not an interior point. A black point p is called an *isolated point* if it forms a singleton object (i.e., all points in $N_k^{*\mathcal{V}}(p)$

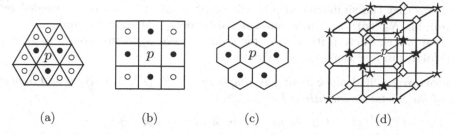

(a)   (b)   (c)   (d)

Fig. 1. The adjacency relations studied on the three possible regular 2D grids (a)–(c). Points that are 1-adjacent to the central point p are marked '•', while points that are 2-adjacent but not 1-adjacent to p are denoted by 'o'. Frequently used adjacency relations on $\mathbb{Z}^3$ (d). The set $N_6^{\mathbb{Z}^3}(p)$ contains point p and the six points marked '★'. The set $N_{18}^{\mathbb{Z}^3}(p)$ contains $N_6^{\mathbb{Z}^3}(p)$ and the twelve points denoted by '◇'. The set $N_{26}^{\mathbb{Z}^3}(p)$ contains $N_{18}^{\mathbb{Z}^3}(p)$ and the eight points marked '⋆'.

are white). A black point p is a *2D-curve-endpoint* if $N_k^{*V}(p) \cap B$ is a singleton set (i.e., p is k-adjacent to exactly one black point).

Let p be a point in the 3D cubic grid $\mathbb{Z}^3$. Let us denote the set of points that are j-adjacent to a point p by $N_j^{\mathbb{Z}^3}(p)$, and let $N_j^{*\mathbb{Z}^3}(p) = N_j^{\mathbb{Z}^3}(p) \setminus \{p\}$ ($j = 6, 18, 26$, see Fig. 1d).

The above defined concepts on the given 2D grids (including path and connectivity) can be extended to $\mathbb{Z}^3$. A $(26, 6)$ *(binary digital) picture* on $\mathbb{Z}^3$ is a quadruple $(\mathbb{Z}^3, 26, 6, B)$ [6], where $B \subseteq \mathbb{Z}^3$ denotes the set of *black points*, and each point in $\mathbb{Z}^3 \setminus B$ is said to be a *white point*. A *black component* or an *object* is a 26-component of B, while a *white component* is a 6-component of $\mathbb{Z}^3 \setminus B$.

A black point p is an *interior point* if all the six points in $N_6^{*\mathbb{Z}^3}(p)$ are black. A black point is said to be a *border point* if it is not an interior point. A black point is a *3D-curve-endpoint* if it is 26-adjacent to exactly one black point.

A reduction in a 2D picture is *topology-preserving* if each object in the input picture contains exactly one object in the output picture, and each white component in the output picture contains exactly one white component in the input picture [6]. There is an additional concept called *tunnel* in 3D pictures [6]. Topology preservation implies that eliminating or creating any tunnel is not allowed.

A black point is said to be *simple* for a set of black points (in a 2D or a 3D picture) if its deletion is a topology-preserving reduction [5,6]. Kardos and Palágyi stated the following characterization of simple points in all the given five types of 2D pictures (i.e., two for $\mathcal{T}$, two for $\mathbb{Z}^2$, and one for $\mathcal{H}$):

Theorem 1. [4] *Let p be a non-isolated border point in a picture $(V, k, \bar{k}, B)$. Then the followings are equivalent:*

1. *p is simple for B.*
2. *p is k-adjacent to exactly one k-component of $N_2^{*V}(p) \cap B$.*
3. *p is $\bar{k}$-adjacent to exactly one $\bar{k}$-component of $N_2^V(p) \setminus B$.*

Note that the simplicity of p is a local property (i.e., it can be decided by examining $N_2^{*\mathcal{V}}(p)$), and only non-isolated border points may be simple.

A useful characterization of simple points on $(26, 6)$ pictures on $\mathbb{Z}^3$ is stated by Malandain and Bertrand as follows:

Theorem 2. [9] *A black point p is simple in picture $(\mathbb{Z}^3, 26, 6, B)$ if and only if all of the following conditions hold:*

1. *The set $N_{26}^{*\mathbb{Z}^3}(p) \cap B$ contains exactly one 26–component.*
2. *The set $N_6^{\mathbb{Z}^3}(p) \setminus B$ is not empty.*
3. *Any two points in $N_6^{\mathbb{Z}^3}(p) \setminus B$ are 6–connected in the set $N_{18}^{\mathbb{Z}^3}(p) \setminus B$.*

Based on Theorem 2, the simplicity of a point p can be decided by examining the set $N_{26}^{*\mathbb{Z}^3}(p)$. We can state that all simple points are non-isolated border points.

3   2D-Simplifier and Weak-3D-Simplifier Points

In order to make computationally efficient implementation of sequential 2D thinning algorithms possible, one of the authors introduced the notion of a 2D-simplifier point for pictures sampled on the square grid [15]. Here we extend that concept to the pictures on the remaining two regular planar grids:

Definition 1. *A point $p \in B$ in a picture $(\mathcal{V}, k, \bar{k}, B)$ is a 2D-simplifier point if p is simple for B, and there is a non-simple and border point $q \in B$, such that q is simple for $B \setminus \{p\}$.*

The following statement is to characterize 2D-simplifier points:

Theorem 3. *If a point $p \in B$ is a 2D-simplifier point in a picture $(\mathcal{V}, k, \bar{k}, B)$, then p is a 2D-curve-endpoint.*

Proof. Let p be a simple point in picture $(\mathcal{V}, k, \bar{k}, B)$. Assume that there is a point $q \in B$, that is a border point in that picture, it is not simple for B, but it is simple for $B \setminus \{p\}$. (In other words, it is assumed that p is a simplifier point.) By Theorem 1, $q \in N_2^{*\mathcal{V}}(p)$.

In [15], one of the authors proved this theorem for $(1, 2)$ and $(2, 1)$ pictures sampled on $\mathbb{Z}^2$. Hence we need to consider the remaining three kinds of pictures on the regular planar grids.

Then the following cases are to be investigated:

– Let us assume that $(k, \bar{k}) = (2, 1)$. (Hence $(2, 1)$ pictures on grids $\mathcal{T}$ and $\mathcal{H}$ are taken into consideration).
  Since q is not simple for B, by Theorem 1, $N_2^{*\mathcal{V}}(q) \cap B$ does not contain exactly one 2-component. As q is simple for $B \setminus \{p\}$, there is just one 2-component in $N_2^{*\mathcal{V}}(q) \cap (B \setminus \{p\})$. Thus $\{p\}$ forms a singleton 2-component in $N_2^{*\mathcal{V}}(q) \cap B$. It means that $N_2^{*\mathcal{V}}(p) \cap N_2^{*\mathcal{V}}(q) \cap B = \emptyset$. Consequently $\{q\}$ forms a singleton 2-component in $N_2^{*\mathcal{V}}(p) \cap B$.
  Since p is simple for B, $N_2^{*\mathcal{V}}(p) \cap B = \{q\}$. Thus, p is a 2D-curve-endpoint.

– Consider $(k, \bar{k}) = (1, 2)$ pictures on $\mathcal{T}$. The proof is carried out with the help of Figs. 2, 3 and 4. In each case p is a 2D-curve-endpoint, or we arrive at a contradiction.

□

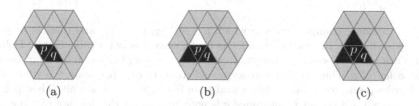

(a)   (b)   (c)

Fig. 2. Three base configurations in which $p \in N_1^{*\mathcal{V}}(q)$. In case (a), p is a 2D-curve-endpoint. In case (b), the simplicity of q does not depend on the 'color' of p. Thus we arrive at a contradiction. In case (c), p is not simple (since it is not a border point). Hence we come into contradiction.

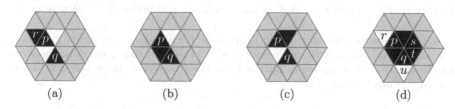

(a)   (b)   (c)   (d)

Fig. 3. Four base configurations in which $p \in N_2^{*\mathcal{V}}(q) \setminus N_1^{*\mathcal{V}}(q)$ and there is a point in $N_1^{*\mathcal{V}}(p) \cap N_1^{*\mathcal{V}}(q)$. In case (a), point r is black, since p is not a (non-simple) isolated point. Thus p is a 2D-curve-endpoint. In both cases (b) and (c), the simplicity of q does not depend on the 'color' of p. Thus we arrive at a contradiction. In case (d), point r is white since p is a border point, and both points s and t are black, since p is simple. Then point u is white since q is a border point. Since q is not simple after the deletion of p (i.e., q is 2-adjacent to two white 2-components), we come into contradiction.

Theorem 3 states that all 2D-simplifier points are 2D-curve-endpoints. Figure 5 illustrates that the contrary statement does not hold:

Proposition 1. *Let p be a 2D-curve-endpoint in picture $(\mathcal{V}, k, \bar{k}, B)$, and let $N_k^{*\mathcal{V}}(p) \cap B = \{q\}$ be a non-simple and border point in that picture. Then q may be non-simple in $(\mathcal{V}, k, \bar{k}, B \setminus \{p\})$ (i.e., p may not be a 2D-simplifier point).*

Now let us examine the 3D case:

Proposition 2. *Let q be a non-simple border point in picture $(\mathbb{Z}^3, 26, 6, B)$. If q is simple in $(\mathbb{Z}^3, 26, 6, B \setminus \{p\})$, point p may be a non-3D-curve-endpoint.*

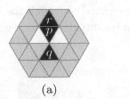 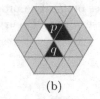 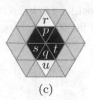

(a)   (b)   (c)

Fig. 4. Three base configurations in which $p \in N_2^{*\mathcal{V}}(q) \setminus N_1^{*\mathcal{V}}(q)$ and there is no point in $N_1^{*\mathcal{V}}(p) \cap N_1^{*\mathcal{V}}(q)$. In case (a), point r is black, since p is not a (non-simple) isolated point. Thus p is a 2D-curve-endpoint. In case (b), the simplicity of q does not depend on the 'color' of p. Thus we arrive at a contradiction. In case (c), point r is white since p is a border point, and both points s and t are black, since p is simple. Then point u is white since q is a border point. Since q is not simple after the deletion of p (i.e., q is 2-adjacent to two white 2-components), we come into contradiction.

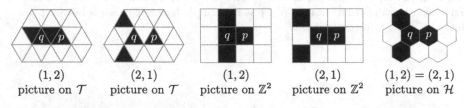

(1, 2)   (2, 1)   (1, 2)   (2, 1)   (1, 2) = (2, 1)
picture on $\mathcal{T}$ picture on $\mathcal{T}$ picture on $\mathbb{Z}^2$ picture on $\mathbb{Z}^2$ picture on $\mathcal{H}$

Fig. 5. Configurations associated with Proposition 1. Point q is a non-simple and border point, and $p \in N_2^{*\mathcal{V}}(q)$ is a 2D-curve-endpoint. We can state that q remains non-simple after the deletion of p. Hence in all the considered five kinds of pictures, 2D-curve-endpoint p is not a simplifier.

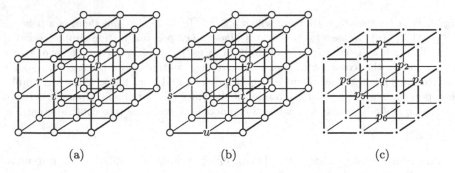

(a)   (b)   (c)

Fig. 6. Configuration assigned to Proposition 2(a): Let $\{p, q, r, s, t\} \subseteq B$. Border point q is not simple for B (since Condition 3 of Theorem 2 is violated). Despite of the fact that p is a simple point for B, and it is not a 3D-curve-endpoint (as $N_{26}^{*\mathbb{Z}^3}(p) \cap B = \{q, r, s\}$), q is simple for $B \setminus \{p\}$. Configuration associated with Proposition 4(b): Consider the picture $(\mathbb{Z}^3, 26, 6, B)$, where $\{p, q, r, s, t, u\} \subseteq B$. Point q is not simple for B (since both Conditions 1 and 3 of Theorem 2 are violated). Despite of the fact that p is a (simple) 3D-curve-endpoint for B (since $N_{26}^{*\mathbb{Z}^3}(p) \cap B = \{q\}$), q remains a non-simple point for $B \setminus \{p\}$ (as Condition 3 of Theorem 2 is still violated). Configuration assigned to Proposition 5(c).

Figure 6a is to illustrate Proposition 2.

Let us now state the following proposition (that is 'much more weaker' than Theorem 3):

Proposition 3. *Let p and q be two black points in picture $(\mathbb{Z}^3, 26, 6, B)$ such that p is simple, and q violates Condition 1 of Theorem 2. If q is simple in $(\mathbb{Z}^3, 26, 6, B \setminus \{p\})$, point p is a 3D-curve-endpoint.*

Proof. It is assumed that q is not simple for B, but q is simple for $B \setminus \{p\}$. Since the simplicity in $(26, 6)$ pictures is a local property, by Theorem 2, $p \in N_{26}^{*\mathbb{Z}^3}(p) \cap B$.

Since Condition 1 of Theorem 2 is not satisfied, $N_{26}^{*\mathbb{Z}^3}(q) \cap B$ does not contain exactly one 26-component. As Condition 1 of Theorem 2 holds for q after the deletion of p, $N_{26}^{*\mathbb{Z}^3}(q) \cap (B \setminus \{p\})$ contains exactly one 26-component. Thus $\{p\}$ forms a singleton 26-component in $N_{26}^{*\mathbb{Z}^3}(q) \cap B$.

It means that $N_{26}^{*\mathbb{Z}^3}(p) \cap N_{26}^{*\mathbb{Z}^3}(q) \cap B = \emptyset$. Consequently $\{q\}$ forms a singleton 26-component in $N_{26}^{*\mathbb{Z}^3}(p) \cap B$.

Since it is assumed that p is simple for B (i.e., Condition 1 of Theorem 2 is satisfied by p in the original picture), $N_{26}^{*\mathbb{Z}^3}(p) \cap B = \{q\}$. Thus p is a 3D-curve-endpoint. □

We are now ready to define the concept of a *weak-3D-simplifier point*:

Definition 2. *A point $p \in B$ in a picture $(\mathbb{Z}^3, 26, 6, B)$ is a* weak-3D-simplifier *point if p is simple for B, and there is a point $q \in B$, such that $N_{26}^{*\mathbb{Z}^3}(q) \cap B$ docs not contain exactly one 26-component (i.e., Condition 1 of Theorem 2 is violated) but q is simple for $B \setminus \{p\}$.*

As an easy consequence of Proposition 3, we can state the following theorem:

Theorem 4. *If a point in a $(26, 6)$ picture on $\mathbb{Z}^3$ is a weak-3D-simplifier point, then it is a 3D-curve-endpoint.*

Similarly to Proposition 1, the converse of Theorem 4 does not hold as it is shown in Fig. 6b. Therefore, we can state:

Proposition 4. *Let p be a 3D-curve-endpoint in picture $(\mathbb{Z}^3, 26, 6, B)$, and let $N_{26}^{*\mathbb{Z}^3}(p) \cap B = \{q\}$ be a non-simple and border point in that picture. Then q may be non-simple in $(\mathbb{Z}^3, 26, 6, B \setminus \{p\})$.*

Lastly, we can state the following proposition:

Proposition 5. *If a (non-simple) point q in a $(26, 6)$ picture on $\mathbb{Z}^3$ violates Condition 1 of Theorem 2, q is a border point.*

Proof. Consider the picture depicted in Fig. 6c. Since $\{p_1, p_2, \ldots, p_6\} \subseteq (N_6^{*\mathbb{Z}^3}(q) \cap B)$, q is an interior point (i.e., it is not a border point) in that picture.

It is easy to check that each point in $\{p_1, p_2, \ldots, p_6\}$ are 26-adjacent to exactly four further black points in $\{p_1, p_2, \ldots, p_6\}$, and each point in $(N_{26}^{\mathbb{Z}^3}(q) \setminus N_6^{\mathbb{Z}^3}(q)) \cap B$ is 26-adjacent to at least three points in $\{p_1, p_2, \ldots, p_6\}$. Consequently, $N_{26}^{*\mathbb{Z}^3}(q) \cap B$ is 26-connected (i.e., Condition 1 of Theorem 2 holds).

Thus we arrive at a contradiction. $\qquad\qquad\qquad\qquad\qquad\qquad\qquad\qquad\square$

Endpoint-based 2D thinning algorithms never delete 2D-curve-endpoints, and endpoint-based 3D thinning algorithms may not alter 3D-curve-end-points. By Theorems 3 and 4, and Proposition 5, we can state the following two propositions:

Proposition 6. *The produced skeleton-like feature of any endpoint-based sequential 2D thinning algorithm contains all non-simple border points in the original input picture (and in the intermediate pictures of the iterative thinning process).*

Proposition 7. *The produced skeleton-like feature of any endpoint-based sequential 3D thinning algorithm contains all non-simple points that violates Condition 1 of Theorem 2 in the original input picture (and in the interim pictures).*

Now let us define the concepts of a 2D-safe point and a 3D-safe point, and state an additional proposition (as an immediate consequence of propositions 6 and 7):

Definition 3. *A border point $p \in B$ in a picture $(\mathcal{V}, k, \bar{k}, B)$ is a 2D-safe point if p is a 2D-curve-endpoint or it is not simple for B.*

Definition 4. *A border point $p \in B$ in a picture $(\mathbb{Z}^3, 26, 6, B)$ is a 3D-safe point if p is a 3D-curve-endpoint or $N_{26}^{*\mathbb{Z}^3}(q) \cap B$ does not contain exactly one 26-component (i.e., Condition 1 of Theorem 2 is violated).*

Proposition 8. *The produced skeleton-like feature of any endpoint-based 2D and 3D sequential thinning algorithm, respectively, contains all 2D-safe points and 3D-safe points in the original input picture (and in the interim pictures).*

However various types of (curve and surface) endpoints have been proposed in 2D and 3D pictures [3,13], each existing endpoint-based (sequential or parallel) 2D and 3D thinning algorithm, respectively, does not delete 2D-curve-endpoints and 3D-curve-endpoints. Hence, Proposition 8 is valid for arbitrary endpoint-based 2D and 3D sequential thinning algorithms.

4   Implementations

One of the authors proposed a general, easy, and computationally efficient implementation scheme for arbitrary sequential thinning algorithms [12]. His method utilizes the following properties of these algorithms:

– Only border points in the current picture are investigated in each reduction/thinning phase (i.e., we do not have to evaluate the deletion rules for interior points).
– Only some simple points in the current picture may be deleted in each thinning phase (since topology preservation is a crucial requirement to be complied with).
– Since supports (i.e., the minimal sets of points whose values determine the new value of a point) of all existing algorithms are local, the Boolean functions associated with thinning deletion rules can be evaluated for all possible configurations, and their results can be stored in (pre-calculated) look-up-tables.

The pseudocode of the 'conventional' implementation is described by Algorithm 1.

Algorithm 1.   'Conventional' Implementation Scheme for Arbitrary Sequential Thinning Algorithms

Input: array A storing the picture to be thinned
Output: array A storing the picture with the produced skeleton-like feature
// collecting border points
$border\_list \leftarrow$ < empty list >
foreach element p in array A **do**
$\quad$ **if** $A[p] = 1$ and p is a border point **then**
$\quad\quad$ $border\_list \leftarrow border\_list + < p >$
$\quad\quad$ $A[p] \leftarrow 2$

// thinning process
repeat
$\quad$ $number\_of\_deleted\_points \leftarrow 0$
$\quad$ **foreach** point p in $border\_list$ **do**
$\quad\quad$ **if** p is 'deletable' **then**
$\quad\quad\quad$ $border\_list \leftarrow border\_list - < p >$
$\quad\quad\quad$ $A[p] \leftarrow 0$
$\quad\quad\quad$ $number\_of\_deleted\_points \leftarrow number\_of\_deleted\_points + 1$
$\quad\quad\quad$ **foreach** point q being 'adjacent' to p **do**
$\quad\quad\quad\quad$ **if** $A[q] = 1$ **then**
$\quad\quad\quad\quad\quad$ $A[q] \leftarrow 2$
$\quad\quad\quad\quad\quad$ $border\_list \leftarrow border\_list + < q >$

until $number\_of\_deleted\_points > 0$;

The 'conventional' method uses a list name $border\_list$ for storing the border points in the input and the interim pictures, thus the repeated scans of the entire array storing the picture are avoided. In input array A, the value '1' corresponds to black points in the picture to be thinned, and the value '0' is assigned to white ones. In order to avoid storing more than one copy of a border point in *border_list*, a three-color picture is assumed in which value of '2' corresponds to border points to be checked in the forthcoming iterations.

If a border point is deleted, all interior points that are 'adjacent' to it become border points. These brand new border points of the resulted picture are added to the *border_list*. In 2D algorithms acting on $(k, \bar{k})$-pictures, 'adjacent' means $\bar{k}$-adjacent. If a 3D algorithm assumes $(26, 6)$-pictures on $\mathbb{Z}^3$, 'adjacent' corresponds to the 6-adjacency relation. Note that some thinning algorithms do not apply the same deletion rule at each iteration [3,12,13].

The thinning process terminates when no more points can be deleted (i.e., stability is reached). After thinning, all points having a nonzero value in array A belong to the produced skeleton-like feature.

With the help of the concepts of a 2D-safe point and a 3D-safe point, a more efficient implementation can be proposed for 2D and 3D endpoint-based sequential thinning algorithms (and for parallel algorithms with equivalent deletion rules [14]), see Algorithm 2.

Algorithm 2. 'Advanced' Implementation Scheme for Endpoint-Based Sequential Thinning Algorithms

---

Input: array A storing the picture to be thinned
Output: array A storing the picture with the produced skeleton-like feature
// collecting border points
border_list ← < empty list >
foreach element p in array A **do**
  if $A[p] = 1$ and p is a border point **then**
    border_list ← *border_list* + < p >
    $A[p]$ ← 2

// thinning process
repeat
  number_of_deleted_points ← 0
  foreach point p in *border_list* **do**
    if p is a 'safe point' **then**
      $A[p]$ ← 3
      border_list ← *border_list* − < p >
    else if p is 'deletable' **then**
      border_list ← *border_list* − < p >
      $A[p]$ ← 0
      number_of_deleted_points ← *number_of_deleted_points* +1
      foreach point q being 'adjacent' to p **do**
        if $A[q] = 1$ **then**
          $A[q]$ ← 2
          border_list ← *border_list* + < q >

  until *number_of_deleted_points* > 0;

In the 'advanced' implementation, array A represents a four-color picture, where

- a value of '0' corresponds to white points,
- a value of '1' is assigned to interior points,
- a value of '2' corresponds to border points to be checked (i.e., elements of the current *border_list*), and
- a value of '3' is assigned to each detected 'safe point'.

By Proposition 8, a 'safe point' belongs to the produced skeleton-like feature. In the 2D case, 'safe point' means 2D-safe point (see Definition 3), and 3D algorithms consider 3D-safe points (see Definition 4).

5   Results

One may think that taking safe points into consideration is absolutely unavailing. This section is to demonstrate that it is far from true.

In the 2D, the 'conventional' and the proposed 'advanced' implementation schemes were compared on a number of thinning algorithms and objects of different shapes.

Table 1. Computation times (in sec.) of algorithm **GH1992** for five test images.

Test image	Size	Number of object points	Number of skeletal points	'conventional' comp. time **C**	'advanced' comp. time **A**	Speed-up **C/A**
	500 × 860	175 229	3 508	0.097	0.041	**2.360**
	624 × 700	108 871	2 557	0.056	0.028	**2.020**
	1266 × 1269	268 560	6 558	0.225	0.078	**2.882**
	700 × 700	159 419	2 831	0.074	0.038	**1.950**
	2050 × 2050	1 040 892	11 564	0.795	0.269	**2.949**

Here we focus on two endpoint-based 2D sequential thinning algorithms called **GH1992** and **NKP2011**. The deletion rule of algorithm **GH1992** was proposed by Guo and Hall [2], and Németh, Kardos, and Palágyi [11] framed the deletion rule of **NKP2011**. Both algorithms act on $(2,1)$-pictures on $\mathbb{Z}^2$.

The efficiency of the proposed 'advanced' implementation scheme over the 'conventional' one is illustrated in Tables 1 and 2 for five test images. The examined algorithms were run on a usual PC under Linux (Fedora 27–64 bit), using a 3.30 GHz 4x Intel Core i5-2500 CPU. (Note, that just the iterative thinning process itself was considered here; reading the input volume, the look-up-table associated to the deletion rule, and writing the output image were not taken into account but the processing involved is not excessive.)

Note that the 'conventional' and the 'advanced' implementation schemes (based on weak-3D-simplifier points) were also compared on various endpoint-based 3D thinning algorithms. We found that the speed-up is not large-scale (merely 10–20%), but it might be remarkable in some applications.

Table 2. Computation times (in sec.) of algorithm **NKP2011** for five test images.

Test image	Size	Number of object points	Number of skeletal points	'conventional' comp. time C	'advanced' comp. time A	Speed-up C/A
	500×860	175 229	3 439	0.098	0.043	**2.271**
	624×700	108 871	2 513	0.057	0.030	**1.916**
	1266×1269	268 560	6 437	0.226	0.084	**2.698**
	700×700	159 419	2 812	0.077	0.040	**1.912**
	2050×2050	1 040 892	11 205	0.787	0.286	**2.755**

Acknowledgments. This research was supported by the project "Integrated program for training new generation of scientists in the fields of computer science", no EFOP-3.6.3-VEKOP-16-2017-0002. The project has been supported by the European Union and co-funded by the European Social Fund.

References

1. Bertrand, G., Couprie, M.: Transformations topologiques discrètes. In: Coeur-jolly, D., Montanvert, A., Chassery, J.-M. (eds.) Géométrie discrète et images numériques, pp. 187–209. Hermès Science Publications, England (2007)
2. Guo, Z., Hall, R.W.: Fast fully parallel thinning algorithms. CVGIP: Image Underst. **55**, 317–328 (1992). https://doi.org/10.1016/1049-9660(92)90029-3
3. Hall, R.W.: Parallel connectivity-preserving thinning algorithms. In: Kong, T.Y., Rosenfeld, A. (eds.) Topological Algorithms for Digital Image Processing, pp. 145–179. Elsevier, Amsterdam (1996)
4. Kardos, P., Palágyi, K.: On topology preservation in triangular, square, and hexagonal grids. In: Proceedings of the 8th International Symposium on Image and Signal Processing and Analysis, ISPA 2013, pp. 782–787 (2013). https://doi.org/10.1109/ISPA.2013.6703844
5. Kong, T.Y.: On topology preservation in 2-D and 3-D thinning. Int. J. Pattern Recognit. Artif. Intell. **9**, 813–844 (1995). https://doi.org/10.1142/S0218001495000341
6. Kong, T.Y., Rosenfeld, A.: Digital topology: introduction and survey. Comput. Vis. Graph. Image Process. **48**, 357–393 (1989). https://doi.org/10.1016/0734-189X(89)90147-3
7. Kovalevsky, V.A.: Geometry of Locally Finite Spaces. Publishing House, Berlin (2008). https://doi.org/10.1142/S0218654308001178
8. Lam, L., Lee, S.-W., Suen, C.Y.: Thinning methodologies - a comprehensive survey. IEEE Trans. Pattern Anal. Mach. Intell. **14**, 869–885 (1992). https://doi.org/10.1109/34.161346
9. Malandain, G., Bertrand, G.: Fast characterization of 3D simple points. In: Proceedings of 11th IEEE International Conference on Pattern Recognition, ICPR 1992, pp. 232–235 (1992). https://doi.org/10.1109/ICPR.1992.201968
10. Marchand-Maillet, S., Sharaiha, Y.M.: Binary Digital Image Processing: A Discrete Approach. Academic Press, New York (2000). https://doi.org/10.1117/1.1326456
11. Németh, G., Kardos, P., Palágyi, K.: 2D parallel thinning and shrinking based on sufficient conditions for topology preservation. Acta Cybernetica **20**, 125–144 (2011). https://doi.org/10.14232/actacyb.20.1.2011.10
12. Palágyi, K., Tschirren, J., Hoffman, E.A., Sonka, M.: Quantitative analysis of pulmonary airway tree structures. Comput. Biol. Med. **36**, 974–996 (2006). https://doi.org/10.1016/j.compbiomed.2005.05.004
13. Palágyi, K., Németh, G., Kardos, P.: Topology preserving parallel 3D thinning algorithms. In: Brimkov, V.E., Barneva, R.P. (eds.) Digital Geometry Algorithms: Theoretical Foundations and Applications to Computational Imaging. LNCVB, vol. 2, pp. 165–188. Springer, Dordrecht (2012). https://doi.org/10.1007/978-94-007-4174-4_6
14. Palágyi, K.: Equivalent sequential and parallel reductions in arbitrary binary pictures. Int. J. Pattern Recognit. Artif. Intell. **28**, 1460009-1–1460009-16 (2014). https://doi.org/10.1142/S021800141460009X
15. Palágyi, K.: Simplifier points in 2D binary images. In: Brimkov, V.E., Barneva, R.P. (eds.) IWCIA 2017. LNCS, vol. 10256, pp. 3–15. Springer, Cham (2017). https://doi.org/10.1007/978-3-319-59108-7_1
16. Suen, C.Y., Wang, P.S.P. (eds.): Thinning Methodologies for Pattern Recognition. Series in Machine Perception and Artificial Intelligence, vol. 8. World Scientific, Singapore (1994). https://doi.org/10.1142/9789812797858_0009

Structuring Digital Plane by Closure Operators Associated with n-ary Relations

Josef Slapal$^{(\boxtimes)}$

Brno University of Technology, 616 69 Brno, Czech Republic
slapal@fme.vutbr.cz
https://www.vutbr.cz/en/people/josef-slapal-1671

Abstract. We associate a closure operator with every n-ary relation ($n > 1$ an integer) on a given set. We focus on certain n-ary relations on the digital line $\mathbb{Z}$ and study the closure operators on the digital plane $\mathbb{Z}^2$ that are associated with special products of pairs of the relations. These closure operators, which include the Khalimsky topology, are shown to provide well behaved connectedness, so that they may be used as background structures on the digital plane for the study of digital images.

Keywords: n-ary relation · Closure operator · Digital plane ·
Khalimsky topology · Jordan curve theorem

1 Introduction and Preliminaries

A basic problem of digital topology is to find a convenient structure on the digital plane $\mathbb{Z}^2$ (or, more generally, digital space $\mathbb{Z}^n$, n a positive integer) that would allow as to study digital images. The convenience means that such a structure satisfies analogues of some basic geometric and topological properties of the Euclidean topology on the real plane $\mathbb{R}^2$. Of these properties, an analogue of the Jordan curve theorem plays a crucial role (recall that the Jordan curve theorem states that every simple closed curve in the Euclidean plane separates this plane into precisely two components). In the classical approach to this problem (see e.g. [6]), graph theoretic tools are used for structuring $\mathbb{Z}^2$, namely the well-known binary relations of 4-adjacency and 8-adjacency. But neither 4-adjacency nor 8-adjacency itself allows for an analogue of the Jordan curve theorem. To eliminate this deficiency, a combination of the two binary relations is usually used or some particular graphs are employed [9]. In [4], a new, purely topological approach to the problem was proposed which utilizes a convenient topology, called Khalimsky topology, for structuring the digital plane. The topological approach to digital topology was then developed by many authors - see, e.g., [5] and [7].

In [8], it was shown that closure operators more general than topologies, i.e., Kuratowski closure operators, may advantageously be used for structuring the digital plane $\mathbb{Z}^2$. In the present note, we continue the study of convenient closure

© Springer Nature Switzerland AG 2019
R. P. Barneva et al. (Eds.): CompIMAGE 2018, LNCS 10986, pp. 16–22, 2019.
https://doi.org/10.1007/978-3-030-20805-9_2

operators on $\mathbb{Z}^2$ (and, more generally, $\mathbb{Z}^n$). We discuss closure operators that are associated, in a certain way, to n-ary relations. We focus on closure operators providing well-behaved connectedness on the digital plane, i.e., allowing for an analogue of the Jordan curve theorem.

By a *graph* we understand an undirected simple graph without loops. We will work with some basic graph-theoretic concepts - we refer to [3] for them.

Throughout the paper, n will denote a natural number (i.e., a finite ordinal) with $n > 1$. Given an n-ary relation R on a set X (i.e., a subset $R \subseteq X^n$), the pair (X, R) will be called an *n-ary relational system* and the elements (n-tuples) $(x_0, x_1, ..., x_{n-1})$ of R will be denoted by $(x_i| \ i < n)$. Further, we denote by $\bar{R}$ the *reflexive hull* of R, i.e., the n-ary relation on X given by $\bar{R} = R \cup \{(x_i| \ i < n) \in X^n; \ x_i = x_j \text{ for all } i, j < n\}$. Let $(X, R), (Y, S)$ be a pair of n-ary relational systems. Recall that the *cartesian product* $R \times S$ of R and S is the n-ary relation on $X \times Y$ given by $R \times S = \{((x_i, y_i)| \ i < n); \ (x_i| \ i < n) \in R \text{ and } (y_i| \ i < n) \in S\}$. We define the *extended product* of R and S to be the n-ary relation $R \otimes S$ on $X \times Y$ given by $R \otimes S = (\bar{R} \times S) \cup (R \times \bar{S})$ (so that $R \times S \subseteq R \otimes R$).

By a *closure operator* u on a set X, we mean a map u: $\exp X \to \exp X$ (where $\exp X$ denotes the power set of X) which is

(i) grounded (i.e., $u\emptyset = \emptyset$),
(ii) extensive (i.e., $A \subseteq X \Rightarrow A \subseteq uA$), and
(iii) monotone (i.e., $A \subseteq B \subseteq X \Rightarrow uA \subseteq uB$).

The pair (X, u) is then called a *closure space*. Closure spaces were studied by Čech [1] (who called them topological spaces).

A closure operator u on X that is

(iv) additive (i.e., $u(A \cup B) = uA \cup uB$ whenever $A, B \subseteq X$) and
(v) idempotent (i.e., $uuA = uA$ whenever $A \subseteq X$)

is called a *Kuratowski closure operator* or a *topology* and the pair (X, u) is called a *topological space*.

For closure spaces, we use some concepts that are natural extensions of certain basic concepts known for topological spaces (see, e.g., [2]). In particular, a closure space (Y, v) is said do be a *subspace* of a closure space (X, u) if $vA = uA \cap Y$ for every subset $A \subseteq X$. We then say that Y is a subspace of (X, u). Further, a closure space (X, u) is *connected* if $\emptyset$ and X are the only subsets of X that are both closed and open. Given a closure space (X, u), a subset $A \subseteq X$ is said to be *connected* in (X, u) if A is a connected subspace of (X, u). And a *component* of a closure space (X, u) is a maximal (with respect to set inclusion) connected subset of the space. We will employ the obvious fact that the union of a sequence of connected subsets of a closure space is connected if every pair of consecutive members of the sequence has a nonempty intersection. A *connectedness graph* of a closure operator u on a set X is a graph with the vertex set X such that vertices $x \in X$ and $y \in Y$ are adjacent if and only if they are different and $\{x, y\}$ is a connected subset of X.

2   Closure Operators Associated with n-ary Relations

Let X be a set and $n > 1$ a natural number. We denote by $\mathcal{R}_n(X)$ the set of all n-ary relations on X.

Let (X, R) be an n-ary relational system ($n > 1$ a natural number). Then, for every subset $A \subseteq X$, we put $f_n(R)A = A \cup \{x \in X;$ there exist $(x_i | \ i < n) \in R$ and a natural number m with $0 < m < n$ such that $\{x_i; \ i < m\} \subseteq A$ and $x_m = x\}$ for every $A \subseteq X$. It may easily be seen that $f_n(R)$ is a closure operator on X. Thus, denoting by $\mathcal{U}(X)$ the set of all closure operators on X, we get a map $f_n : \mathcal{R}_n(X) \to \mathcal{U}(X)$. The closure operator $f_n(R)$ will be said to be *associated* with R. It is evident that, for every $(x_i | \ i < n) \in R$, the set $\{x_i | \ i < m\}$ is connected in the closure space $(X, f_n(R))$ whenever m is a natural number with $0 < m \leq n$.

We will focus on closure operators on the digital plane $\mathbb{Z}^2$ associated with certain n-ary relations. We will start with introducing particular n-ary relations on the digital line $\mathbb{Z}$.

For every natural number $n > 1$, we denote by R the n-ary relation on $\mathbb{Z}$ given as follows:

$R = \{(x_i | \ i \leq n);$ there exists an odd integer k such that $x_i = k(n-1) + i$ for all i, $0 \leq i < n$, or $x_i = k(n-1) - i$ for all i, $0 \leq i < n\}$.

The n-ary relational system $(\mathbb{Z}, R)$ is demonstrated in Fig. 1 where only the points $k(n-1)$, $k \in \mathbb{Z}$, are marked out (by bold dots). The n-tuples belonging to R are represented by line segments oriented from the first to the last members of the n-tuples. It is evident that $(\mathbb{Z}, f_n(R))$ is a connected closure space.

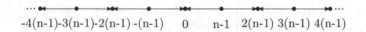

-4(n-1) -3(n-1) -2(n-1) -(n-1)   0   n-1   2(n-1) 3(n-1) 4(n-1)

Fig. 1. The relational system $(\mathbb{Z}, R)$

The closure operator $f_2(R)$ coincides with the well-known Khalimsky topology on $\mathbb{Z}$, i.e., the topology on $\mathbb{Z}$ generated by the subbase $\{\{2k - 1, 2k, 2k + 1\}; \ k \in \mathbb{Z}\}$ - cf. [4].

In the sequel, we will discuss the n-ary relational systems $(\mathbb{Z}^2, R \otimes R)$, $n > 1$. The systems are demonstrated in Figure 2 where, similarly to Fig. 1, only the points $(k(n - 1), l(n - 1))$, $k, l \in \mathbb{Z}$, are marked out and only the n-tuples in $R \otimes R$ whose end points are among the marked out points are displayed (as line segments oriented from the first to the last members of the n-tuples). Thus, between any pair of neighboring parallel horizontal or vertical line segments (having the same orientation), there are $n-2$ more parallel line segments with the same orientation that are not displayed in order to make the Figure transparent.

It may easily be seen that the closure space $(\mathbb{Z}^2, f_n(R \otimes R))$ is connected.

Let, for every natural number $n > 1$, G_n be the graph with the vertex set $\mathbb{Z}^2$ and with the set of edges E_n such that, for any $(x_1, y_1), (x_2, y_2) \in \mathbb{Z}^2$,

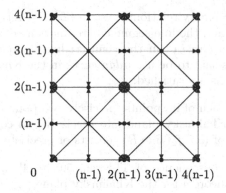

Fig. 2. The n-ary relational system $(\mathbb{Z}^2, R \otimes R)$.

$\{(x_1, y_1), (x_2, y_2)\} \in E_n$ if and only if there is $((t_i, z_i)| \ i < n) \in R \otimes R$ and a natural number m, $0 \leq m < n - 1$ such that $(x_1, y_1) = (t_m, z_m)$, $(x_2, y_2) = (t_{m+1}, z_{m+1})$ and one of the following four conditions is satisfied for some $k \in \mathbb{Z}$:

$x_1 - y_1 = x_2 - y_2 = 2k(n-1)$,
$x_1 + y_1 = x_2 + y_2 = 2k(n-1)$,
$x_1 = x_2 = 2k(n-1)$,
$y_1 = y_2 = 2k(n-1)$.

The graph G_n is demonstrated in Fig. 3 where only the vertices $(2k(n-1), 2l(n-1))$, $k, l \in \mathbb{Z}$, are marked out. Note that every circle C in G_n is a connected subset of $(\mathbb{Z}^2, f_n(R \otimes R))$. Indeed, C consists (is the union of) a finite sequence of n-tuples belonging to $R \otimes R$ such that every pair of consecutive n-tuples in the sequence has a point in common.

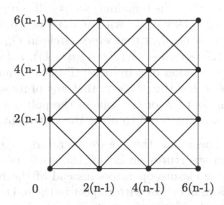

Fig. 3. A section of the graph G_n.

The closure operator $f_2(R \otimes R)$ coincides with the *Khalimsky topology* on $\mathbb{Z}^2$. The connectedness graph of the Khalimsky topology on $\mathbb{Z}^2$ coincides with the symmetrization of the binary relational system $(\mathbb{Z}^2, R \otimes R)$, i.e., with the graph in Fig. 2 where $n = 2$ and the line segments are unoriented.

According to [4], a circle C in the connectedness graph of the Khalimsky topology $f_2(R \otimes R)$ is said to be a *Jordan curve* in the Khalimsky plane if the following two conditions are satisfied:

(1) C contains, with each of its points, precisely two points adjacent to it,
(2) C separates the Khalimsky plane into precisely two components (i.e., the subspace $\mathbb{Z}^2 - C$ of $(\mathbb{Z}^2, f_2(R \otimes R))$ consists of precisely two components).

As an immediate consequence of Theorem 5.6 in [4], we get the following digital Jordan curve theorem for the Khalimsky plane $(\mathbb{Z}^2, f_2(R \otimes R))$: A circle C in the graph G_2 is a Jordan curve in the Khalimsky plane if and only if it does not turn, at any of its points, under the acute angle $\frac{\pi}{4}$.

For every natural number $n > 2$, we define (*digital*) Jordan curves in $(\mathbb{Z}^2, f_n(R \otimes R))$ to be just the circles C in G_n that separate $(\mathbb{Z}^2, f_n(R \otimes R))$ into precisely two components. Now the problem arises to determine, for every $n > 2$, those circles in G_n that are Jordan curves in $(\mathbb{Z}^2, f_n(R \otimes R))$. The following statement gives a solution of the problem.

Theorem 1. *Every circle in G_n that does not turn at any of the points $((2k + 1)(n-1), (2l+1)(n-1))$, $k, l \in \mathbb{Z}$, is a Jordan curve in $(\mathbb{Z}^2, f_n(R \otimes R))$ whenever $n > 2$.*

Sketch of Proof. In the graph G_n, every square $\{(p, q) \in \mathbb{Z}^2; \ 2kn \leq p \leq 2(k + 1)n, \ 2ln \leq q \leq 2(l+1)n\}$, $k, l \in \mathbb{Z}$, gives rise to four right triangles - the perimeter of each of them consists of a diagonal and a pair of neighboring sides of the square. These triangles will be called fundamental. It may easily be shown that every fundamental triangle is connected and, if we subtract from a fundamental triangle some of its sides, then the remaining set is still connected. One may also see that every connected subset of $\mathbb{Z}^2$ with at most two points is a subset of a fundamental triangle. It is obvious that every circle in G_n that does not turn at any of the points $((2k + 1)(n - 1), (2l + 1)(n - 1))$, $k, l \in \mathbb{Z}$, is a perimeter of a polygon which is the union of a finite set $\mathcal{T}$ of fundamental triangles such that every triangle $T \in \mathcal{T}$ has the property that any of its sides is also a side of another triangle belonging to $\mathcal{T}$ or is a side of the polygon (hence, a subset of the perimeter). These facts are used to prove the statement. $\square$

In consequence of Theorem 1, the closure operators $f_n(R \otimes R)$, $n > 2$, may be used as background structures on $\mathbb{Z}^2$ for the study of digital images. The advantage of using these closure operators instead of the Khalimsky topology $f_2(R \otimes R)$ is that the Jordan curves with respect to them, i.e., circles in G_n, may turn under the acute angle $\frac{\pi}{4}$ at some points - see the following example:

Example 1. Consider the set of points of $\mathbb{Z}^2$ demonstrated in Fig. 4, which represents the (border of) letter M. This set is not a Jordan curve in the Khalimsky plane $(\mathbb{Z}^2, f_2(R \otimes R))$. For it to be a Jordan curve in the Khalimsky plane, we have to delete the eight points that are ringed. But that would cause a certain deformation (loss of sharpness) of the letter. On the other hand, the set is a circle in the graph G_3 satisfying the assumption of Theorem 1 1 and, therefore, it is a Jordan curve in $(\mathbb{Z}^2, f_3(R \otimes R))$.

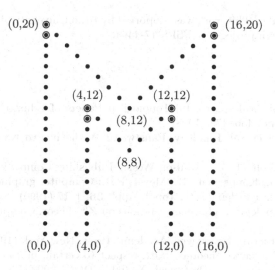

Fig. 4. A digital image of M.

3 Conclusion

Digital images may be regarded as approximations of real ones and so, to be able to study them, we need to provide the digital plane (and, more generally, digital space) with a structure that would conveniently model the Euclidean plane (Euclidean space). For the digital plane, an important criterion of such a convenience is the validity of a digital analogue of the Jordan curve theorem. In two-dimensional digital images, digital Jordan curves represent borders of objects. In this paper we associated a closure operator with each n-ary relation on a given set ($n > 1$ an integer). For every integer $n > 1$, we introduced a particular n-ary relation R on the digital line $\mathbb{Z}$ and focused on the closure operator $f_n(R \otimes R)$ on the digital plane $\mathbb{Z}^2$ associated with a special product $R \otimes R$ of two copies of R. By Theorem 1, the closure operators $f_n(R \otimes R)$ satisfy a digital analogue of the Jordan curve theorem so that they may be used as convenient backgrounds (connectedness models) on the digital plane $\mathbb{Z}^2$ for studying and processing of digital images. For $n = 2$, we obtain the well-known Khalimsky topology on $\mathbb{Z}^2$. An advantage of the closure operators $f_n(R \otimes R)$ with $n > 2$ over the Khalimsky topology is that Jordan curves with respect to them may turn under the acute angle $\frac{\pi}{4}$ so that they provide a more flexible variety of Jordan curves than the Khalimsky topology.

Our further research will be focused on proving a generalization of the Jordan curve theorem formulated in Theorem 1 to digital spaces of all dimensions greater than 1, i.e., to the closure spaces $(\mathbb{Z}^m, f_n(\underbrace{R \otimes \ldots \otimes R}_{m-times}))$ with $m > 1$. In particular, we will aim to obtaining a digital version of the Jordan curve theorem for $m = 3$ (the so-called Jordan-Brouwer separation theorem).

Acknowledgments. This work was supported by Brno University of Technology from the Specific Research project no. FSI-S-17-4464.

References

1. Čech, E.: Topological spaces. In: Topological Papers of Eduard Čech. Academia, Prague ch. 28, pp. 436–472 (1968)
2. Engelking, R.: General Topology. Państwowe Wydawnictwo Naukowe, Warszawa (1977)
3. Harrary, F.: Graph Theory. Addison-Wesley Publishing Company, Reading (1969)
4. Khalimsky, E.D., Kopperman, R., Meyer, P.R.: Computer graphics and connected topologies on finite ordered sets. Topol. Appl. **36**, 1–17 (1990)
5. Kong, T.Y.: Topological adjacency relations on Z^n. Theor. Comput. Sci. **283**, 3–28 (2002)
6. Rosenfeld, A.: Picture Languages. Academic Press, New York (1979)
7. Šlapal, J.: Jordan curve theorems with respect to certain pretopologies on $\mathbb{Z}^2$. In: Brlek, S., Reutenauer, C., Provençal, X. (eds.) DGCI 2009. LNCS, vol. 5810, pp. 252–262. Springer, Heidelberg (2009). https://doi.org/10.1007/978-3-642-04397-0_22
8. Šlapal, J.: Convenient closure operators on $\mathbb{Z}^2$. In: Wiederhold, P., Barneva, R.P. (eds.) IWCIA 2009. LNCS, vol. 5852, pp. 425–436. Springer, Heidelberg (2009). https://doi.org/10.1007/978-3-642-10210-3_33
9. Šlapal, J.: Graphs with a path partition for structuring digital spaces. Inf. Sci. **233**, 305–312 (2013)

Maximal P-simple Sets on (8,4) Pictures

Péter Kardos[✉] and Kálmán Palágyi

University of Szeged, Szeged, Hungary
{pkardos,palagyi}@inf.u-szeged.hu

Abstract. Bertrand proposed the notion of a P-simple set for constructing topology-preserving reductions. In this paper, we define the maximalness of a P-simple set, give a new sufficient condition for topology-preserving reductions acting on (8,4) pictures on the square grid, and it is proved that this condition designates a maximal P-simple set.

Keywords: Digital geometry · Topology preservation · P-simple set

1 Introduction

A binary picture on a grid is a mapping that assigns a color of black or white to each grid element called point. A regular partitioning of the 2D Euclidean space is formed by a tessellation of regular polygons [8,9]. In this work, our attention is focused only on the square grid. A reduction transforms a binary picture only by changing some black points to white ones which is referred to as deletion [3]. Reductions are mostly used in thinning algorithms which iteratively peel the boundary of objects to extract skeleton-like shape features in a topology-preserving way [2,7,8]. An important notion called P-simple set was introduced by Bertrand [1]. He showed that the deletion of arbitrary P-simple sets provides a topology-preserving reduction. His approach makes us possible not only to verify topological correctness but also to design parallel thinning algorithms. However, it remains still an open question how can we find a 'maximal' P-simple set in a picture, i.e., a P-simple set that cannot be extended with any other point such that the resulting set is still P-simple. By deleting a maximal P-simple set in each iteration step of a thinning algorithm we could produce a 'minimal' skeleton-like shape feature in a topology-preserving way. The aim of this work is to answer the above question. We give a new sufficient condition for topology-preserving reductions, and we prove that this condition yields a maximal P-simple set.

2 Basic Notions and Results

In this paper, we apply the fundamental concepts of digital topology as reviewed by Kong and Rosenfeld [8].

The elements of the 2D digital space $\mathbb{Z}^2$ are called *points*, which can be represented by the elements of the square grid due to its duality to $\mathbb{Z}^2$. Two

© Springer Nature Switzerland AG 2019
R. P. Barneva et al. (Eds.): CompIMAGE 2018, LNCS 10986, pp. 23–32, 2019.
https://doi.org/10.1007/978-3-030-20805-9_3

points are 4-*adjacent* if they share an edge and they are 8-*adjacent* if they share an edge or a vertex, see Fig. 1. A point p is j-adjacent to a non-empty set of points X if there is a point $q \in X$ such that p and q are j-adjacent. Let us denote by $N_j(p)$ the set of points being j-adjacent to a point p in $\mathbb{Z}^2$, and let $N_j^*(p) = N_j(p) \setminus \{p\}$ $(j = 4, 8)$.

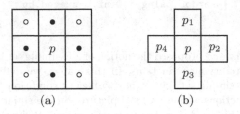

(a)   (b)

Fig. 1. The studied two adjacency relations on the square grid (a). Points that are 4-adjacent to the central point p are marked "•", while points being 8-adjacent but not 4-adjacent to p are depicted by "∘". Distinct notations of the four points in $N_4^*(p)$ (b).

A sequence of distinct points $\langle p_0, p_1, \ldots, p_m \rangle$ is called a j-*path* from p_0 to p_m in a non-empty set of points $X \subseteq \mathbb{Z}^2$ if each point of the sequence is in X and p_i is j-adjacent to p_{i-1} for each $i = 1, 2, \ldots, m$. Two points are said to be j-*connected* in a set X if there is a j-path in X between them. A set of points X is j-*connected* in the set of points $Y \supseteq X$ if any two points in X are j-connected in Y. A j-*component* of a set of points X is a maximal (with respect to inclusion) j-connected subset of X.

An (8,4) *binary digital picture* is a quadruple $(\mathbb{Z}^2, 8, 4, B)$ [8], where set $\mathbb{Z}^2$ contains all points of the considered grid, $B \subseteq \mathbb{Z}^2$ denotes the set of *black points*, and each point in $\mathbb{Z}^2 \setminus B$ is said to be a *white point*. A *black component* or *object* is an 8-component of B, while a *white component* is a 4-component of $\mathbb{Z}^2 \setminus B$. An object is said to be *small*, if it is composed of mutually 8-adjacent points but it is not constituted by an isolated point or by two 4-adjacent points, see Fig. 2.

The *lexicographical order relation* $\prec$ between two distinct points $p = (p_x, p_y)$ and $q = (q_x, q_y)$ is defined as follows:

$$p \prec q \quad \Leftrightarrow \quad p_y < q_y \lor (p_y = q_y \land p_x < q_x).$$

Let $Q \subset \mathbb{Z}^2$. Then, point $p \in Q$ is the *smallest element* of Q if for any $q \in Q \setminus \{p\}$, $p \prec q$. The smallest elements of the possible small objects are indicated in Fig. 2.

A black point is said to be a *border point* if it is 4-adjacent to at least one white point. Furthermore, a border point p is called an m-*border point* $(m \in 1, 2, 3, 4)$ if m is the lowest index such that $p_m \in \mathbb{Z}^2 \setminus B$ (see Figs. 1b and 3). By careful examination of the configurations depicted in Fig. 3, we can state the following property of m-border points:

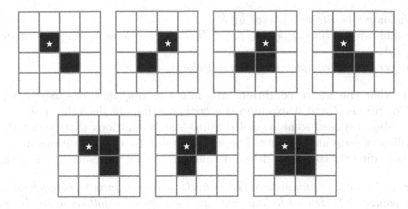

Fig. 2. All the seven possible small objects. Their smallest elements (with respect to relation $\prec$) of them are marked stars.

Proposition 1. *If a point is m-border, then it is not n-border for* $m \neq n$ $(m, n = 1, 2, 3, 4)$.

A border point p is called an *isolated point* if all points in $N_8^*(p)$ are white (i.e., $\{p\}$ is a singleton object).

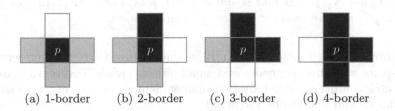

(a) 1-border   (b) 2-border   (c) 3-border   (d) 4-border

Fig. 3. The four types of border points. Points depicted in gray can be either black or white points. Note that such a three-color configuration having n gray elements represents a set of 2^n binary configurations (having only black and white positions). For example, there are $2^3 = 8$ kinds of 1-border points, as configuration (a) contains three gray positions.

A 2D reduction is *topology-preserving* if each object in the input picture contains exactly one object in the output picture, and each white component in the output picture contains exactly one white component in the input picture [8]. A black point is said to be *simple* for a set of black points (or in a picture) if its deletion is a topology-preserving reduction [7,8].

For (8,4) pictures, the authors gave the following sufficient conditions for topology-preserving reductions [4]. Note that it is a simplified version of Ronse's result [10].

Theorem 1. [4] *A reduction* $\mathcal{R}$ *is topology-preserving, if all of the following conditions hold for any picture* $(\mathbb{Z}^2, 8, 4, B)$.

1. *Only simple points are deleted by* $\mathcal{R}$.
2. *For any two 4-adjacent points,* $p, q \in B$ *that are deleted by* $\mathcal{R}$, *p is simple for* $B \setminus \{q\}$.
3. $\mathcal{R}$ *never deletes completely any small object.*

Note that the above condition falls into the *configuration-based* category since Conditions 2 and 3 examine the configurations of deletable points. The authors also proposed some so-called *point-based* conditions that deal with the deletability of individual points. The following point-based conditions make use possible to directly construct deletion rules for topology-preserving algorithms:

Theorem 2. [5] *For any picture* $(\mathbb{Z}^2, 8, 4, B)$, *a reduction is topology-preserving if each point* $p \in B$ *deleted by that reduction satisfies the following conditions:*

1. *Point p is simple for B.*
2. *For any* $q \in N_4^*(p) \cap B$ *that is simple for B, p is simple for* $B \backslash \{q\}$.
3. *Point p does not belong to a small object.*

Theorem 3. [5] *For any picture* $(\mathbb{Z}^2, 8, 4, B)$, *a reduction is topology-preserving if each point* $p \in B$ *deleted by that reduction satisfies the following conditions:*

1. *Point p is simple for B.*
2. *For any* $q \in N_4^*(p) \cap B$ *that is simple for B, p is simple for* $B \backslash \{q\}$, *or* $q \prec p$.
3. *Point p is not the smallest element of a small object.*

Theorem 2 offers a *symmetric* condition, since it ensures the total preservation of two-point wide line segments and small objects, while Theorem 3 states an *asymmetric* condition, since only the smallest elements of the sets considered in Conditions 2 and 3 are to be preserved.

In order to construct topology-preserving reductions and provide a verification method, Bertrand introduced the notion of a *P-simple set*:

Definition 1. [1] *Let* $Q \subset B$ *be a set of black points in a picture. A set* Q *is called a P-simple set if any point* $q \in Q$ *is simple for* $B \setminus R$ *for any* $R \subseteq Q \setminus \{q\}$. *Furthermore, the elements in a P-simple set are called P-simple points.*

Bertrand's approach provides the following sufficient condition for topology preservation:

Theorem 4. [1] *A reduction that deletes a P-simple set is topology-preserving.*

The authors of this paper presented both formal and easily visualized local characterizations of P-simple points for (8,4) pictures [6]. Furthermore, they linked the concept of P-simplicity with their configuration-based condition:

Theorem 5. [5] *A reduction satisfies all conditions of Theorem 1 if and only if it deletes only P-simple points.*

Notice that there may be numerous P-simple sets in a picture. That is why we introduce the concept of a maximal P-simple set:

Definition 2. *A P-simple set $Q \subset B$ is a* maximal P-simple set *for B if for any $q \in (B \setminus Q)$, $Q \cup \{q\}$ is not a P-simple set for B.*

Here we note that both reductions that delete all points satisfying the above mentioned symmetric and asymmetric conditions (see Theorems 2 and 3) do not guarantee the deletion of maximal P-simple sets. As a counterexample to show this, let us consider the two-point wide diagonal line segment shown in Fig. 4.

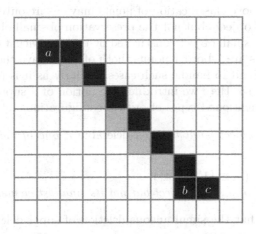

Fig. 4. A counterexample to demonstrate that both reductions that delete all points satisfying the conditions of Theorems 2 and 3 do not determine maximal P-simple sets. A reduction fulfilling the symmetric condition deletes only points a and c, while the asymmetric condition allows only the deletion of points a, b, and c. Note that all points in this object are simple, and if we expand the set $\{a, b, c\}$ with any subsets of points depicted in gray, then the resulting set remains P-simple.

3   A New Sufficient Condition

In this section we introduce an asymmetric point-based condition for topology-preserving reductions acting on (8,4) pictures that rests on the classification of simple border points into four groups with different priorities. Let p be a simple m-border point ($m \in \{1, 2, 3, 4\}$). The lower m is, the higher priority is assigned to p. If p has the highest priority among all points in $N_4(p)$, then it can be safely deleted. However, if there is one or more simple points in $N_4^*(p)$ that have higher priority than p, then we must further examine the neighborhood of those points. A typical critical configuration in an (8,4) binary picture is constituted by two 4-adjacent simple points, whose complete deletion would lead to splitting an object. We make use of the following notion to unambiguously decide which points can be deleted in such cases.

Definition 3. *Let p be a simple m-border point in picture $(\mathbb{Z}^2, 8, 4, B)$ ($m \in \{1, 2, 3, 4\}$). Point p is m-deletable, if for any $1 \leq n < m$ and any simple n-border point $q \in N_4^*(p)$, p is simple for $B \setminus \{q\}$ or q is not n-deletable.*

The following two statements are easy consequences of Definition 3.

Proposition 2. *If a point is m-deletable, then it is not n-deletable for $m \neq n$ ($m, n = 1, 2, 3, 4$).*

Proposition 3. *A 1-border simple point is 1-deletable.*

Note that the above classification of points may ensure only the preservation of connectedness of objects but not the preservation of small objects. Let us, for instance, consider a small object constituted by two 8-adjacent object points. As both of those points are 1-border points, both of them have the highest priority for deletion. We intend to handle such cases similarly as it is regulated in Condition 3 of Theorem 5. Here we introduce the notion of a super-deletable point which takes both mentioned types of critical configurations into consideration:

Definition 4. *An object point is super-deletable if one of the following conditions hold:*

1. *It is m-deletable ($m \in \{1, 2, 3, 4\}$).*
2. *It is an element of a small object but not its smallest element.*

First we show that the simultaneous deletion of super-deletable points preserves topology.

Theorem 6. *A reduction is topology-preserving if it deletes only super-deletable points.*

Proof. Let $\mathcal{R}$ be a reduction that deletes only super-deletable pixels. It is sufficient to prove that all conditions of Theorem 1 hold.

- By Definition 3, all points that satisfy Condition 1 of Definition 4 are simple. If p fulfills Condition 2 of Definition 4, then, by examining the 3×3 neighborhood of p, it can be seen that p is a simple point. If p is an isolated point, then it is not simple and it is also the smallest element of the object, hence it is not super-deletable. Thus, $\mathcal{R}$ deletes only simple points, which means that Condition 1 of Theorem 1 is satisfied.
- Let us assume that $\mathcal{R}$ deletes the set of two 4-adjacent points $\{p, q\}$ such that p is not simple for $B \setminus \{q\}$. Both points p and q may be elements of a small object only if that object is formed by these two points, or else p would be simple for $B \setminus \{q\}$. One of these points is the smallest element of the object, which is not deleted by $\mathcal{R}$. However, this is not possible, therefore, Condition 2 of Definition 4 may not hold for p and q, hence Condition 1 is satisfied, i.e., p and q are m_p-deletable and m_q-deletable points, respectively ($m_p, m_q \in \{1, 2, 3, 4\}$). If $m_p = m_q$, then, by examining the arrangement of points in $N_4^*(p)$ and $N_4^*(q)$, we can observe that the deletion of p does not

influence the simplicity of q and vice versa, thus p is simple for $B \setminus \{q\}$, which contradicts our initial assumption. Therefore $m_p \neq m_q$. Without loss of generality, we can suppose that $m_p > m_q$. By Definition 3, p is simple for $B \setminus \{q\}$ or q is not m_q-deletable. The first of these two situations contradicts the initial assumption on set $\{p, q\}$, the other one is a contradiction with the m_q-deletable property of q. Hence, $\mathcal{R}$ does not delete completely the set $\{p, q\}$. Therefore, $\mathcal{R}$ satisfies Condition 2 of Theorem 1.

- By Definitions 3 and 4, super-deletable points being not m-deletable are not the smallest element of any small object, and m-deletable points cannot be elements of small objects. Hence $\mathcal{R}$ fulfills Condition 3 of Theorem 1.   □

Lastly, we state the main theorem of this paper.

Theorem 7. *Let Q denote the set of super-deletable points of an (8,4) picture. Then Q is a maximal P-simple set in this picture.*

Proof. Let B be the set of black points in an (8,4) picture, and let $\mathcal{R}$ be a reduction that deletes Q. In the proof of the previous theorem we saw that $\mathcal{R}$ satisfies the conditions of Theorem 1, hence by Theorem 5, Q is a P-simple set of the picture.

To prove the maximality of Q, let us indirectly suppose that set $Q \cup \{q\}$ is P-simple for a point $q \in B \setminus Q$. By Definition 1, q is a simple point, hence it is an m-border point ($m \in \{1, 2, 3, 4\}$). As $\mathcal{R}$ does not delete q, point q does not satisfy any condition of Definition 4. Thus, q is not m-deletable, and it may only be the smallest element of a small object. However, in the latter case, $\mathcal{R}$ deletes every point besides p, which means that the deletion of set $Q \cup \{q\}$ would cause the removal of an object, and this would contradict the P-simplicity of this set. As q is not m-deletable and not an element of a small object, by Definition 4, q is not a 1-border point (i.e., $m > 1$), and there exists an n-deletable ($n < m$) simple point $r \in N_4^*(q)$ such that q is not simple for $B \setminus \{r\}$. The n-deletable property of r implies that $r \in Q$. However, by Definition 1, this contradicts the P-simplicity of set $Q \cup \{q\}$.   □

Let us compare the different behaviours of reductions derived from the symmetric, asymmetric and the super-deletable point-based conditions through an example. Let $\mathcal{R}_1$ and $\mathcal{R}_2$ be the reductions that delete all points satisfying the conditions of Theorems 4 or 5, respectively, and let $\mathcal{R}_3$ be the reduction that deletes all super-deletable points. In Fig. 5 we can observe the difference of these reductions on a small (8,4) binary picture.

Lastly, let us examine the support of $\mathcal{R}_3$ (i.e. the minimal sets of points whose values determine the super-deletable property):

- Let p be a point in picture $(\mathbb{Z}^2, 8, 4, B)$. The simplicity of p can be decided by investigating the set $N_8^*(p)$, i.e. the 3×3 neighborhood of p [8].
- It is easy to see that the support for the detection of elements of small objects covers the 5×5 neighbourhood of p, which coincides with the support of $\mathcal{R}_1$ (see Fig. 6a), while detection of non-small elements of small objects (i.e. the points that fulfill Condition 2 of Definition 4) requires the smaller support of $\mathcal{R}_2$ (see Fig. 6b).

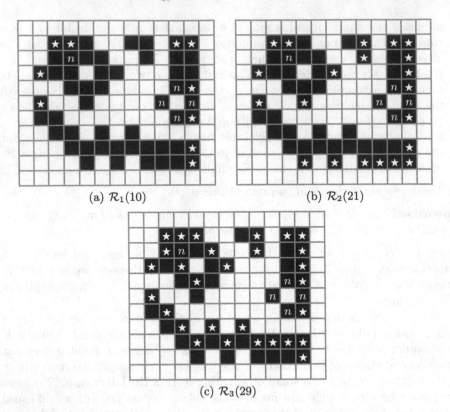

(a) $\mathcal{R}_1(10)$ (b) $\mathcal{R}_2(21)$

(c) $\mathcal{R}_3(29)$

Fig. 5. Comparison of reductions $\mathcal{R}_1$ (a), $\mathcal{R}_2$ (b), and $\mathcal{R}_3$ (c) for an (8,4) picture, where non-marked black points are non-deletable simple points. Deleted points and non-simple points are marked stars and 'n', respectively. Numbers in parentheses mean the count of deletable points. Note that all the three sets of deletable points are P-simple ones, but only the third one is a maximal P-simple set.

- Let us focus on Condition 1 of Definition 4. For 1-border points, this condition is equivalent to the simplicity of p (see Definition 2 and Proposition 3). For 2-, 3-, and 4-border points, we must also take into account the sequences $\langle p = p^1, p^2, \dots, p^s \rangle$ of at least two simple border points such that the following conditions hold:

  ○ p^s is super-deletable,
  ○ p^i is 4-adjacent to p^{i+1} $(0 \le i < s)$,
  ○ p^i is not simple for $B \setminus \{p^{i+1}\}$, and
  ○ if p^i is an m_i-border point, then $m_i > m_{i+1}$.

Let us call such structures *critical sequences*. It is obvious from the above definition that the last point in such a sequence directly or indirectly influences the super-deletable property of p. Note that critical sequences may contain at most four points, due to the four different types of border points. If the length of the sequence is two (i.e., $s = 2$), then we must only verifiy if p^1 is simple for $B \setminus \{p^2\}$, which can be done by the investigation of the points in

$N_8(p^1) \cup N_8(p^2)$. We note that for reductions $\mathcal{R}_1$ and $\mathcal{R}_2$, the investigation of such cases does not require larger support than the above mentioned ones for detecting the (smallest) elements of small objects. Thus, the verification of Conditions 2 and 3 of Theorems 2 and 3 can be carried out with the supports in Fig. 6a and b, respectively. However, unlike $\mathcal{R}_1$ and $\mathcal{R}_2$, $\mathcal{R}_3$ also handles the possible situations for $s = 3$ and $s = 4$, which are shown in Fig. 7.

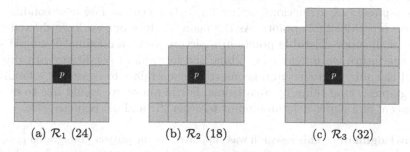

(a) $\mathcal{R}_1$ (24)   (b) $\mathcal{R}_2$ (18)   (c) $\mathcal{R}_3$ (32)

Fig. 6. The supports of the three discussed reductions derived from point-based conditions. Numbers in parentheses mean the count of points in the supports.

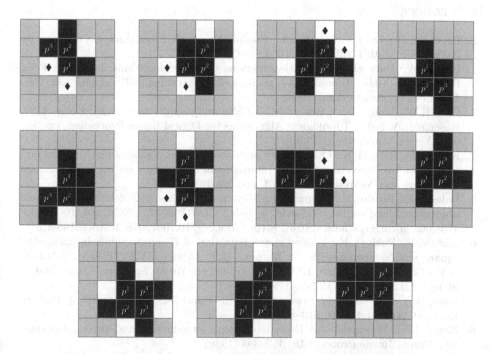

Fig. 7. The possible cases when $p = p^1$ is an element of a critical sequence with the length of three or four points. At least one of the points marked ♦ is white. Points shown in gray can be either black or white as long as they do not influence the simplicity of the points marked p^i.

Taking all of the above statements into consideration, we can conclude that the support for detecting super-deletable points (i.e., the support of $\mathcal{R}_3$) contains 32 elements in the arrangement as shown in Fig. 6c.

4   Conclusions

In this paper we proposed an asymmetric point-based sufficient condition for topology-preserving reductions acting on (8,4) pictures. The new condition is based on super-deletable points. As the main result of our work we showed that the set of all super-deletable points in a picture forms a maximal P-simple set.

In the future we intend to combine the introduced condition with diverse parallel thinning strategies and geometrical constraints to construct a family of topology-preserving thinning algorithms. Furthermore, we would like to extend the concept of a super-deletable point to other 2D and 3D regular grids.

Acknowledgments. This research was supported by the project "Integrated program for training new generation of scientists in the fields of computer science", no EFOP-3.6.3-VEKOP-16-2017-0002. The project has been supported by the European Union and co-funded by the European Social Fund.

References

1. Bertrand, G.: On P-simple points. Compte Rendu de l'Académie des Sciences de Paris, Série Math **I**(321), 1077–1084 (1995)
2. Hall, R.W.: Parallel connectivity-preserving thinning algorithms. In: Kong, T.Y., Rosenfeld, A. (eds.) Topological Algorithms for Digital Image Processing, pp. 145–179. Elsevier, Amsterdam (1996)
3. Hall, R.W., Kong, T.Y., Rosenfeld, A.: Shrinking binary images. In: Kong, T.Y., Rosenfeld, A. (eds.) Topological Algorithms for Digital Image Processing, pp. 31–98. Elsevier, Amsterdam (1996)
4. Kardos, P., Palágyi, K.: On topology preservation in triangular, square, and hexagonal grids. In: Proceedings of 8th International Symposium on Image and Signal Processing and Analysis, ISPA 2013, pp. 782–787 (2013)
5. Palágyi, K., Kardos, P.: A single-step 2D thinning scheme with deletion of P-simple points. In: Mendoza, M., Velastín, S. (eds.) CIARP 2017. LNCS, vol. 10657, pp. 475–482. Springer, Cham (2018). https://doi.org/10.1007/978-3-319-75193-1_57
6. Kardos, P., Palágyi, K.: Unified characterization of P-simple points in triangular, square, and hexagonal grids. In: Barneva, R.P., Brimkov, V.E., Tavares, J.M.R.S. (eds.) CompIMAGE 2016. LNCS, vol. 10149, pp. 79–88. Springer, Cham (2017). https://doi.org/10.1007/978-3-319-54609-4_6
7. Kong, T.Y.: On topology preservation in 2-D and 3-D thinning. Int. J. Pattern Recognit. Artif. Intell. **9**, 813–844 (1995)
8. Kong, T.Y., Rosenfeld, A.: Digital topology: introduction and survey. Comput. Vis. Graph. Image Process. **48**, 357–393 (1989)
9. Marchand-Maillet, S., Sharaiha, Y.M.: Binary Digital Image Processing - A Discrete Approach. Academic Press, New York (2000)
10. Ronse, C.: Minimal test patterns for connectivity preservation in parallel thinning algorithms for binary digital images. Discrete Appl. Math. **21**, 67–79 (1988)

An Immersed Boundary Approach for the Numerical Analysis of Objects Represented by Oriented Point Clouds

László Kudela[1]([⊠]), Stefan Kollmannsberger[1], and Ernst Rank[1,2]

[1] Chair for Computation in Engineering, Technische Universität München,
Arcisstr. 21, 80333 München, Germany
laszlo.kudela@tum.de
[2] Institute for Advanced Study, Technische Universität München,
München, Germany

Abstract. This contribution presents a method for numerical analysis of solids whose boundaries are represented by oriented point clouds. In contrast to standard finite elements that require a boundary-conforming discretization of the domain of interest, our approach works directly on the point cloud representation of the geometry. This is achieved by combining the inside-outside information that is inferred from the members of the point cloud with a high order immersed boundary technique. This allows for avoiding the challenging task of surface fitting and mesh generation, simplifying the image-based analysis pipeline drastically. We demonstrate by a numerical example how the proposed method can be applied in the context of linear elastostatic analysis of solids.

Keywords: Image-based finite element analysis · Point clouds · Finite Cell Method

1 Introduction

A core challenge in the context of image-based finite element analysis revolves around the question of how to derive an analysis-suitable finite element model from the point cloud data that describes the shape of the domain of interest. Examples include the structural analysis of statues [5], historical structures [2,3, 20] and the coupling of finite element computations to *in vitro* measurements of biological tissues [15]. In order to construct a finite-element mesh that resolves the boundaries of the geometry, the usual approach is to process the point cloud data through a multi-step pipeline that results in a mesh of boundary-conforming finite elements. Generally, the main steps of such cloud-to-analysis pipelines can be characterized as follows:

1. *Geometry recovery*
   A geometric model is derived from the point cloud information using geometric segmentation and surface fitting techniques.

© Springer Nature Switzerland AG 2019
R. P. Barneva et al. (Eds.): CompIMAGE 2018, LNCS 10986, pp. 33–41, 2019.
https://doi.org/10.1007/978-3-030-20805-9_4

2. *Mesh generation*
   Once the geometric representation of the object is recovered, the model is subdivided into a set of boundary-conforming finite elements.
3. *Finite Element Analysis*
   The mesh from the previous step together with the necessary material parameters and boundary conditions is handed over to a finite element solver.

These steps are difficult to automate, as a solution which is tailored to a specific class of geometries is usually not directly applicable on other types of objects. Moreover, because the pipeline requires the interplay of many techniques from computational science and engineering, the analyst performing the above steps needs to be experienced with a wide variety of softwares and has to be aware of their respective pitfalls. For example, even if the geometry of the object is available through a CAD model, the preparation of an analysis-suitable finite element mesh may require a great amount of human interaction and can take up to 80% of the total analysis time [7].

In recent years, research efforts aiming at avoiding the difficult task of mesh generation brought forth many approaches, such as the Finite Cell Method (FCM) introduced in [17]. The FCM relies on the combination of approaches well-known in computational mechanics: immersed boundary (IB) methods [18] and high-order finite elements (p-FEM) [26]. While initially suffering from low accuracy and high computational costs, IB methods have seen a complete revival in recent years. New numerical technologies addressing issues related to discretization [25], stability [6,19], boundary conditions [21] and numerical integration [11,14,16] allowed for the application of IB approaches in non-trivial fields. Examples include geometrically non-linear problems [24], plasticity [1], simulation of biomechanical structures [9], flow problems [29] and contact simulation [4].

Instead of generating a boundary-conforming discretization, FCM extends the physical domain of interest by a so-called fictitious domain, such that their union forms a simple bounding box that can be meshed easily. To keep the consistency with the original problem, the material parameters in the fictitious domain are penalized by a small factor α. The introduction of α shifts the analysis effort from mesh generation to numerical integration. The biggest advantage of the FCM lies in high convergence rates with almost no meshing costs.

In its simplest implementation, the only information that FCM needs from a geometric model is inside-outside state: given a point in space, does this point lie in the physical or the fictitious part of the domain? A wide variety of geometric representations is able to provide such *point membership tests* and have been shown to work well in combination with the FCM, ranging from simple shapes to models as complex as metal foams.

In this contribution, the Finite Cell Method is combined with geometries that are represented by oriented point clouds. The members of the point cloud and the vectors associated to them provide enough information for point membership tests, allowing for simulating objects directly on their cloud representation. This way, the tedious tasks of recovering a geometric model and generating a boundary conforming mesh can be avoided. This allows for significant simplifications in the cloud-to-analysis pipeline.

2 The Finite Cell Method Combined with Oriented Point Clouds

In the following, the essential ideas of the Finite Cell Method for steady linear elastic problems are discussed. For further details, see [8,17].

2.1 A Brief Overview of FCM

As mentioned in the introduction, the FCM aims at circumventing the problem of mesh generation by extending the boundaries of the physical domain of interest Ω_{phy} by a fictitious part Ω_{fict}. The union of these two parts $\Omega_{\text{phy}} \cup \Omega_{\text{fict}}$ forms the embedding domain $\Omega_{\cup}$. This possesses a simple, box-like geometry that can be meshed easily. The concept is depicted in Fig. 1.

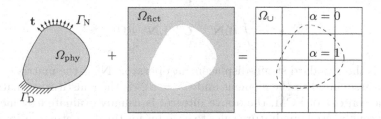

Fig. 1. The core concept of the FCM. The physical domain Ω_{phy} is extended by the fictitious domain Ω_{fict}. Their union, the embedding domain $\Omega_{\cup}$ can be meshed easily. The influence of the fictitious domain is penalized by the scaling factor α.

The derivation of FCM is based on the principle of virtual work [13]:

$$\delta W(\mathbf{u}, \delta\mathbf{u}) = \int_{\Omega} \boldsymbol{\sigma} : (\nabla_{\text{sym}}\delta\mathbf{u}) \, dV - \int_{\Omega_{\text{phy}}} \delta\mathbf{u} \cdot \mathbf{b}dV - \int_{\Gamma_{\text{N}}} \delta\mathbf{u} \cdot \mathbf{t}dA = 0, \quad (1)$$

where $\boldsymbol{\sigma}, \mathbf{b}, \mathbf{u}, \delta\mathbf{u}$ and ∇_{sym} denote the Cauchy stress tensor, the body forces, the displacement vector, the test function and the symmetric part of the gradient, respectively. The traction vector $\mathbf{t}$ specifies the Neumann boundary conditions on Γ_{N}. Stresses and strains are related through the constitutive tensor $\mathbf{C}$:

$$\boldsymbol{\sigma} = \alpha\mathbf{C} : \boldsymbol{\varepsilon}, \quad (2)$$

where α is an indicator function defined as:

$$\alpha(\boldsymbol{x}) = \begin{cases} 1 & \forall \boldsymbol{x} \in \Omega_{phy} \\ 10^{-q} & \forall \boldsymbol{x} \in \Omega_{fict}. \end{cases} \quad (3)$$

In practice, the value of q is chosen between 6 and 12.

Homogeneous Neumann boundary conditions are automatically satisfied by the formulation. Nonhomogeneous Neumann boundary conditions can be realized by evaluating the contour integral over Γ_N in Eq. 1. Dirichlet boundary conditions are generally formulated in the weak sense, e.g. using the penalty method or Nitsche's method [21].

The unknown quantities $\delta\mathbf{u}$ and $\mathbf{u}$ are discretized by a linear combination of N_i shape functions with unknown coefficients $\mathbf{u}_i$:

$$\mathbf{u} = \sum_i N_i \mathbf{u}_i; \; \delta\mathbf{u} = \sum_i N_i \delta\mathbf{u}_i, \tag{4}$$

leading to the discrete finite cell representation:

$$\mathbf{Ku} = \mathbf{f}. \tag{5}$$

In the standard version of FCM, integrated Legendre polynomials known from high-order finite elements are employed as shape functions [8].

The stiffness matrix $\mathbf{K}$ results from a proper assembly of the element stiffness matrices:

$$\mathbf{k}^e = \int_{\Omega^e} [\mathbf{LN}^e]^T C^\alpha [\mathbf{LN}^e] \, d\Omega^e, \tag{6}$$

where $\mathbf{L}$ is the standard strain-displacement operator, $\mathbf{N}^e$ is the matrix of shape functions associated to the element and $C^\alpha = \alpha C$ is the constitutive matrix.

In the context of FCM, the above integral is usually evaluated by means of specially constructed quadrature rules to account for the discontinuous integrand due to the scaling factor α. The most popular method is based on composed Gaussian quadrature rules combined with a recursive subdivision of the elements cut by the boundary of the physical domain. In this process, every intersected element is subdivided into equal subcells, until a pre-defined depth is reached. Quadrature points are then distributed on the domains of the leaf cells of this integration mesh.

To compute the value of C^α for a given quadrature point, the indicator function in Eq. 3 needs to be evaluated. This requires the geometric model that represents Ω_{phy} to provide point-membership tests: given a quadrature point, does this point belong to Ω_{phy} or not? Many geometric representations are able to answer such inside-outside queries and have been successfully applied in combination with the FCM. Examples include voxel models from CT-scans [22], constructive solid geometries [27], boundary representations [16] and STL descriptions [10].

2.2   Point Membership Tests on Oriented Point Clouds

In the context of point cloud based simulations, the domain Ω_{phy} is represented by a set of sample points $\mathbf{p}_i$ and their associated normal vectors $\mathbf{n}_i$. Assuming that no outliers are present, the set of pairs $S = \{\mathbf{p}_i, \mathbf{n}_i\}$ constitute a discrete sampling of the boundary $\partial\Omega_{\text{phy}}$ of the domain.

Each element in S defines a hyperplane that separates the space in two half spaces: the open half-space Ω_i^- lying on the side of the hyperplane where the direction vector $\mathbf{n}_i$ points, and the closed half-space Ω_i^+ lying on the other side. This concept is depicted in Fig. 2. For every $\mathbf{x} \in \Omega_i^+$, the following holds:

$$(\mathbf{p}_i - \mathbf{x}) \cdot \mathbf{n}_i \geq 0. \tag{7}$$

Therefore, to determine whether a quadrature point $\mathbf{q}$ lies inside or outside the domain, it suffices to find the $\mathbf{p}_i$ and the associated $\mathbf{n}_i$ in S that lies closest to $\mathbf{q}$ and evaluate the scalar product of Eq. 7. The algorithm requires an efficient nearest neighbor query. In our examples, we use the k-d tree implementation from the Point Cloud Library [23]. The point membership classification method is summarized in Algorithm 1.

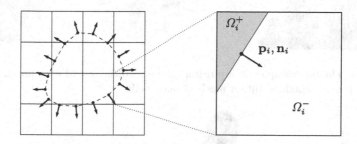

Fig. 2. Point membership classification on oriented point clouds. The domain is represented by a set of points $\mathbf{p}_i$ and associated normals $\mathbf{n}_i$. Every such pair locally separates the space along a hyperplane into two half-spaces: Ω_i^- and Ω_i^+.

Algorithm 1. Point membership test for oriented point clouds

---

1 function isPointInside $(\mathbf{q}, S)$;
    Input   : Quadrature point $\mathbf{q}$ and oriented point cloud $S = \{\mathbf{p}_i, \mathbf{n}_i\}$
    Output: Boolean true if $\mathbf{q}$ lies inside the domain represented by S, false
            otherwise
2 $\mathbf{p}_i, \mathbf{n}_i = \text{getClosestPointInCloud}(\mathbf{q}, S)$;
3 $\mathbf{v} = \mathbf{p}_i - \mathbf{q}$;
4 $d = \mathbf{v} \cdot \mathbf{n}_i$;
5 if $d \geq 0$ then
6 | return true;
7 end
8 return false;

---

3   Numerical Example

To demonstrate how the combination of the FCM and the proposed algorithm can be applied to solve linear elastostatic problems, a statue from the museum

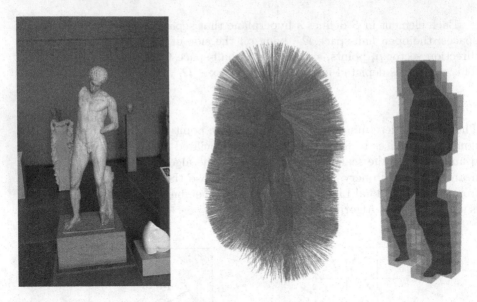

Fig. 3. Linear elastic example: an input image, the resulting cloud with normal vectors and the structure embedded into a mesh of finite cells

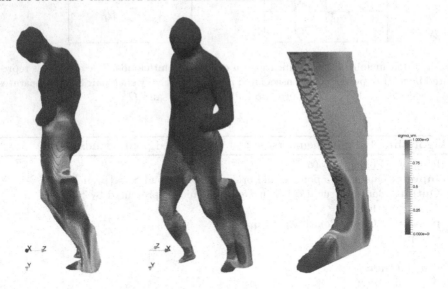

Fig. 4. Linear elastic example: the resulting von Mises stresses over the structure with a cross-sectional view on the left foot

"Glypthotek" in Munich was recorded by a simple cell phone camera from 36 different views. The input images were processed by the popular structure-from-motion toolbox VisualSFM [28], and the multi-view reconstruction algorithm of [12]. The images and the resulting point cloud are depicted in Fig. 3. The cloud was embedded in a regular mesh of 325 finite cells that were using integrated Legendre polynomials of order $p = 5$ for the discretization of the displacement field. The structure was loaded under its own weight and homogeneous Dirichlet (no displacement) boundary conditions were prescribed on the two feet. The value of α was chosen as 10^{-6}. The resulting field of von Mises stresses on the deformed structure is plotted in Fig. 4.

4   Conclusion and Outlook

This contribution presented a method for simulation of objects represented by oriented point clouds. The technique is based on the Finite Cell Method, which, in its simplest implementation, only requires inside-outside information from the geometric model of interest. It was shown that oriented point clouds—if no outliers are present—are able to provide such point membership tests. As demonstrated by a numerical example, this allows for computations in the context of linear elastostatics, without the need for a boundary conforming finite element mesh or the reconstruction of a geometric model. This way, a seamless connection between photogrammetric shape measurements and high order numerical simulations can be established. In an upcoming paper we will report on an extension to more complex boundary conditions and focus on the robustness of the method, in particular on cases, when point clouds include outliers or yield incomplete information of some parts of the surface.

References

1. Abedian, A., Parvizian, J., Düster, A., Rank, E.: The finite cell method for the J2 flow theory of plasticity. Finite Elem. Anal. Des. **69**, 37–47 (2013)
2. Almac, U., Pekmezci, I.P., Ahunbay, M.: Numerical analysis of historic structural elements using 3D point cloud data. Open Constr. Building Technol. J. **10**(1), 233–245 (2016)
3. Barsanti, S.G., Guidi, G., De Luca, L.: Segmentation of 3D models for cultural heritage structural analysis-some critical issues. ISPRS Ann. Photogrammetry Remote Sens. Spatial Inf. Sci. **4**, 115 (2017)
4. Bog, T., Zander, N., Kollmannsberger, S., Rank, E.: Weak imposition of frictionless contact constraints on automatically recovered high-order, embedded interfaces using the finite cell method. Comput. Mech. **61**(4), 385–407 (2018)
5. Borri, A., Grazini, A.: Diagnostic analysis of the lesions and stability of Michelangelo's David. J. Cult. Heritage **7**(4), 273–285 (2006)
6. Burman, E., Claus, S., Hansbo, P., Larson, M.G., Massing, A.: CutFEM: discretizing geometry and partial differential equations. Int. J. Numer. Methods Eng. **104**(7), 472–501 (2015)
7. Cottrell, J.A., Hughes, T.J., Bazilevs, Y.: Isogeometric Analysis: Toward Integration of CAD and FEA. Wiley, London (2009)
8. Düster, A., Rank, E., Szabó, B.: The p-version of the finite element and finite cell methods. Encyclopedia of Computational Mechanics, 2nd edn. Wiley, London (2017)

9. Elhaddad, M., et al.: Multi-level hp-finite cell method for embedded interface problems with application in biomechanics. Int. J. Numer. Methods Biomed. Eng. **34**(4), e2951 (2018)
10. Elhaddad, M., Zander, N., Kollmannsberger, S., Shadavakhsh, A., Nübel, V., Rank, E.: Finite cell method: high-order structural dynamics for complex geometries. Int. J. Struct. Stab. Dyn. **15**, 1540018 (2015)
11. Fries, T.P., Omerović, S.: Higher-order accurate integration of implicit geometries. Int. J. Numer. Methods Eng. **106**(5), 323–371 (2016)
12. Furukawa, Y., Ponce, J.: Accurate, dense, and robust multiview stereopsis. IEEE Trans. Pattern Anal. Mach. Intelli. **32**(8), 1362–1376 (2010)
13. Hughes, T.J.R.: The Finite Element Method: Linear Static and Dynamic Finite Element Analysis. Dover Publications, Mineola (2000)
14. Joulaian, M., Hubrich, S., Düster, A.: Numerical integration of discontinuities on arbitrary domains based on moment fitting. Comput. Mech. **57**(6), 979–999 (2016)
15. Kudela, L., Frischmann, F., Yossef, O.E., Kollmannsberger, S., Yosibash, Z., Rank, E.: Image-based mesh generation of tubular geometries under circular motion in refractive environments. Mach. Vis. Appl. **29**, 719–733 (2018)
16. Kudela, L., Zander, N., Kollmannsberger, S., Rank, E.: Smart octrees: accurately integrating discontinuous functions in 3D. Comput. Methods Appl. Mech. Eng. **306**, 406–426 (2016)
17. Parvizian, J., Düster, A., Rank, E.: Finite cell method. Comput. Mech. **41**(1), 121–133 (2007)
18. Peskin, C.S.: The immersed boundary method. Acta Numerica **11**, 479–517 (2002)
19. de Prenter, F., Verhoosel, C., van Zwieten, G., van Brummelen, E.: Condition number analysis and preconditioning of the finite cell method. Comput. Methods Appl. Mech. Eng. **316**, 297–327 (2017)
20. Riveiro, B., Caamaño, J., Arias, P., Sanz, E.: Photogrammetric 3D modelling and mechanical analysis of masonry arches: an approach based on a discontinuous model of voussoirs. Autom. Constr. **20**(4), 380–388 (2011)
21. Ruess, M., Schillinger, D., Bazilevs, Y., Varduhn, V., Rank, E.: Weakly enforced essential boundary conditions for NURBS-embedded and trimmed NURBS geometries on the basis of the finite cell method. Int. J. Numer. Methods Eng. **95**(10), 811–846 (2013)
22. Ruess, M., Tal, D., Trabelsi, N., Yosibash, Z., Rank, E.: The finite cell method for bone simulations: verification and validation. Biomech. Model. Mechanobiol. **11**(3–4), 425–437 (2012)
23. Rusu, R.B., Cousins, S.: 3D is here: point cloud library (PCL). In: IEEE International Conference on Robotics and Automation (ICRA), Shanghai, China, 9–13 May 2011
24. Schillinger, D., Düster, A., Rank, E.: The hp-d-adaptive finite cell method for geometrically nonlinear problems of solid mechanics. Int. J. Numer. Methods Eng. **89**(9), 1171–1202 (2012)
25. Schillinger, D., Ruess, M., Zander, N., Bazilevs, Y., Düster, A., Rank, E.: Small and large deformation analysis with the p-and B-spline versions of the finite cell method. Comput. Mech. **50**(4), 445–478 (2012)
26. Szabó, B., Düster, A., Rank, E.: The p-version of the finite element method. Encyclopedia of Computational Mechanics. Wiley, London (2004)

27. Wassermann, B., Kollmannsberger, S., Bog, T., Rank, E.: From geometric design to numerical analysis: a direct approach using the finite cell method on constructive solid geometry. Comput. Math. Appl. **74**(7), 1703–1726 (2017)
28. Wu, C., et al.: VisualSFM: a visual structure from motion system (2011)
29. Xu, F., Schillinger, D., Kamensky, D., Varduhn, V., Wang, C., Hsu, M.C.: The tetrahedral finite cell method for fluids: immersogeometric analysis of turbulent flow around complex geometries. Comput. Fluids **141**, 135–154 (2016)

Pure Hexagonal Context-Free Grammars Generating Hexagonal Patterns

Pawan Kumar Patnaik[1(⊠)], Venkata Padmavati Metta[1], Jyoti Singh[2], and D. G. Thomas[3]

[1] Department of Computer Science and Engineering,
Bhilai Institute of Technology, Durg, India
pawanpatnaik37@gmail.com
[2] Chhattisgarh Professional Examination Board, Raipur, India
[3] Department of Mathematics, Saveetha School of Engineering,
SIMATS, Chennai, India

Abstract. A new syntactic model, called pure hexagonal context free grammar is introduced based on the notion of pure two-dimensional context-free grammar. These grammars generate hexagonal picture arrays on triangular grids. We also examine certain closure properties of pure hexagonal context free languages.

Keywords: Hexagonal arrays · Array grammars · Pure grammars · Two-dimensional CFGs

1 Introduction

Picture generation using formal grammars is one of the most explored fields of theoretical computer science. Pattern generation has several applications especially in picture processing and image analysis. Large variety of grammars were used to generate linear, rectangular, 3D, hexagonal pattern. Different formal models for generating hexagonal patterns are introduced and investigated [16,17]. Siromoney and Siromoney [11] proposed grammatical models for generating hexagonal pictures by introducing a very natural notion of "arrowhead catenation" and using left or right linear rules. In [16], properties of hexagonal array grammars containing context free and context sensitive rules are studied. All these models are motivated by the fact that hexagonal arrays on triangular grids can be treated as two-dimensional representations of three-dimensional blocks thus are extensions of grammars generating two dimensional rectangular arrays.

Pure grammars played an important role in the generation of two dimensional rectangular patterns. In [13], pure two-dimensional CFGs are used for generating rectangular patterns. But the limitation of pure 2D picture grammar is that rectangular array can be generated only at the x and y direction.

© Springer Nature Switzerland AG 2019
R. P. Barneva et al. (Eds.): CompIMAGE 2018, LNCS 10986, pp. 42–55, 2019.
https://doi.org/10.1007/978-3-030-20805-9_5

Pure hexagonal context-free grammar generates 3D pattern by rewriting all the symbols in x, y and z direction which can be used in image analysis and bioinformatics. There exist two basic variants of array grammars (i) isometric array grammars in which geometric shape of the rewritten portion of the array is preserved (ii) non-isometric array grammars that can alter the geometric shape. These grammars used table of context free rules and all symbols of the patterns are rewritten in parallel by strings of equal length. In this paper, we discuss pure hexagonal context free grammar which is related to (i). The notion of pure hexagonal context free grammar involves only terminal symbols as in any pure grammar [4] and tables of context free rules. Here we introduce a new hexagonal context free grammar based on pure context free rules, called pure hexagonal context free grammar for hexagonal picture array generation. In this model we allow rewriting from upper left vertex to upper right vertex, upper right to right most vertex and upper left to left most vertex of the hexagonal rewriting unlike the models in [9,10,12]. In [9] a generative two dimensional rectangular array models have been proposed. Special classes of these models where the distinction between terminals and nonterminals are removed, provide for rectangular development array; the hierarchy within these classes has been studied. In [12], a linguistic model to generate matrices (arrays of terminals) have been presented. In [10], parallel/sequential generative models with tables have been introduced and properties studied. We compare the generative power of the family of pure hexagonal context free language with $(r/lr/ll)$. Certain closure properties of this model are also obtained. Pure hexagonal context-free grammar can be applied in the field of image analysis, picture processing and pattern recognition.

This paper is organized as follows. Section 2 introduces hexagonal array, pure hexagonal context free grammar and notions of pure hexagonal context free grammar pertaining to hexagonal array. Section 3 deals with pure hexagonal context free grammar with $(r/lr/ll)$ mode of derivations and provides some illustrative examples and comparison of the generative power of the family of pure hexagonal context free languages with $(r/lr/ll)$. Finally conclusions have been drawn in Sect. 4.

2 Preliminaries

For notions related to formal language theory, we refer to [7,8] and for pure array grammar and pure two - dimensional context free grammar generating picture languages, we refer to [3].

In this section, we review the definitions of hexagonal arrays, pure hexagonal context free grammars and notations of pure hexagonal context free grammars pertaining to hexagonal arrays. The following notations and definition are mainly from [2,11].

We consider a triangular grid made up of lines equally inclined and parallel to three fixed directions (right ($\rightarrow$), lower right ($\searrow$), lower left ($\swarrow$)).

Let Σ be a finite alphabet of symbols. A hexagonal array of symbols of Σ over the triangular grid is a hexagonal pattern over Σ where the x, y and z co-ordinates of each symbol can be fixed.

A regular hexagonal pattern contains equal number of symbols along the edges of the pattern on triangular grid with axis. In this paper we discuss only about regular hexagonal patterns. The set of all hexagonal arrays over the alphabet Σ is represented by Σ^{***H} and the set of all non-empty hexagonal arrays over Σ is denoted by Σ^{+++H}. A hexagonal array language L over Σ is a subset of Σ^{***H}.

A hexagonal picture over the alphabet $\{a, b, c, d, e, f, g\}$ on triangular grid with axis is shown in Fig. 1.

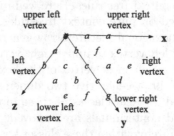

Fig. 1. A regular hexagonal picture p on a traingular grid

The coordinates of each element of the hexagonal picture in Fig. 1 with respect to the triad of triangular axes x, y and z are shown in Fig. 2.

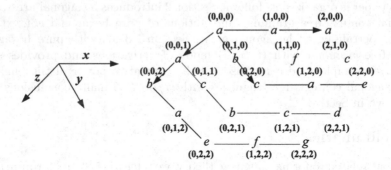

Fig. 2. Coordinates of elements of hexagonal picture of Fig. 2

Given a picture $p \in \Sigma^{+++H}$, let $|p|_x$ denotes the number of elements in the border of p from the upper left vertex to upper right vertex in the x-direction ($\rightarrow$), $|p|_y$ denotes the number of elements in the border of p from the upper right vertex to the right most vertex in the y-direction ($\searrow$) and $|p|_z$ denotes the number of elements in the border of p from the upper left vertex to the left most vertex in the z-direction ($\swarrow$). The triplet ($|p|_x, |p|_y, |p|_z$) is called the size of a hexagonal picture p. The directions are fixed with the origin of reference as the upper left vertex, having co-ordinates $(0,0,0)$. Let $p_{i,j,k}$ denotes the symbol in

p called a pixel, with the coordinates (i, j, k) where $0 \leq i \leq |p|_x, 0 \leq j \leq |p|_y,$
$0 \leq k \leq |p|_z$. Let $\Sigma^{(l,m,n)H}$ be the set of all hexagonal pictures of size (l, m, n).
A typical hexagonal array of size (l, m, n) can be denoted by $[p_{i,j,k}]^{(l,m,n)}$.

Now we define a pure hexagonal context free grammar.

Definition 1. *A pure hexagonal context-free grammar is a 5-tuple $G = (\Sigma, P_r,$*
$P_{lr}, P_{ll}, H_0)$ where

- *Σ is a finite alphabet of symbols*
- *P_r is a finite set of right vertex i.e. P_r denotes the number of elements in the*
  border of p from the upper left vertex to upper right vertex in the x-direction
  $(\rightarrow)$
- *P_{lr} is a finite set of lower right vertex i.e. P_{lr} denotes the number of elements*
  in the border of p from the upper right vertex to the right most vertex in the
  y-direction $(\searrow)$
- *P_{ll} is a finite set of lower left vertex i.e. P_{ll} denotes the number of elements*
  in the border of p from the upper left vertex to the left most vertex in the
  z-direction $(\swarrow)$.

The set of context free rules of the form $a \rightarrow \alpha, a \in \Sigma, \alpha \in \Sigma^{***H}$.

- *$H_0 \subseteq \Sigma^{***H} - \{\Lambda\}$ is a finite set of hexagonal axiom arrays.*

Example 1. Consider a pure hexagonal context free grammar $G_1 = (\Sigma, P_r,$
$P_{lr}, P_{ll}, H_0)$ where $\Sigma = \{a, b, e\}, p_r = \{r\}, p_{lr} = \{lr\}, p_{ll} = \{ll\}$. We consider
only the axiom hexagonal array and the table rules. The axiom hexagonal array
H_0 is shown in Fig. 3. The table rules are given by $r = \{e \rightarrow ea, a \rightarrow a, b \rightarrow bb\}$,
$lr = \{e \searrow ea, a \searrow ab, b \searrow bb\}, ll = \{a \swarrow a, b \swarrow bb, e \swarrow ea\}$.

$$
H_0 \;=\; \begin{matrix} e & & a \\ a & a & b \\ & b & b \end{matrix}
$$

Fig. 3. Axiom hexagonal array

G_1 generates a picture language L_1 consisting of picture arrays p of size
$(l, m + 2, n), l \geq 2, m \geq 0, n \geq 2$ has the following properties: $p(0, 0, 0) =$
$e; p(i, 0, 0) = a$, for $i \geq 1; p(0, j, 0) = a$ for $j = 1; p(0, 0, k) = a$, for $k \geq 1$,
$p(i, j, k) = b$ otherwise. A generated pure hexagonal context free grammar is
shown in Fig. 4.

We note that the element at the top in x direction are $eaa\ldots\ldots$, the elements
in y direction are e_a, the elements in z direction are a^{a^e}, and remaining all
elements are b (Fig. 5).

$$H_0 = \begin{matrix} & e & & a \\ a & & a & & b \\ & b & & b \end{matrix} \overset{r}{\Rightarrow} \begin{matrix} & e & & a & & a \\ a & & a & & b & & b \\ & b & & b & & b \end{matrix} \overset{lr}{\Rightarrow} \begin{matrix} & e & & a & & a \\ a & & a & & b & & b \\ & b & & b & & b & & b \\ & & b & & b & & b \end{matrix} \overset{ll}{\Rightarrow} \begin{matrix} & & e & & a & & a \\ & a & & a & & b & & b \\ a & & b & & b & & b & & b \\ & b & & b & & b & & b \\ & & b & & b & & b \end{matrix}$$

Fig. 4. Sample derivation of a hexagonal picture

$$\begin{matrix} & e & & a & & a \\ & a & & a & & b & & b \\ a & & b & & b & & b & & b \\ & b & & b & & b & & b \\ & & b & & b & & b \end{matrix}$$

Fig. 5. A picture in the language L_1

3   Pure Hexagonal Context-Free Grammar with $(r/lr/ll)$ Mode of Derivations

We introduce a variant of PHCFG. The leftmost and the rightmost derivation modes in context-free grammar in string language theory, are well known [7,8], especially in the context of the study of parsers. It is also known that these derivation modes are equivalent to the "ordinary" erivations in a CFG in the sense of generating the same language class. Motivated to consider a corresponding notion of "leftmost kind" of derivation in pure 2D context-free grammars, the (l/u) P2DCFG with an (l/u) mode of derivation was introduced in [3]. In this paper the idea is to rewrite from upper left vertex to upper right vertex of a picture array by x-rule table or upper right vertex to rightmost vertex by y-rule table or upper left to left most vertex z-rule table(if an x-rule or y-rule or z-rule table is applicable) in a pure hexagonal context free grammar.

Definition 2. *Let* $G = (\Sigma, P_r, P_{lr}, P_{ll}, H_0)$ *be a pure hexagonal context free grammar with the components as in Definition 1. An $(r/lr/ll)$ mode of derivation of a picture array in G denoted by $\Rightarrow_{(r/lr/ll)}$, is a derivation in G such that only the right or lower right or lower left is rewritten. The generated picture language is defined as in the case of a PHCFG but with $\Rightarrow_{(r/lr/ll)}$ derivations. The family of picture languages generated by PHCFG under $\Rightarrow_{(r/lr/ll)}$ derivations is denoted by $(r/lr/ll)$ PHCFL. For convenience, we write $(r/lr/ll)$ PHCFG to refer to PHCFG with $\Rightarrow_{(r/lr/ll)}$ derivations.*

  We illustrate with an example.

Example 2. Consider an $(r/lr/ll)$ pure hexagonal context free grammar $G_2 = (\Sigma, P_r, P_{lr}, P_{ll}, H_0)$ where $\Sigma = \{a, b\}$, $p_r = \{r\}$, $p_{lr} = \{lr\}$ and $p_{ll} = \{ll\}$ with $r = \{a \rightarrow aa, b \rightarrow bb\}$, $l_r = \{a \searrow ab, b \searrow bb\}$, $ll = \{a \nearrow a, b \nearrow ba\}$ and

$$H_0 = \begin{matrix} & a & & a \\ a & & b & & b \\ & a & & b \end{matrix}$$

G_2 generates a picture language L_2 consisting of picture arrays p of size $(l, m+2, n)$, $l \geq 2, m \geq 0, n \geq 2$ has the following properties: $p(0,0,0) = $ a; $p(i,0,0) = a$; for $i \geq 1$; $p(0,0,k) = $ a, for $k \geq 1$; $p(0,j,k) = $ a, for $j \geq 1$, $k \geq 1$; $p(i,j,k) = b$ otherwise. A member of L_2 is shown in Fig. 6. A sample derivation in $(r/lr/ll)$ pure hexagonal context free grammar starting from H_0 and using the context free grammar rules r, lr, r, ll, ll in this order is shown in Fig. 6. We note that in this derivation the application of x-direction rule table r rewrites all symbols from upper left vertex to upper right vertex in parallel and likewise, the application of the y direction rule table lr rewrites all symbols from upper right vertex to right most vertex,the application of the z direction rule table ll rewrites all symbols from upper left vertex to left most vertex.

We now compare the generative power of $(r/lr/ll)$PHCFL with PHCFL. Here comparisons of the generative power of the family of pure hexagonal context free language with $(r/lr/ll)$.

Theorem 1. *The families of PHCFL and $(r/lr/ll)$PHCFL are incomparable but not disjoint, when the alphabet contains at least two symbols.*

Proof. The non-trivial picture language L_{Hexa} of all hexagonal picture arrays over $\{a, b\}$ belongs to both of PHCFL, $(r/lr/ll)$PHCFL.

The picture language L_2 in Example 2 which belongs to $(r/lr/ll)$PHCFL can not generated by any PHCFG, since top element (including the bottom elements) in picture arrays of L_2 involves the symbol 'a' only and so in order to generate the picture arrays of L_2 starting from an axiom array, we have to specify context free rules for both a, b. In the $(r/lr/ll)$ mode of derivation, from upper left vertex to upper right vertex will require a x-direction rule table r that will rewrite a into $a....aa$ and b into $b...bb$, but the table with these rules can be applied to any x-direction rule in a PHCFG. This will result in picture arrays not in the language L_2.

On the other hand the picture language L_1 in Example 1 belongs to PHCFL but it can not be generated by any $(r/lr/ll)$PHCFG.

Theorem 2. *The family of $(r/lr/ll)$ pure hexagonal context free languages is not closed under union.*

Proof. Let $L_3 \subseteq \{a, b, d\}^{***}$ be a picture language such that each $p \in$ L_3 of size $(l, m+2, n)$, $l \geq 2$, $m \geq 0$ and $n \geq 2$ has the following properties: $p(0,0,0) = $ b; $p(i,0,0) = $ a, for $i \geq 1$; $p(0,j,0) = $ a, for $j = 1$; $p(0,0,k) = $ a, for $k \geq 1$, $p(i,j,k) = $ d otherwise.

Let $L_4 \subseteq \{a, b, e\}^{***}$ be a picture language such that each $p \in$ L_4 of size $(r, s+2, t)$, $r \geq 2$, $s \geq 0$ and $t \geq 2$ has the following properties: $p(0,0,0) = b$; $p(i,0,0) = a$, for $i \geq 1$; $p(0,j,0) = a$, for $j = 1$; $p(0,0,k) = a$, for $k \geq 1$, $p(i,j,k) = e$ otherwise. The language L_3 and L_4 are generated by $(r/lr/ll)$ pure hexagonal context free grammar G_3 and G_4 respectively. We mention here only the tables of rules and axiom arrays of these grammars. The other components are understood from the tables of rules.

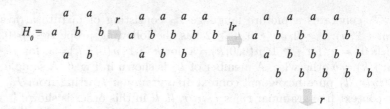

$$
H_0 =
\begin{matrix}
a & a \\
a & b & b \\
& a & b
\end{matrix}
\xrightarrow{r}
\begin{matrix}
a & a & a & a \\
a & b & b & b & b \\
& a & b & b
\end{matrix}
\xrightarrow{lr}
\begin{matrix}
a & a & a & a \\
a & b & b & b & b \\
a & b & b & b & b \\
b & b & b & b & b
\end{matrix}
$$

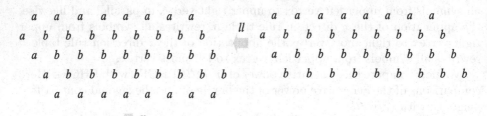

$$
\begin{matrix}
a & a & a & a & a & a & a & a \\
a & b & b & b & b & b & b & b & b \\
a & b & b & b & b & b & b & b \\
a & b & b & b & b & b & b & b & b \\
a & a & a & a & a & a & a
\end{matrix}
\xleftarrow{ll}
\begin{matrix}
a & a & a & a & a & a & a & a \\
a & b & b & b & b & b & b & b & b \\
a & b & b & b & b & b & b & b & b \\
b & b & b & b & b & b & b & b & b
\end{matrix}
$$

ll

$$
\begin{matrix}
a & a & a & a & a & a & a & a \\
a & b & b & b & b & b & b & b & b \\
a & b & b & b & b & b & b & b \\
a & b & b & b & b & b & b & b & b \\
a & a & a & a & a & a & a
\end{matrix}
$$

Fig. 6. A sample derivations under $(r/lr/ll)$ mode

The context free rule table of G_3 is
$r_1 = \{b \rightarrow ba, a \rightarrow a, d \rightarrow dd\}$
$lr_1 = \{b \searrow ba, a \searrow ad, d \searrow dd\}$
$ll_1 = \{a \nearrow a, b \nearrow ba, d \nearrow dd\}$

The context free rule table of G_4 is
$r_2 = \{b \rightarrow ba, a \rightarrow a, e \rightarrow ee\}$
$lr_2 = \{b \searrow ba, a \searrow ae, e \searrow ee\}$
$ll_2 = \{a \nearrow a, b \nearrow ba, e \nearrow ee\}$

The axiom pictures of G_3 and G_4 are

$$
\begin{matrix}
& b & a \\
a & a & d \\
& d & d
\end{matrix}
$$

and

$$
\begin{matrix}
& b & a \\
a & a & e \\
& e & e
\end{matrix}
$$

respectively. Now the union picture language $L_3 \cup L_4$ cannot be generated by any $(r/lr/ll)$ pure hexagonal context free grammar. Since the smallest picture in $L_3 \cup L_4$ are

$$\begin{matrix} & b & a \\ a & a & d \\ & d & d \end{matrix}$$

and

$$\begin{matrix} & b & a \\ a & a & e \\ & e & e \end{matrix}$$

both of these will be the axiom arrays in any $(r/lr/ll)$ pure hexagonal context free grammar that could be formed to generate $L_3 \cup L_4$. Also in order to generate the pictures of L_3, x-direction rules r of the form $d \rightarrow dd...d$ will be required while to generate the pictures L_4, x-direction rules r of the form $e \rightarrow ee...e$ will be needed. Likewise for y-direction and z-direction rules. But then there is no restriction on the application of the tables of rules which will therefore generate pictures not in $L_3 \cup L_4$.

Theorem 3. *The family of $(r/lr/ll)$ pure hexagonal context free languages is not closed under intersection.*

Proof. Let $L_5 \subseteq \{x, d, b\}^{***}$ be a picture language such that each $p \in L_5$ of size $(l, m + 2, n)$, $l \geq 2$, $m \geq 0$ and $n \geq 2$ has the following properties: $p(0,0,0) = x$; $p(i,0,0) = d$, for $i \geq 1$; $p(0,j,0) = d$, for $j = 1$; $p(0,0,k) = d$, for $k \geq 1$, $p(i,j,k) = b$ otherwise.

Let $L_6 \subseteq \{x, e, b\}^{***}$ be a picture language such that each $p \in L_6$ of size $(r, s + 2, t)$, $r \geq 2$, $s \geq 0$ and $t \geq 2$ has the following properties: $p(0,0,0) = x$; $p(i,0,0) = e$, for $i \geq 1$; $p(0,j,0) = e$, for $j = 1$; $p(0,0,k) = b$, for $k \geq 1$, $p(i,j,k) = b$ otherwise. The language L_5 and L_6 are generated by $(r/lr/ll)$ pure hexagonal context free grammar G_5 and G_6 respectively. We mention here only the tables of rules and axiom arrays of these grammars. The other components are understood from the tables of rules.

The context free rule table of G_5 is
$r_1 = \{x \rightarrow xd, d \rightarrow d, b \rightarrow bb\}$
$lr_1 = \{x \searrow xd, d \searrow db, b \searrow bb\}$
$ll_1 = \{x \swarrow xd, d \swarrow d, b \swarrow bb\}$

The context free rule table of G_6 is
$r_2 = \{x \rightarrow xe, e \rightarrow e, b \rightarrow bb\}$
$lr_2 = \{x \searrow xe, e \searrow eb, b \searrow bb\}$
$ll_2 = \{x \swarrow xe, e \swarrow e, b \swarrow bb\}$

The axiom pictures of G_5 and G_6 are

```
  x   d
d   d   b
  b   b
```

and

```
  x   e
e   e   b
  b   b
```

respectively. Now it can be seen that $L_5 \cap L_6$ can not generated by any $(r/lr/ll)$ PHCFG since the application of the rule tables are independent and hence can not insure hexagonal size of the pictures generated. Analogous to (R)PHCFG, we can define a controlled $(r/lr/ll)$PHCFG.

Theorem 4. *The families of $(r/lr/ll)$ PHCFL is not closed under intersection and complementation.*

Proof. Consider the following pure context free grammar:
$$G_5 = (\{x, b, d\}, \{r_1\}, \{lr_1\}, \{ll_1\}, H_0)$$
$$G_6 = (\{x, e, b\}, \{r_2\}, \{lr_2\}, \{ll_2\}, H_0)$$

Clearly it can be seen that $L_5 \cap L_6$ cannot generated by any $(r/lr/ll)$ PHCFG which was shown in Theorem 3. This proves that the family of $(r/lr/ll)$ PHCFG is not closed under intersection. if it were closed under complementation, then, because it is closed under union, the language.
$$L(G_5) \cap L(G_6) = \sim ((\sim L(G_5)) \cup (\sim L(G_6)))$$ would be pure context-free, which is inappropriate.

Definition 3. *A pure hexagonal context free grammar with regular control ((R) PHCFG) is a tuple $G_r = (G, \Gamma, C)$, where*

1. *G is a PHCFG*
2. *Γ is the control alphabet, the set of labels of the rule tables in $P_r \cup P_{lr} \cup P_{ll}$*
3. *$C \subseteq \Gamma^*$ is the regular control associates with the G_r.*

If $H \in \Sigma^{***H}$ and $H_0 \in M_0$, H is derived from H_0 in G_r by means of a control word $w = w_1 w_2 \ldots w_m \in C$, in symbols $C \Rightarrow_w H$, if H is obtained from H_0 by applying the table rules as in the sequence of tables $w_1 w_2 \ldots w_m$. The language $L(G)$ generated by (R) PHCFG G_r is the set of pictures $\{H/H_0 \Rightarrow_w H \in \Sigma^{+++H}$ for some $w \in C\}$. We denote by (R) PHCFL the family of hexagonal picture languages generated by PHCFG with regular control. The applications of the tables in an $(r/lr/ll)$ derivation in G are regulated by the control words of C, called the control language. An $(r/lr/ll)$ PHCFG with a regular and context-free control language is denoted by (R) $(r/lr/ll)$ PHCFG and (CF) $(r/lr/ll)$ PHCFG, respectively. In addition, the family of picture languages generated by (R) $(r/lr/ll)$ PHCFG and (CF) $(r/lr/ll)$ PHCFG is denoted by (R) $(r/lr/ll)$ PHCFL and (CF) $(r/lr/ll)$ PHCFL, respectively.

Theorem 5. *$(r/lr/ll)$ PHCFL $\subset$ (R) $(r/lr/ll)$ PHCFL $\subset$ (CF) $(r/lr/ll)$ PHCFL.*

Proof. The inclusions follow by noting that a $(r/lr/ll)$ PHCFG is an (R) $(r/lr/ll)$ PHCFG on setting the regular control language as Γ^* where Γ is the set of labels of the rule tables of the $(r/lr/ll)$ PHCFG and the well known fact [8] that the class of regular string languages is included in the class of context free languages.

The proper inclusion of (R) $(r/lr/ll)$ PHCFL in (CF)$(r/lr/ll)$ PHCFL can be shown by considering a picture language of L_7 consisting of picture arrays p as in Example 1 but of sizes $(l, m+2, n)$, $l \geq 2$, $m \geq 0$, $n \geq 2$.

The (CF) $(r/lr/ll)$ PHCFG $G^c = \{G_7, \Gamma, c\}$ generates L_7, where $G_7 = (\Sigma, P_r, P_{lr}, P_{ll}, H_0)$, where $\Sigma = \{a, b, e\}$, $p_r = \{r\}$, $p_{lr} = \{lr\}$, $p_{ll} = \{ll\}$

$r = \{e \rightarrow ea, a \rightarrow a, b \rightarrow bb\}$

$lr = \{e \searrow ea, a \searrow ab, b \searrow bb\}$

$ll = \{a \diagup a, e \diagup ea, b \diagup bb\}$,

$$H_0 \;=\; \begin{matrix} & e & a & \\ a & a & b \\ & b & b & \end{matrix}$$

and $\Gamma = (r, lr, ll)$ with r, lr, ll themselves being considered as the levels of the corresponding tables. The CF control language is $C = \{(rlr)^n\, ll(lr)^n \mid n \geq 0\}$. The grammar G_7 generates the picture arrays of L_7, in the $(r/lr/ll)$ derivation mode according to the control words of C. Starting from the axiom array

$$H_0 \;=\; \begin{matrix} & e & a & \\ a & a & b \\ & b & b & \end{matrix}$$

the x-direction of H_0 is rewritten using the x-rule table r immediately followed by y-rule table lr. This is repeated n times (for some $n \geq 0$) and then the z-rule table ll is applied once, followed by application of the y-rule table lr, the same number of times as r followed by lr was done, thus yielding a picture array in L_7. But L_7 can not be generated by any $(r/lr/ll)$ PHCFG with regular control. The notion of a control symbol or control character was considered in [1] while dealing with RPHCFG. The idea is that in an (R)PHCFG, the alphabet may contain some symbols called control symbols [1] which might not be ultimately involved in the picture arrays of language generated.

For example, the (R)$(r/lr/ll)$PHCFG with the PHCFG$(\Sigma, P_r, P_{lr}, P_{ll}, H_0)$, where $\Sigma = \{a, b, e\}$

$r_1 = \{e \rightarrow ea, a \rightarrow a, b \rightarrow bb\}$

$lr = \{e \searrow ea, a \searrow ab, b \searrow bb\}$

$ll = \{a \diagup a, b \diagup bb, e \diagup ea\}$

$r_2 = \{e \rightarrow a, a \rightarrow a, b \rightarrow b\}$ and

$$H_0 \;=\; \begin{matrix} & e & a & \\ a & a & b \\ & b & b & \end{matrix}$$

and the control language $\{(r_1 lr)^n ll r_2 \mid n \geq 0\}$ generates picture arrays p such that the top most element (i.e. from upper left vertex to upper right vertex) and all the element from upper left vertex to left most vertex of p involve only the symbol a while all other position have the symbol b. But the alphabet contains a

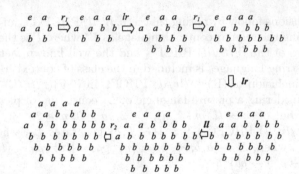

Fig. 7. Control language $\{(r_1lr)^n llr_2 \mid n \geq 0\}$ generates hexagonal picture array

symbol e which ultimately does not appear in the picture arrays of the language, Such a symbol is referred to as a control symbol or a control character in the context of an R $(r/lr/ll)$PHCFG. A picture language L_d was considered in [1] given by $L_d = \{p \in \{a,b\}^{++} \mid \mid p \mid_{col}=\mid p \mid_{row}, p(i,j) = a$, for $i= j$, $p(i,j) = b$, for $i \neq j\}$. It was shown in [1], that atleast two control symbols are require to generate L_d using (R) P2DCFG.

In [3], it was proved that L_d can be generated with a single control character using (R) (l/u)P2DCFG. We show here that an analogous result holds in the case of (R) $(r/lr/ll)$ PHCFG.

Theorem 6. *The picture arrays language consisting of hexagonal arrays over the alphabet is generated by a (R)(r/lr/ll) PHCFG with a regular control.*

Proof. The $(R)(r/lr/ll)$ $(\{e, a, b\}$ p_r, p_{lr}, p_{ll}, $H_0)$ where $p_r =\{r_1, r_2\}$, $p_{lr} = \{lr\}$, $p_{ll} = \{ll\}$, $\Sigma = \{a, b, e\}$

$r_1 = \{e \rightarrow ea, a \rightarrow a, b \rightarrow bb\}$

$lr = \{e \searrow ea, a \searrow ab, b \searrow bb\}$

$ll = \{a \nearrow a, b \nearrow bb, e \nearrow ea\}$

$r_2 = \{e \rightarrow a, a \rightarrow a, b \rightarrow b\}$ *and*

$$
H_0 = \begin{matrix} & e & a & \\ a & a & b \\ & b & b & \end{matrix}
$$

With the regular control language $\{(r_1lr)^n llr_2 \mid n \geq 0\}$ where r_1, lr, ll, r_2 are respectively the labels of p_r, p_{lr}, p_{ll} can be seen to generate the picture arrays language consisting of hexagonal arrays over the alphabet which is shown in Fig. 7.

Lemma 1. *[1] The language L_d cannot be defined by using less than two control characters and a P2DCFG with a regular control language.*

We show in the following theorem that in an $(R)(r/lr/ll)$PHCFG the picture language L_d can be generated with a single control character.

Theorem 7. *The language L_d can be defined by an (R) (r/lr/ll) PHCFG that uses a single control characters. Moreover, L_d is not in (r/lr/ll) PHCFL.*

Proof. A picture language L_d is considered in given $L_d = \{p \in \{0,1\}^{+++} \mid p \mid_x = \mid p \mid_y = \mid p \mid_z, p(i,j,k) = 1, \text{for } i = j = k, p(i,j,k) = 0, \text{otherwise.}\}$ It is shown to require at least two control symbols to generate with a single character using a Pure hexagonal context grammar and a regular control language.

The ((R) PHCFG) with the (r/lr/ll) PHCFG given by ($\{0,1,2\}, \{r\}, \{lr\}, \{ll\}, \{H_0\}$) where $r = \{1 \rightarrow 10, 0 \rightarrow 0\}$, $lr = \{1 \searrow 12, 2 \searrow 21, 0 \searrow 00\}$, $ll = \{1 \swarrow 10, 0 \swarrow 0, 0 \swarrow 01, 2 \swarrow 10\}$, and control language ($\{r/lr/ll\}^*$) generates L_d. The idea in the generation of the picture arrays of L_d is that the symbol '2' in the alphabet acts as the control character. It is clear that if there are only two symbols 0, 1 in the alphabet, then for example, there need to be two ll rules $\{0 \swarrow 00, 0 \swarrow 01\}$ in a table to maintain the diagonal of 1's but this will yield pictures not in L_d. A similar reason holds for lr rules. It can be seen that L_d can not be generated by any (r/lr/ll)PHCFL (Fig. 8).

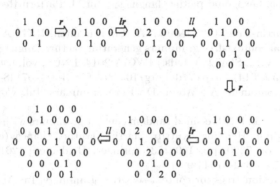

Fig. 8. Control language (r/lr/ll) generates L_d

Theorem 8. *The families of (r/lr/ll)PHCFL and HLOC are incomparable but their intersection is not empty.*

Proof. The language of hexagonal picture arrays over a one letter alphabet $\{a\}$ is clearly in *(r/lr/ll)PHCFL* and is also known [2] to be in HLOC. On the other hand, the language L_d in Theorem 7 is in HLOC but again by Theorem 7, L_d is not in *(r/lr/ll)PHCFL*.

4   Conclusion

In this work it has been concluded that another variant of pure hexagonal context free grammar rewriting only the x-direction rules or y-direction rules or z-direction rules of a picture array is considered and properties of the resulting family $(r/lr/ll)$ pure hexagonal context free language of picture languages are obtained. We can also consider and examine other variants of PHCFG having a mixed mode of derivation. In [1], membership problem and the effect of substitution rules of the form $a \rightarrow \alpha$ have been explored for the class P2DCFL. It will also be of interest to allow eliminating rules of the form $a \rightarrow \alpha$ and examines the effect of using these rules in the derivation of the picture arrays.

The variant of PHCFG can generate a wide variety of digitized hexagonal pictures and patterns. The application of this research in picture processing tasks and pattern recognition should be investigated in future.

References

1. Bersani, M.M., Frigeri, A., Cherubini, A.: Expressiveness and complexity of regular pure two dimensional context free languages. Int. J. Comput. Math. **90**, 1708–1733 (2013)
2. Dersanambika, K.S., Krithivasan, K., Martin-vide, C., Subramanian, K.G.: Local and recognizable hexagonal picture languages. Int. J. Pattern Recognit. **19**, 853–871 (2005)
3. Křivka, Z., Martín-Vide, C., Meduna, A., Subramanian, K.G.: A variant of pure two-dimensional context-free grammars generating picture languages. In: Barneva, R.P., Brimkov, V.E., Šlapal, J. (eds.) IWCIA 2014. LNCS, vol. 8466, pp. 123–133. Springer, Cham (2014). https://doi.org/10.1007/978-3-319-07148-0_12
4. Maurer, H.A., Salomaa, A., Wood, D.: Pure grammars. Inf. Control **44**, 47–72 (1980)
5. Meduna, A., Zemek, P.: One-sided random context grammars with leftmost derivations. In: Bordihn, Henning, Kutrib, Martin, Truthe, Bianca (eds.) Languages Alive. LNCS, vol. 7300, pp. 160–173. Springer, Heidelberg (2012). https://doi.org/10.1007/978-3-642-31644-9_11
6. Nagy, B.: Derivation trees for context-sensitive grammars. In: Automata, Formal Languages and Algebraic Systems (AFLAS 2008), pp. 179–199. World Scientific Publishing, Singapore (2010)
7. Rozenberg, G., Salomaa, A. (eds.): Handbook of Formal Languages, vol. 13. Springer, Berlin (1997)
8. Salomaa, A.: Formal Languages. Academic Press, Reading (1973)
9. Siromoney, R., Siromoney, G.: Extended controlled tabled L-arrays. Inf. Control **35**, 119–138 (1977)
10. Siromoney, R., Subramanian, K.G., Rangarajan, K.: Parallel/sequential rectangular arrays with tables. Int. J. Comput. Math. **6A**, 143–158 (1977)
11. Siromoney, G., Siromoney, R.: Hexagonal arrays and rectangular blocks. Comput. Graph. Image Process. **5**, 353–381 (1976)
12. Siromoney, G., Siromoney, R., Krithivasan, K.: Abstract families of matrices and picture languages. Comput. Graph. Image Process. **1**, 234–307 (1972)
13. Subramanian, K.G., Ali, R.M., Geetahlakshmi, M., Nagar, A.K.: Pure 2D picture grammars and languages. Discrete Appl. Math. **157**, 3401–3411 (2009)
14. Subramanian, K.G., Nagar, A.K., Geethalakshmi, M.: Pure 2D picture grammars (P2DPG) and P2DPG with regular control. In: Brimkov, V.E., Barneva, R.P., Hauptman, H.A. (eds.) IWCIA 2008. LNCS, vol. 4958, pp. 330–341. Springer, Heidelberg (2008). https://doi.org/10.1007/978-3-540-78275-9_29

15. Subramanian, K.G., Rangarajan, K., Mukund, M. (eds.): Formal Models, Languages and Applications. Series in Machine Perception and Artificial Intelligence, vol. 66. World Scientific Publishing, Singapore (2006)
16. Subramanian, K.G.: Comput. Graph. Image Process. Hexagonal array grammars **10**, 388–394 (1979)
17. Wang, P.S.-P. (ed.): Array Grammars, Patterns and Recognizers. Series in Computer Science, vol. 18. World Scientific Publishing, Singapore (1989)

Multimaterial Tomography: Reconstruction from Decomposed Projection Sets

László G. Varga[✉]

Department of Image Processing and Computer Graphics, University of Szeged,
Árpád tér 2, Szeged 6720, Hungary
vargalg@inf.u-szeged.hu

Abstract. We propose a reconstruction method for a theoretic projection acquisition technique, where we assume that the object of study consists of a finite number of materials, and we can separately measure the amount of materials along the paths of projection beams. The measurement decomposes the projections for separating materials, i.e., we get a separate projection set for each material (called decomposed projections), and each projection set holds information on one material only. We describe a mathematical formulation where the newly proposed reconstruction problem is formalised by an equation system and show that the model can be solved by equation system-based reconstruction techniques like the SIRT method while maintaining convergence. We test the theoretic setup on simulated data by reconstructing phantom images from simulated projections and compare the results to reconstructions from classical X-ray projections. We show that using decomposed projections can lead to better results from 20 times less number of projections than the classical X-Ray tomography.

Keywords: Tomography · Reconstruction · Decomposed projections · GPGPU

1 Introduction and Motivation

Tomography [1,4] is a collection of imaging and image processing techniques for discovering the inner structure of objects from their projections. In *transmission tomography* projections are gathered by exposing the object of study to some kind of electromagnetic or particle radiation, and measuring the loss of energy of the beams passing through it. Provided that sufficient data of measurements is available, one can determine the attenuation coefficient at each point of the object.

In *discrete tomography* [2,3] we assume that the object to be reconstructed consists of only few different materials with known attenuation coefficients. Moreover, in the special case called *binary tomography* our aim is to detect the presence or absence of one single material at each position. With this prior

© Springer Nature Switzerland AG 2019
R. P. Barneva et al. (Eds.): CompIMAGE 2018, LNCS 10986, pp. 56–69, 2019.
https://doi.org/10.1007/978-3-030-20805-9_6

information it is possible to accurately reconstruct objects from only few (usually not more than 10–12) projections.

In this paper, we outline the mathematical formulation and a reconstruction technique for measuring set-ups, where it is possible to measure separately the of amount of different materials on volumetric areas. For example, by Prompt Gamma Neutron Activation Analysis [8], one can expose a partial volume of a sample to neutron radiation. Afterwards, the material will emit its own radiation (different materials with different characteristics) that can be used for measuring the ratio of separate materials along the path of the neutron rays. Furthermore, in some cases of crystallography, we can get separated images of grains, that might be refined to be used as different projections (see, e.g., The BoxScan technique described in [7]).

Based on the above ideas, we are giving a mathematical model for the reconstruction of volumes from *decomposed projections* of objects, i.e., where we can deduce the amount of each material separately along the path of the beams. We provide combined models for using both decomposed and classical X-ray projections (where the projection is the mixture of the attenuation coefficients of the materials) in one reconstruction as well. We also show that the new model can be solved by well-known reconstruction techniques like the Simultaneous Iterative Reconstruction Technique (SIRT, [10]) while maintaining convergence of the algorithm. Finally, we evaluate the methods and plot the differences between classical reconstructions, the reconstruction from separated projections and results gained from combining both types of projections. According to our results, if projection acquisition techniques for decomposed imaging were available, they can lead to better reconstructions from significantly less (i.e., from 8 instead of 176) projections as the classical X-ray projections.

Similar reconstruction techniques in different areas already exist. E.g., dual energy CT reconstructions measure different characteristics of the material of investigation by using two X-Ray energies [14]. Also there are previous experiments in combining Prompt Gamma Neutron Activation Analysis with neutron tomography [11]. Our presented approach, however, is different from previous studies in the structure of the data, and the formulated model as well.

The paper is structured as follows. In Sect. 2 we give a brief formulation of the reconstruction problem from classical projections. Then, in Sect. 3 we provide an extension of the mathematical model of reconstruction to the decomposed projections, and provide an extension of the SIRT method, that can solve the problem. In Sect. 4, we outline an experimental framework we use for testing the provided tools, and in Sect. 5 we give the numerical results. Finally, Sect. 6 is for the conclusion.

2   Classical Formulation of Discrete Tomography

We present our results for the two-dimensional case of binary tomography, with parallel beam line projections. The reader should note, that the results can be extended to any image dimensions and any projection geometry that can be formulated as a system of linear equations.

In the sequel, we will use the algebraic formulation of tomography (see, e.g., Chapter 7 of [4]) and assume that the object to be reconstructed is represented on a two dimensional image. Without the loss of generality, we will assume that the image is of size $n \times n$, and the projection values are given by a finite number of projection rays which interact with the reconstructed pixels. With these assumptions, the noiseless reconstruction problem can be written in a form of a linear equation system

$$\mathbf{Ax} = \mathbf{b}, \qquad \mathbf{x} \in (\mathbb{R}_0^+)^{n^2}, \qquad\qquad (1)$$

where

- $\mathbf{x}$ is the vector of all n^2 unknown image pixels,
- $\mathbf{b}$ is the vector of all m projection values,
- $\mathbf{A}$ is a projection coefficient matrix of size $m \times n^2$, that describes the projection geometry by all a_{ij} elements representing the intersection of the i-th projection line through the j-th pixel.

This model of formulation is illustrated in Fig. 1.

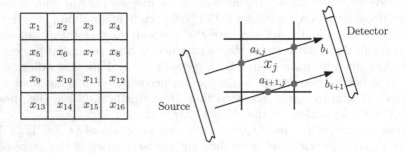

Fig. 1. Illustration of the equation-system based representation of the projections.

With this formulation, the noiseless reconstruction problem gains a versatile description, since any projection geometry (e.g., the well-known parallel beam or fan beam, or even more complex ones) can be applied, as long as the relation between the projections and the image pixels is linear, i.e., a corresponding $\mathbf{A}$ projection coefficient matrix exists.

From this point, we will only be using the equation system of the projections, and omit the actual projection geometry.

If there is a reconstruction satisfying the projections, then one can acquire a solution to the noiseless reconstruction problem by solving (1). Although this model is quite straightforward, finding the solution can be hard because of the huge number of pixels. Furthermore, the equation system is usually also underdetermined due to the low amount of data. Also, the projections can be corrupted by noise leading to an inconsistent equation system. A common way for coping with the problem is using iterative equation system solvers for approximating the results (see, e.g., [1,4,10]).

3   Methodology

In this paper, we provide an extended model of the classical equation system-based formulation of the reconstruction problem.

Let l be the number of homogeneous materials present in the investigated object, that build up the entire volume (depending on the application: empty space, air, bone, iron, copper, etc.). Assume that $\Omega = \{\omega_1, \omega_2, \ldots, \omega_l\}$ is the set of absorption coefficients of the materials in the object. Each ω_i value gives the intensity of the material as it appears on the pixels of the reconstruction. Without loss of generality, we can assume, that $\omega_i \in [0, 1]$, with $\omega_1 = 0$ and $\omega_l = 1$.

In a reconstruction we can say, that each pixel shows a mixture of the materials. If we try to decompose the reconstruction to these materials, we can get another formulation, where materials are shown in a set of separate images

$$\mathbf{Y} = \left\{ \mathbf{y}^i | \mathbf{y}^i \in [0, 1]^{n^2} , \ i \in \{1, 2, \ldots, l\} \right\} . \tag{2}$$

Here, each y_k^i takes a value of 0 if the i-th material is not present in the k-th pixel and 1 if it fully covers the pixel. From this representation, the $\mathbf{x}$ classical reconstructed image can be given in the form

$$\mathbf{x} = \sum_{i=1}^{l} \left(\omega_i \cdot \mathbf{y}^i \right) . \tag{3}$$

3.1   Problem Formulation with Decomposed Materials

With the decomposed reconstructed images $\mathbf{y}^i$ we can design an equation system, that formulates the reconstruction of the layers.

Assume, that we want to reconstruct the set of images $\mathbf{Y}$. Assuming, that we can take projections containing information on each material separately. Therefore, for each material we can write an equation system

$$\mathbf{V}^i \mathbf{y}^i = \mathbf{c}^i , \ i \in \{1, 2, \ldots, l\} , \tag{4}$$

where $\mathbf{y}^i$ is the image of the i-th material, $\mathbf{c}^i$ is a vector of projection values, holding information on the i-th material, and $\mathbf{V}^i$ is a projection matrix describing the connection between the $\mathbf{y}^i$ reconstruction and the $\mathbf{c}^i$ projection values.

The equation systems of (4) can be combined into one single equation system

$$\begin{pmatrix} \mathbf{V}^1 & 0 & \cdots & 0 \\ 0 & \mathbf{V}^2 & \cdots & 0 \\ \vdots & \vdots & \ddots & \vdots \\ 0 & 0 & \cdots & \mathbf{V}^l \end{pmatrix} \begin{pmatrix} \mathbf{y}^1 \\ \mathbf{y}^2 \\ \vdots \\ \mathbf{y}^l \end{pmatrix} = \begin{pmatrix} \mathbf{c}^1 \\ \mathbf{c}^2 \\ \vdots \\ \mathbf{c}^l \end{pmatrix} \tag{5}$$

In addition, we also know, that the materials together fill all the pixels, and the coverage of the pixels is exactly 100%, that is

$$\sum_{i=1}^{l} y_k^i = 1 , \quad k \in \{1, 2, \ldots, n^2\} . \tag{6}$$

This leads us to an extended equation system

$$\begin{pmatrix} \mathbf{V}^1 & 0 & \cdots & 0 \\ 0 & \mathbf{V}^2 & \cdots & 0 \\ \vdots & \vdots & \ddots & \vdots \\ 0 & 0 & \cdots & \mathbf{V}^l \\ \hline \mathbf{I} & \mathbf{I} & \mathbf{I} & \mathbf{I} \end{pmatrix} \begin{pmatrix} \mathbf{y}^1 \\ \mathbf{y}^2 \\ \vdots \\ \mathbf{y}^l \end{pmatrix} = \begin{pmatrix} \mathbf{c}^1 \\ \mathbf{c}^2 \\ \vdots \\ \mathbf{c}^l \\ \hline \mathbf{1} \end{pmatrix} , \tag{7}$$

where $\mathbf{I}$ and $\mathbf{1}$ are, respectively, the identity matrix and a column vector with all elements having a value of 1.

By solving (7), we can gain reconstructions of the separated materials in the examined volume. This can be done by any type of linear equation system solvers which can handle the size of the system.

3.2   Combined Model of Classical and Separated Projections

We also note that if we have classical and separated projections as well, we can easily combine the information content of the two types in one single equation system. From (3) we know the connection between the $\mathbf{x}$ pixels of the classical equation system and the decomposed images $\mathbf{y}$ is

$$\sum_{i=1}^{l} \omega_i \mathbf{A} \mathbf{y}^i = \mathbf{A} (\sum_{i=1}^{l} \omega_i \mathbf{y}^i) = \mathbf{A} \mathbf{x} = \mathbf{b} . \tag{8}$$

This leads us to a new equation system

$$\mathbf{W} \mathbf{z} = \mathbf{d} , \tag{9}$$

where

$$\mathbf{W} = \begin{pmatrix} \omega_1 \cdot \mathbf{A} & \omega_2 \cdot \mathbf{A} & \cdots & \omega_l \cdot \mathbf{A} \\ \hline \mathbf{V}^1 & 0 & \cdots & 0 \\ 0 & \mathbf{V}^2 & \cdots & 0 \\ \vdots & \vdots & \ddots & \vdots \\ 0 & 0 & \cdots & \mathbf{V}^l \\ \hline \mathbf{I} & \mathbf{I} & \cdots & \mathbf{I} \end{pmatrix} , \tag{10}$$

is the combined matrix of the classical and decomposed projections

$$\mathbf{d} = \begin{pmatrix} \mathbf{b} \\ \hline \mathbf{c}^1 \\ \mathbf{c}^2 \\ \vdots \\ \mathbf{c}^l \\ \hline \mathbf{1} \end{pmatrix} , \tag{11}$$

is the sequence of all projection values, and

$$z = \begin{pmatrix} \mathbf{y}^1 \\ \mathbf{y}^2 \\ \vdots \\ \mathbf{y}^l \end{pmatrix}. \tag{12}$$

is gained by combining the $\mathbf{y}^i$ vectors.

One interesting property of this equation system is that it does not require the projection geometries of the classical and the decomposed materials to be the same. We can take different projections for each material, and still have a solution. The only thing required is that the pixels of the classical and the decomposed reconstructions correspond to each other.

3.3   Adaptation of the SIRT Algorithm to the Decomposed Reconstruction Problem

After creating the mathematical model, we also need numerical tools for solving the equation system. This can be done by various techniques. Here we will show that the Simultaneous Iterative Reconstruction Technique (SIRT [10]), is suitable in the following way. Let $\mathbf{W}$, $\mathbf{z}$, and $\mathbf{d}$ be as defined in (9), (10), (11) and (12).

With the above formalism, the reconstruction problem can be solved by SIRT given in Algorithm 1.

Algorithm 1. Simultaneous Iterative Reconstruction Technique

Input: $\mathbf{W}$ projection matrices; $\mathbf{d}^i$ expected projection values; $\mathbf{z}^{(0)}$ initial solution; ϵ step size bound; k_{max} maximal iteration count

1: $k \leftarrow 0$
2: **repeat**
3:    $\mathbf{v}^{(k)} \leftarrow (\mathbf{W}\mathbf{z}^{(k)} - \mathbf{d})$
4:    **for all** $i \in 1, \ldots, n^2$ **do**
5:       $z_i^{(k+1)} \leftarrow z_i^{(k)} - \frac{1}{\sum_{j=1}^m w_{ji}} \sum_{j=1}^m \frac{w_{ji} v_j^{(k)}}{\sum_{l=1}^n w_{jl}}$
6:    **end for**
7:    $k \leftarrow k + 1$
8: **until** $\|\mathbf{z}^{(k+1)} - \mathbf{z}^{(k)}\|_2^2 < \epsilon$ or $k > k_{max}$
9: **return** $\mathbf{z}^{(k)}$

Convergence of the Optimization

We can also assure the convergence of the SIRT method. From [10] we have the following theorem.

Theorem 1. *The iteration*

$$\mathbf{z}_j^{q+1} = \mathbf{z}_j^q - \frac{\beta}{\gamma_j} \sum_i \frac{\mathbf{W}_{ij}(\mathbf{Wz} - c)}{\rho_i} \tag{13}$$

is convergent with the parameters

$$\gamma_j = \sum_i |\mathbf{W}_{ij}|^\alpha; \quad \rho_i = \sum_k |\mathbf{W}_{ik}|^{2-\alpha}, \quad 0 \leq \alpha \leq 2, \quad 0 \leq \beta \leq 2. \tag{14}$$

From this, we come to the following proposition.

Proposition 1. *Algorithm 1 is convergent.*

Proof. The equation system given in (9), (10), (11) and (12) satisfy all preliminaries of Theorem 1. Therefore, making the choices of $\alpha = 1$, and $\beta = 1$, we get Algorithm 1, with an α, and β, pair satisfying Theorem 1.

Algorithm 1 is only an example for solving the equation system. Several other classes of optimization methods, and discrete reconstruction methods can be applied for optimizing (9) (see, e.g., [6,9,12,13]), most of which can be used without any modification.

4   Experimental Evaluation of the Model

For the evaluation of the given concept we performed software simulations. The main questions were if it is possible to reconstruct the objects from decomposed projection sets and if using them can improve the result of reconstructions.

We took a set of software phantoms holding different types of intensity sets, we simulated projection sets of the phantoms and performed the reconstruction from the simulated projections. Reconstructions were carried out on the decomposed projections, classical projections and combined projection sets.

We wanted to have various phantom sets for the reconstructions, therefore we used images of high variability. The images contained 2 to 5 intensities (including the background) simulating different types of materials. Within the intensity counts, we used various images where the intensity sets were distributed. For each intensity count, the first set of phantoms were generated with intensity sets equally distributed on the $[0, 1]$ interval.

On the second set of phantoms, the intensity values were placed closer to each other (i.e.: we changed the intensities from $\{0, 0.5, 1\}$ to $\{0, 0.75, 1\}$). This lead to phantoms with less distinguishable object contours. In practice such phantoms pose a challenge to reconstruction algorithms, because intensities close to each other are harder to reconstruct. The final set of phantoms were generated with intensity sets even closer to each other to make the reconstruction task even harder. The intensity lists are summarized in Table 1. In total, we had 70 phantom images some of which are shown in Fig. 2.

Table 1. Intensity lists in the Groups of phantom images.

	2. intensities
Group 1.	0 1
Group 2.	0 0.25
Group 3.	0 0.75

	3. intensities
Group 1.	0 0.5 1
Group 2.	0 0.95 1
Group 3.	0 0.75 1

	4. intensities
Group 1.	0 0.33 0.66 1
Group 2.	0 0.45 0.5 1
Group 3.	0 0.25 0.5 1

	5. intensities
Group 1.	0 0.25 0.5 0.75 1
Group 2.	0 0.25 0.33 0.95 1
Group 3.	0 0.25 0.67 0.75 1

After generating the projection sets, we performed reconstructions. In all the cases we used the SIRT algorithm for the reconstruction. Then, we evaluated the results by comparing the outputs to the original phantoms by three types of error measures.

The first measure was the classical Relative Mean Error measure [5], which is given by the formula

$$RME(\mathbf{x}^*, \hat{\mathbf{x}}) = \frac{\sum_i |x_i^* - \hat{x}_i|}{\sum_i \lceil x_i^* \rceil} \;, \tag{15}$$

by $\mathbf{x}^*$ denoting the expected image, and $\hat{\mathbf{x}}$ the reconstruction result.

This RME value is suitable for both the classical, and decomposed reconstructions, but it has a drawback in not considering all the properties of the decomposed results. Namely, the decomposed reconstructions provide density information on each material in the image. Therefore, we created a multivalued version of the Relative Mean Error measure by the formula

$$mRME(\mathbf{Y}^*, \hat{\mathbf{Y}}) = \frac{\sum_{k=1...l} \sum_i |y_{ki}^* - \hat{y}_{ki}|}{l \cdot \sum_{k,\omega_k \neq 0} \sum_i \lceil y_{ki}^* \rceil} \;. \tag{16}$$

This measure gave a tool for comparing multivalued reconstructions while it is still compatible with the RME value. (Note, that if we have two materials, then the RME and $mRME$ values are equivalent.)

The RME does not take the separation of materials into account, e.g., if a pixel is determined by the value 0.5 it can be a material with an $\omega_i = 0.5$ density, or the mixture of two materials with $\omega_j = 0$ and $\omega_k = 1$ densities. The

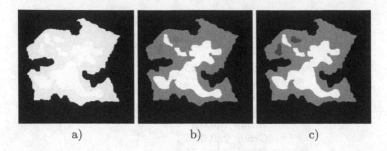

a)   b)   c)

Fig. 2. Some of the software phantoms used in the examination of the algorithms. (a) is from Group 2 of 3 intensities; (b) from Group 2 of 4 intensities; (c) from Group 3 with 4 intensities.

decomposed model formulates such mixtures, but the simple model, and the RME values do not. The $mRME$ values on the other hand handle mixed pixel values but are not applicable for the results of classical reconstruction methods. Therefore, we created another variant of the RME measure, that is similar to the $mRME$ but is applicable to the classical reconstructions. This measure was based on the decomposition of the results of classical reconstructions. Given an $\hat{\mathbf{x}}$ reconstruction the decomposed RME value can be calculated as

$$dRME(\mathbf{Y}^*, \hat{\mathbf{x}}) = mRME(\mathbf{Y}^*, \mathcal{D}_\Omega(\hat{\mathbf{x}})^*) \ , \tag{17}$$

where $\mathcal{D}_\Omega : \mathbb{R}^{n^2} \to [0,1]^{n^2 \times l}$ is a function such that

$$(\mathcal{D}_\Omega(\mathbf{x}))_{ij} = \begin{cases} \frac{x_i - \omega_{j-1}}{\omega_j - \omega_{j-1}} & \text{if } x_i \in [\omega_{j-1}, \omega_j) \ , \\ \frac{\omega_{j+1} - x_i}{\omega_j - \omega_{j+1}} & \text{if } x_i \in [\omega_j, \omega_{j+1}] \ , \\ 0 & \text{otherwise.} \end{cases} \tag{18}$$

Practically, this measure determines the amount of materials in each pixel of the classical reconstruction by the linear combination of the closest (ω_j, ω_{j+1}) intensity values.

5   Results

With the above tools, we performed reconstructions of the phantom images from various projection sets, using the SIRT algorithm, and evaluated the results with the three error measures. The projection sets were created by combinations of projection pairs containing $\{0, 2, 4, 8, 16\}$ classical, and $\{0, 2, 4, 8, 16\}$ decomposed projections. We also produced classical reconstructions with projection counts $\{32, 48, 64, 80, 96, 112, 128, 144, 160, 176\}$. The reconstructions were performed by two approaches. When the projection sets contained decomposed projections we used the modified SIRT algorithm described in Sect. 3.3. In case of projection sets containing only classical projections, we used the general SIRT method, for producing only the classical $\hat{\mathbf{x}}$ reconstructions. The parameters of the SIRT method were chosen $\epsilon = 0.05$ and $k_{max} = 5000$. The starting images were generated with all pixels having a value of 0.5. Some of the resulting reconstructions can be seen in Fig. 3.

After performing the reconstructions, we evaluated the data with the RME, $mRME$ and $cRME$ measures. Unfortunately, the $mRME$ value could only be evaluated for the models containing decomposed projection sets, since the classical SIRT reconstruction did not provide separated density maps. On the other hand, we could calculate the classical RME of the decomposed reconstructions after creating a composed image by (3). The results are summarized in Table 2.

| Figure 2a | Figure 2b | Figure 2c |

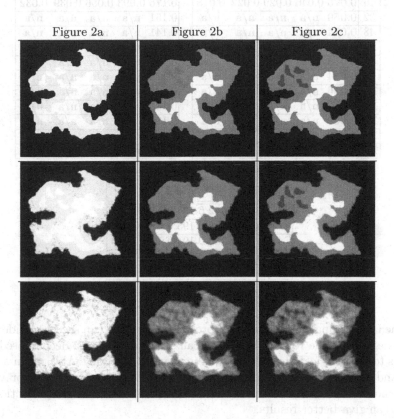

Fig. 3. Reconstructions of the software phantoms of Fig. 2. Top row is reconstructed from 0 classical, and 16 decomposed projections; middle row from 8 classical, and 8 decomposed projections; bottom row from 16 classical, and 0 decomposed projections.

Observing the tables we can find various tendencies. First of all, when we used only classical projection sets we found, that the error of the reconstructions decreases by the increasing number of projections. This is a quite straightforward tendency, since the increasing amount of information enables the algorithm to compute a more accurate result. This tendency is also visible when only decomposed projection sets are used.

Table 2. Average *RME dRME* and *mRME* values of the reconstructions according to the numbers of classical (increasing in rows) and decomposed (increasing in columns) projections.

	RME						dRME				
	0	2	4	8	16		0	2	4	8	16
0	n/a	0.517	0.153	0.029	0.005		n/a	0.660	0.221	0.046	0.010
2	0.601	0.522	0.164	0.040	0.021		0.770	0.668	0.237	0.063	0.036
4	0.356	0.242	0.163	0.039	0.019		0.515	0.345	0.236	0.062	0.033
8	0.121	0.082	0.052	0.038	0.018		0.236	0.139	0.086	0.061	0.032
16	0.076	0.046	0.029	0.022	0.018		0.176	0.093	0.056	0.039	0.032
32	0.059	n/a	n/a	n/a	n/a		0.151	n/a	n/a	n/a	n/a
48	0.054	n/a	n/a	n/a	n/a		0.141	n/a	n/a	n/a	n/a
64	0.053	n/a	n/a	n/a	n/a		0.138	n/a	n/a	n/a	n/a
80	0.052	n/a	n/a	n/a	n/a		0.135	n/a	n/a	n/a	n/a
96	0.054	n/a	n/a	n/a	n/a		0.135	n/a	n/a	n/a	n/a
112	0.056	n/a	n/a	n/a	n/a		0.135	n/a	n/a	n/a	n/a
128	0.057	n/a	n/a	n/a	n/a		0.135	n/a	n/a	n/a	n/a
144	0.059	n/a	n/a	n/a	n/a		0.136	n/a	n/a	n/a	n/a
160	0.060	n/a	n/a	n/a	n/a		0.136	n/a	n/a	n/a	n/a
176	0.061	n/a	n/a	n/a	n/a		0.137	n/a	n/a	n/a	n/a

	mRME				
	0	2	4	8	16
0	n/a	0.542	0.184	0.034	0.007
2	n/a	0.548	0.195	0.046	0.022
4	n/a	0.283	0.194	0.045	0.020
8	n/a	0.113	0.065	0.045	0.020
16	n/a	0.078	0.042	0.026	0.020

When combining the two types of projections sets we can see two tendencies. When we look at the rows of table, we can see that adding 2 decomposed projections to the classical ones result in an increase of accuracy. Also, when adding more and more decomposed projections to the projection set the error values monotonously decrease, indicating that adding new decomposed projections to the set can give better results.

On the other hand, when we look at the table rows we can see, that the error increases when we add 2 classical projections to the decomposed ones. After this, when increasing the number of classical projections the errors start to decrease, and can eventually reach a level, where the accuracy is better than without the classical projections, but this might need several new projection sets.

The explanation of this phenomena might be, that adding classical projection sets makes the equations system more complex (i.e., it bring new connections between variables), while not giving a significant amount of new information to improve the results. This means a more complex problem to solve leading to a worse reconstruction. When increasing the number of classical projections we

Table 3. Average running times of the reconstructions (in seconds) according to the numbers of classical (increasing in rows) and decomposed (increasing in columns) projections.

	0	2	4	8	16
0	n/a	6.134	12.867	8.021	4.199
2	0.103	10.073	17.718	18.501	19.045
4	0.388	16.153	16.248	17.955	19.111
8	0.554	17.281	18.077	19.724	17.928
16	0.444	20.648	22.572	21.585	18.278
32	0.709	n/a	n/a	n/a	n/a
48	1.118	n/a	n/a	n/a	n/a
64	1.556	n/a	n/a	n/a	n/a
80	2.017	n/a	n/a	n/a	n/a
96	2.472	n/a	n/a	n/a	n/a
112	2.914	n/a	n/a	n/a	n/a
128	3.369	n/a	n/a	n/a	n/a
144	3.829	n/a	n/a	n/a	n/a
160	4.304	n/a	n/a	n/a	n/a
176	4.788	n/a	n/a	n/a	n/a

bring new information to solving the problem, which helps the reconstruction method to find an accurate result. In this way, the benefit of the new information will eventually outweigh the unwanted effect of solving a more complex problem, and the results will get better.

Finally, the general performance of the methods showed, that using decomposed projection sets can greatly benefit the accuracy of the reconstruction. For example, with any applicable error measure, on average, using 8 decomposed projections gave a result more accurate than classical projections could provide with 176 projections. This is due to the combined effect of many factors.

First of all, decomposed projections hold more data and more information. While 8 classical projections with 3 materials hold information from 8 measurements, the amount of measured data is tripled in decomposed projections. This increases the information amount we have. Second, in general, binary reconstruction is an easier task than continuous tomography. Thus, by reconstructing a combination of [0, 1] images the decomposed problem can lead to better results. Finally, in case of intensities close to each other, classical reconstruction methods do not have the means of distinguishing between materials, whereas decomposed projection still have a clear distinction.

Concerning the computational requirement of the methods we measured the average running times with different projection numbers. The results are given in Table 3. The implementation was done in Matlab (R2017a) using the in-built GPU accelerated functionality. The experiments were carried out by an Intel Core i7-6700 CPU and an Nvidia Tesla K40 GPU.

Concerning the running times we can state that using decomposed projections severely increases the computational requirement. In turn we can get significantly better reconstruction which can be preferable in some applications.

6   Conclusion and Further Work

We gave a theoretical model for formulating the reconstruction problem using two types of projections. One type of projections is the classical one, where the projection lines give a sum of the material densities of all the material together along their paths. The other type of projection is given by decomposed projections, where we assume that the projection beams give a vector of values that provide information on the materials separately. Such projections are not so common, but possible to be taken with, e.g., Prompt Gamma Neutron Activation Analysis, or other advanced imaging techniques.

We also showed that the SIRT method can be extended for performing the reconstruction from such hybrid projection sets, and proved, that the extended algorithm is still convergent. Furthermore, we gave an experimental evaluation of the methods by comparing reconstructions of software phantoms with different projection sets. We found that the decomposed projections hold more information than classical ones, and if scanners were available for producing such projection sets we could greatly improve the accuracy of the reconstructions. In out evaluation using 8 decomposed projections lead to better result, than it is possible with 176 classical projections.

Although we do not know of any projection acquisition devices following the proposed models, there are some similar acquisition techniques in theory and in practice [7,11] which are promising for gaining decomposed projections. Finally, one should note, that the proposed method is not only suitable for combining different types of projection sets, but also can be used for incorporating extra information into the model. One such information can be volumetric information on the object localizing the presence of some material, or stating the proportion of materials in a given part of the volume. Furthermore, the extension of the given methods can be used for combining different projection geometries that is subject to further studies.

Acknowledgements. The author would like to thank Péter Balázs and Antal Nagy for their help and advice during the writing process.

This research was supported by the project "Integrated program for training new generation of scientists in the fields of computer science", no EFOP-3.6.3-VEKOP-16-2017-0002. The project has been supported by the European Union and co-funded by the European Social Fund. We gratefully acknowledge the support of NVIDIA Corporation with the donation of a Tesla K40 GPU used for this research. The Author would like to thank Antal Nagy for providing test images for the evaluation.

References

1. Herman, G.T.: Fundamentals of Computerized Tomography: Image Reconstruction from Projections. Springer, Heidelberg (2009). https://doi.org/10.1007/978-1-84628-723-7
2. Herman, G.T., Kuba, A. (eds.): Discrete Tomography: Foundations, Algorithms, and Applications, 1st edn. Birkhäuser Basel, New York (1999). https://doi.org/10.1007/978-1-4612-1568-4
3. Herman, G.T., Kuba, A. (eds.): Advances in Discrete Tomography and Its Applications, 1st edn. Birkhäuser, Basel (2007). https://doi.org/10.1007/978-0-8176-4543-4
4. Kak, A.C., Malcolm, S.: Principles of Computerized Tomographic Imaging. IEEE Press, New York (1999)
5. Kuba, A., Herman, G.T., Matej, S., Todd-Pokropek, A.: Medical Applications of Discrete Tomography. DIMACS Series in Discrete Mathematics and Theoretical Computer Science, vol. 55, pp. 195–208 (2000)
6. Lukić, T.: Discrete tomography reconstruction based on the multi-well potential. In: Aggarwal, J.K., Barneva, R.P., Brimkov, V.E., Koroutchev, K.N., Korutcheva, E.R. (eds.) IWCIA 2011. LNCS, vol. 6636, pp. 335–345. Springer, Heidelberg (2011). https://doi.org/10.1007/978-3-642-21073-0_30
7. Lyckegaard, A.: Development of tomographic reconstruction methods in materials science with focus on advanced scanning methods. Ph.D. thesis, January 2011
8. Paul, R.L., Lindstrom, R.M.: Prompt gamma-ray activation analysis: fundamentals and applications. J. Radioanal. Nucl. Chem. **243**(1), 181–189 (2000). https://doi.org/10.1023/A:1006796003933
9. Schüle, T., Weber, S., Schnörr, C.: Adaptive reconstruction of discrete-valued objects from few projections. Electron. Notes Discrete Math. **20**(0), 365–384 (2005). http://www.sciencedirect.com/science/article/pii/S157106530505078X. Proceedings of the Workshop on Discrete Tomography and its Applications Workshop on Discrete Tomography and its Applications
10. van der Sluis, A., van der Vorst, H.: SIRT- and CG-type methods for the iterative solution of sparse linear least-squares problems. Linear Algebra Appl. **130**, 257–303 (1990). http://www.sciencedirect.com/science/article/pii/002437959090215X
11. Söllradl, S.: Developments in prompt gamma-ray neutron activation analysis and cold neutron tomography and their application in non-destructive testing. Ph.D. thesis, Department of Chemistry and Biochemistry, University of Bern (2014)
12. Varga, L., Péter, B., Nagy, A.: Discrete tomographic reconstruction via adaptive weighting of gradient descents. Comput. Methods Biomech. Biomed. Eng. Imaging Vis., 1–9 (2014). https://doi.org/10.1080/21681163.2013.853624
13. Weber, S., Nagy, A., Schüle, T., Schnörr, C., Kuba, A.: A benchmark evaluation of large-scale optimization approaches to binary tomography. In: Kuba, A., Nyúl, L.G., Palágyi, K. (eds.) DGCI 2006. LNCS, vol. 4245, pp. 146–156. Springer, Heidelberg (2006). https://doi.org/10.1007/11907350_13
14. Zhang, H., et al.: Iterative reconstruction for dual energy CT with an average image-induced nonlocal means regularization. Phys. Med. Biol. **62**(13), 5556–5574 (2017)

Sequential Projection Selection Methods for Binary Tomography

Gábor Lékó$^{(\boxtimes)}$ and Péter Balázs

Department of Image Processing and Computer Graphics, University of Szeged,
Árpád tér 2, Szeged 6720, Hungary
{leko,pbalazs}@inf.u-szeged.hu

Abstract. Binary tomography reconstructs binary images from a low number of their projections. Often, there is a freedom how these projections can be chosen which can significantly affect the quality of reconstructions. We apply sequential feature selection methods to find the 'most informative' projection set based on a blueprint image. Using various software phantom images, we show that these methods outperform the previously published projection selection algorithms.

Keywords: Binary tomography · Reconstruction ·
Projection selection · Feature selection · Optimization

1 Introduction

The aim of binary tomography [5,6] is to reconstruct cross-sections of objects made or consisting of a single homogeneous material, in a non-destructive way, usually by X-ray projections. The 2D slices of the objects can be represented by binary images, where 1 and 0 stand for the presence and absence of the material, respectively, whereas the projections can be regarded as line-sums along different lines in different directions. Due to practical considerations the number of accessible projections is often very low, which ensures a high freedom how to choose them. It has been shown in [10,13] that the choice of projection angles can have a significant influence on the quality of the reconstruction, in many cases. Thus, further attention has been paid on how the 'most informative' projections can be found. Projection selection methods can be classified as online and offline ones. In the former case, a new projection angle is added to the already existing angle set, based on the information content of the previously acquired projections (see, e.g., [1–3]). In the latter case, a blueprint image of the object to be reconstructed is given (which is rather typical, e.g., in industrial non-destructive testing), on which the whole projection data can be simulated, and the proper projection set can be identified. Even though this is easier than finding the angles on-the-fly, the excessive search space of the possible projection sets makes the problem computationally challenging, as an exhaustive search is often not feasible. In [12], several approaches have been published to find good

© Springer Nature Switzerland AG 2019
R. P. Barneva et al. (Eds.): CompIMAGE 2018, LNCS 10986, pp. 70–81, 2019.
https://doi.org/10.1007/978-3-030-20805-9_7

projections angles for binary tomography, all of them reducing the search space of projection sets in a certain way.

In this paper, we suggest sequential search methods [11] to find projection angles with high information content and show that these methods outperform the former ones both in providing better image quality. The structure of the paper is the following. In Sect. 2 we describe the reconstruction problem and an algebraic approach how to solve it. In Sect. 3 we recall some previously published projection selection methods and present the ones based on sequential search strategies. In Sect. 4 we give details about the experimental frameset, while in Sect. 5 we present the experimental results. Finally, Sect. 6 is for the conclusion.

2   The Reconstruction Problem

We consider the algebraic formulation of the reconstruction problem. The goal is to construct a binary image from its parallel-beam projections. Without the loss of generality we can assume that the image is of size $n \times n$. Thus, the aim is to solve

$$\mathbf{A}\mathbf{x} = \mathbf{b}, \quad \mathbf{x} \in \{0,1\}^{n^2}, \tag{1}$$

where $\mathbf{x}$ is the vector of all n^2 unknown image pixels; $\mathbf{b}$ is the vector of all m projection values; and $\mathbf{A}$ is a projection coefficient matrix of size $m \times n^2$ according to the projection geometry. For all $(i,j) \in \{1,\ldots,m\} \times \{1,\ldots,n^2\}$ element a_{ij} represents the proportion of the i-th projection line in the j-th pixel (see Fig. 1). In binary tomography, an approximate solution of (1) is often found by a thresholded version of the Simulated Iterative Reconstruction Technique (SIRT) and we also will use this algorithm [4].

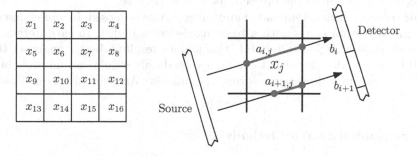

Fig. 1. Equation system-based representation of the parallel-beam projection geometry.

When a blueprint image is available, the quality of the reconstructions can be measured by the Relative Mean Error (RME) defined as

$$RME(\mathbf{x}^*, \mathbf{y}) = \frac{\sum_i |x_i^* - y_i|}{\sum_i x_i^*}, \tag{2}$$

where $\mathbf{x}^*$ is the blueprint and $\mathbf{y}$ is the reconstructed image.

3   Projection Selection Algorithms

In this section we first recall two projection selection strategies from [12] that will serve as references for comparison with our suggested methods. Then, we present our sequential search based approaches.

3.1   Equiangular Approaches

One of the simplest methods is when the projection angles are distributed proportionally, with equiangular spacing. One can distinguish two variants. In the first case the starting angle is positioned to $0°$. As an improved version, in the second case, all the integer starting angles are analysed between $0°$ and $\left[\frac{180}{p}\right]°$ (with a certain quantization), where p is the number of projections. At the end, the angle set ensuring the best quality (the smallest RME value) is kept. The authors of [12] referred to these methods as **Naive** and **EquiAng** angle selections, respectively, and so do we in this paper.

3.2   Simulated Annealing

When arbitrary angles can serve as candidates for taking projections from, the problem of projection selection becomes intractable, an exhaustive search is most often no longer possible. To handle this issue, in [12] the authors represented the problem as an energy minimization task. An optimal list of angles must satisfy

$$RME(\mathbf{x}^*, \mathbf{x}_{L^*}) = \min_{L} RME(\mathbf{x}^*, \mathbf{x}_L), \tag{3}$$

where L is an arbitrary list of angles, L^* is the optimal list of angles, and $\mathbf{x}_L$ is the reconstruction from the projections with L angle set.

For the minimization simulated annealing [8] was proposed. In a brief description, the algorithm starts with a basic fixed-size angle list. In each iteration a randomly chosen angle is altered. If this update results a better angle set then it will be accepted, otherwise it can be accepted only with a certain probability which is constantly decreasing during the process. We refer to this method as **SA**.

3.3   Sequential Search Methods

By the observation that projections can serve as features of the image to reconstruct, we examined numerous types of feature selection algorithms, following the summary of [9]. Among these, the floating search methods [11] seem to be the best option, in this area. Other algorithms contain too much randomization, use exhaustive search or tree structure which, makes them hardly applicable for the task. In the following, we propose four different projection selection algorithms using sequential (floating) search methods.

SFS - Sequential Forward Selection. The process starts with the initialization of a feature subset. Then it iteratively adds features to the initial subset.

The feature to be added is chosen based on the improvement it gives to a certain measure. A certain feature is added if it gives the biggest improvement from all the available features. The process stops when no improvements happen in the evaluation measure in the last t steps, where t is a predefined threshold variable, or all the features have been added to the set. In Algorithm 1 one can see the SFS algorithm for our purpose. At the end of the process the suggested angle set is stored in array A.

Algorithm 1. Angle selection with SFS algorithm

let $A = \{\theta_1, \theta_2\}$ where θ_1 and θ_2 are randomly chosen integer angles
repeat
    for each angle $\theta \in \{0, 1, \ldots, 179\} \setminus A$ **do**
        calculate $RME(A \cup \{\theta\})$
        $\theta_{min} \leftarrow$ angle corresponding to the smallest RME value
    end for
    $A \leftarrow A \cup \{\theta_{min}\}$
until the predefined number of projections is reached

SBS - Sequential Backward Selection. SBS is the backward counterpart of SFS. The initial feature set contains all the features. Then, iteratively, one feature will be removed from the set, namely whose deletion causes the less loss in the evaluation measure. The process also stops when no improvements happen in the evaluation measure in the last t steps, where t is a predefined threshold variable, or all the necessary number of features has been deleted from the set. In Algorithm 2 one can see the SFS algorithm for our purpose. At the end of the process the suggested angle set is stored in array A.

Algorithm 2. Angle selection with SBS algorithm

let $A = \{0, 1, \ldots, 179\}$
repeat
    for each angle $\theta \in A$ **do**
        calculate $RME(A \setminus \{\theta\})$
        $\theta_{min} \leftarrow$ angle corresponding to the smallest RME value
    end for
    $A \leftarrow A \setminus \{\theta_{min}\}$
until the predefined number of projections is reached

SFFS - Sequential Forward Floating Search. Both SFS and SBS suffer from so-called "nesting effect". It means that in SFS the features once selected cannot be later discarded while in SBS the discarded features cannot be reselected. The result is that the methods are only suboptimal. The SFFS is a so-called bottom-up search procedure. It starts with an SFS step. If the desired size of the solution is not reached yet then an SBS can be applied to exclude features. A feature will be excluded permanently if it yields the best subset found so far, otherwise the excluded feature is put back and the process continues again with the SFS step. This process iterates until the desired size of the feature set is reached.

SBFS - Sequential Backward Floating Search. The SBFS is the backward counterpart of SFFS, i.e., it is a top-down search procedure. The basic idea is the same as it was in the case of SFFS, but the SFS and SBS steps are swapped.

The original SFFS and SBFS methods both contain a deviation constant, which allows the algorithm to exceed the desired size of the solution during the searching process and even to end with more or less features. In our case, when these algorithms are used for projection selection, we do not allow the algorithm to finish with more or less projections than the predefined number.

Based on the idea of SFFS and SBFS we propose a Refinement algorithm, which is an extended version of SFS and SBS. In our interpretation the algorithm starts with an SFS or an SBS step and then we apply the Refinement. Depending on which algorithm is used as the first step, we refer to these algorithms as SFSR and SBSR (R is for Refinement). The Refinement algorithm can be seen in Algorithm 3. It is the extended form of the one published in [7] capable of refining the result of both SFS and SBS, or the output of any other algorithm.

Algorithm 3. Angle selection with Refinement

1: **function** REFINEMENT(A)   ▷ A - set of the actual angles, output of SFS or SBS
2:     fix$\Theta \leftarrow$ the last element inserted into A
3:     **repeat**
4:         **for each** angle $\theta \in A \setminus \{fix\Theta\}$ **do**
5:             calculate RME($A \setminus \{\theta\}$)
6:             $\theta_{min} \leftarrow$ angle corresponding to the smallest RME value
7:         **end for**
8:         $A \leftarrow A \setminus \{\theta_{min}\}$
9:         **for** $\theta \leftarrow 0$ to 179 **do**
10:            calculate RME($A \cup \{\theta\}$)
11:            $\theta_{min} \leftarrow$ angle corresponding to the smallest RME value
12:        **end for**
13:        $A \leftarrow A \cup \{\theta_{min}\}$
14:        fix$\Theta \leftarrow \theta_{min}$
15:    **until** the RME cannot be decreased any more.
16: **end function**

As a brief explanation of Algorithm 3: We fix the last element inserted to the projection set (Line 2). Then, we eliminate, one by one, the non-fixed projection angles and compute the RME (Line 4–7). We keep the angle combination with the smallest RME (Line 8). In the second part, we take again all the integer angles between 0 and 179 and compute the RME value by adding each of them to the current set of projections (Line 9–12). We insert the angle with the smallest

RME value into the projection set (Line 13) and fix it (Line 14). Lines 4–14 are repeated until the RME value cannot be decreased any more.

4   Test Frameset and Phantom Images

To compare the performance of the given algorithms we performed experimental tests on a set of binary software phantoms. Our image database consisted of 22 phantoms of different structural complexity, each with 256×256 pixels. Some of them can be seen in Fig. 2.

We used parallel beam geometry. In every projection we set the distance of the beams and detector elements to 1 pixel and used $256 \cdot \sqrt{2}$ of them to cover the whole image. The rotation center was placed into the center of the image.

The reconstructions were performed by the thresholded SIRT algorithm [4], implemented in C++ with GPU acceleration using the CUDA sdk[1], on a machine powered by 4 pieces of NVIDIA Tesla K10 G2 8GB GPUs. The number of iterations in SIRT was set to infinite and the iteration stopped when the difference between two iterations decreased to 0.01. Based on experiments, below 0.01 the change in the quality between two iterations was negligible.

Due to their stochastic nature, in the case of SA, SFS and SFSR, to find the best possible result we used a multistart strategy, but in a different way. We used exactly the same parametrization for SA that was used in [12], i.e., the random angle changes stopped after 200 iterations or when the RME decreased to zero and after 5 restarted runnings we chose the projection set with the smallest RME value.

In case of SFS and SFSR, we started the process 18 times from different random integer angle pairs in order to try to avoid to get stuck into a local minimum. In this way, assuming uniform random distribution, each angle region of 5° can be covered with high probability by at least one angle in at least one initialization. We used angle pairs instead of just a single starting angle since – after experiments – we noticed that in the latter case the process could still very likely stick into a local minimum.

5   Results

In Table 1 we present the RME values of the different projection selection methods, in case of projection sets with 4 angles. The smallest RME values are highlighted in every row. We can observe that SFSR performed the best, in almost every cases. Only in case of Phantom6 was SFSR beaten, by SBSR. The reason can be found in the stochastic nature of SFSR, that was restarted 18 times for each phantom. With further two restarts we achieved a value of 0.0582 with SFSR, which is much better than for SBSR. It is also worth to be noticed, that in case of the rotation independent Phantom2, even the naive method can find the best solution, as for this image all the projections have the same information content.

---

[1] https://www.developer.nvidia.com/cuda-zone.

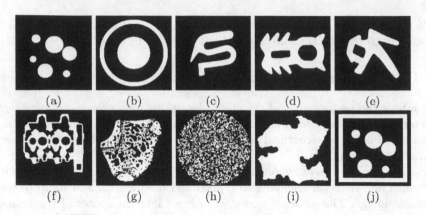

Fig. 2. Some of the software phantoms used for testing (randomly chosen). Figures from (a) to (j) are in Tables 1 and 2 Phantom 1, 2, 6, 8, 11, 14, 16, 17, 19 and 20, respectively.

In Table 2 one can follow the running times of the different methods. We notice that equiangular methods are fast but provide really weak quality reconstructions, while in case of SBS and SBSR the running time is enormous. SA, SFS and SFSR performed well (in most cases in this improving order) and the running time is also acceptable. We emphasize that in the case of SA we took 5, and in the case of SFS and SFSR 18 multistart runnings. This means that one SA run is 1/5 times shorter, and one SFS and SFSR run is 1/18 times shorter than the corresponding values in Table 2.

We summarize the results of Tables 1 and 2 in Fig. 3. The RME values and running times are proportionally normalized between 0 and 1, for better visualization.

For a further comparison, we tested the algorithms on one of the phantoms (Fig. 2e) with more than 4 projections (6, 9, 12, 15). The RME values and the running time can be seen in Tables 3 and 4, respectively. Figures 4 and 5 display the same results in diagrams. Based on these two diagrams, we can conclude that in case of smaller amount of projections SFSR is the absolute winner considering the quality of the reconstructions. Nevertheless, if we increase the number of projections the RME values are getting more and more similar. In case of many projections it is less relevant which strategy we choose. Considering the running time, one can see that in the cases of Naive, EquiAng, SA, SBS, and SBSF the running times are slightly changing, while for SFS and SFSR the running time is significantly increasing with more and more projections.

Finally, we mention that the equiangular methods are exhaustive searches in their own forms (in the restricted search space). SA is non-deterministic due to the fully randomized changes, so it is driven by fortune. SFS and SFSR are deterministic, except the initialization step, i.e., with a fixed initialization they provide the same output every time. SBS and SBSR are fully-deterministic, they do not contain any random steps.

Table 1. RME values belonging to different methods in case of 4 projections

	Naive	EquiAng	SA	SBS	SBSR	SFS	SFSR
Phantom1	0.2694	0.1353	0.1408	0.1302	0.0604	0.0597	**0.0562**
Phantom2	**0.0672**	**0.0672**	0.1982	0.3068	0.1155	0.2487	**0.0672**
Phantom3	0.0409	0.0409	0.0363	0.0842	0.0428	0.0428	**0.0358**
Phantom4	0.2366	0.1523	0.1028	0.1261	0.1103	0.0670	**0.0621**
Phantom5	0.3980	0.1844	0.1324	0.1665	0.1279	0.1043	**0.0912**
Phantom6	0.3708	0.1912	0.0808	0.0757	**0.0665**	0.0673	0.0673
Phantom7	0.1085	0.1056	0.1272	0.1040	0.1006	0.0808	**0.0745**
Phantom8	0.1599	0.1537	0.1366	0.1523	0.1365	0.1228	**0.1192**
Phantom9	0.2056	0.1915	0.0611	0.0813	0.0705	0.0508	**0.0422**
Phantom10	0.0727	0.0727	0.0618	0.0673	0.0475	0.0338	**0.0312**
Phantom11	0.3572	0.2837	0.1035	0.1478	0.1478	0.1132	**0.0891**
Phantom12	0.0080	0.0080	0.0123	0.0144	0.0113	0.0097	**0.0079**
Phantom13	0.0894	0.0894	0.0705	0.0777	0.0623	0.0628	**0.0577**
Phantom14	0.4459	0.4459	0.4252	0.4360	0.4313	0.4054	**0.4048**
Phantom15	0.4813	0.4542	0.4333	0.3792	0.3531	0.3531	**0.3500**
Phantom16	0.5164	0.5164	0.4912	0.4956	0.4790	0.4831	**0.4778**
Phantom17	0.8789	0.8789	0.8892	0.8885	0.8800	0.8736	**0.8664**
Phantom18	0.4721	0.4721	0.4743	0.4536	0.4377	0.4253	**0.4108**
Phantom19	0.0918	0.0918	0.0871	0.0845	0.0675	0.0605	**0.0512**
Phantom20	0.1055	0.1055	0.0422	0.0879	**0.0360**	0.0811	**0.0360**
Phantom21	0.3442	0.3442	0.1590	0.2125	0.1780	0.1591	**0.1337**
Phantom22	0.5244	0.5244	0.4814	0.4848	0.4743	0.4773	**0.4376**
Average	0.2838	0.2504	0.2158	0.2298	0.2017	0.1992	0.1804

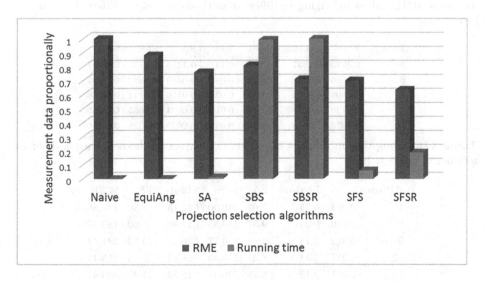

Fig. 3. Diagram for Tables 1 and 2

Table 2. Running time in minutes belonging to different methods in case of 4 projections

	Naive	EquiAng	SA	SBS	SBSR	SFS	SFSR
Phantom1	0.010	0.32	7.52	499.15	504.28	40.70	128.12
Phantom2	0.012	0.25	6.77	668.35	672.40	33.15	96.87
Phantom3	0.010	0.26	10.13	625.62	637.92	47.75	164.63
Phantom4	0.006	0.31	7.29	467.02	471.15	39.45	116.18
Phantom5	0.007	0.32	6.56	486.33	492.28	35.78	120.07
Phantom6	0.004	0.23	7.49	519.15	523.32	40.02	139.15
Phantom7	0.009	0.40	7.37	544.13	548.20	42.18	123.42
Phantom8	0.006	0.22	6.63	606.77	609.12	37.17	117.98
Phantom9	0.006	0.26	7.88	524.92	527.65	45.60	130.48
Phantom10	0.008	0.28	8.16	466.93	471.57	45.35	140.18
Phantom11	0.004	0.25	7.62	510.90	512.15	38.30	137.88
Phantom12	0.006	0.36	7.27	390.28	394.57	50.32	116.80
Phantom13	0.007	0.22	7.82	543.42	547.45	44.17	117.15
Phantom14	0.005	0.17	5.43	822.45	825.10	29.45	89.85
Phantom15	0.005	0.24	4.84	418.23	420.77	23.45	73.48
Phantom16	0.004	0.19	5.64	1007.82	1012.08	31.08	92.13
Phantom17	0.003	0.09	3.96	1402.65	1403.63	25.57	76.60
Phantom18	0.005	0.16	5.19	672.07	674.08	28.03	94.18
Phantom19	0.009	0.25	8.55	609.32	614.80	44.65	144.22
Phantom20	0.008	0.13	6.75	781.28	786.72	23.48	119.75
Phantom21	0.006	0.21	7.78	522.92	531.82	39.85	138.60
Phantom22	0.007	0.27	6.12	565.78	570.72	30.98	104.65
Average	0.007	0.24	6.95	620.70	625.08	37.11	117.38

Table 3. RME values belonging to different methods in case of different number of projections

#Projs.	Naive	EquiAng	SA	SBS	SBSR	SFS	SFSR
4	0.3572	0.2837	0.1035	0.1478	0.1478	0.1132	**0.0891**
6	0.0506	0.0469	0.0403	0.0488	0.0440	0.0382	**0.0321**
9	0.0308	0.0202	0.0184	0.0214	0.0176	0.0144	**0.0126**
12	0.0120	0.0098	0.0099	0.0109	0.0074	0.0065	**0.0059**
15	0.0076	0.0053	0.0050	0.0059	0.0035	0.0028	**0.0020**

Table 4. Running time in minutes belonging to different methods in case of different number of projections

#Projs.	Naive	EquiAng	SA	SBS	SBSR	SFS	SFSR
4	0.004	0.25	7.62	510.90	512.15	38.30	137.88
6	0.010	0.29	9.37	510.85	514.40	96.60	183.80
9	0.012	0.19	8.68	510.77	520.78	174.72	241.17
12	0.011	0.14	8.38	510.65	518.65	251.25	315.43
15	0.011	0.12	8.76	510.48	518.53	331.45	403.62

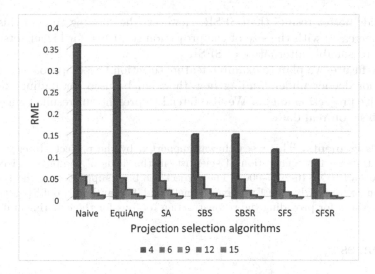

Fig. 4. Diagram for Table 3

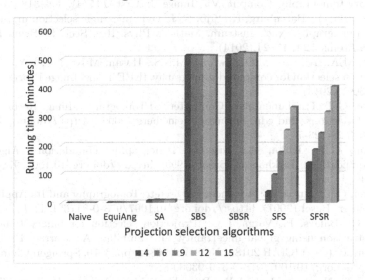

Fig. 5. Diagram for Table 4

6   Conclusion

In this paper we presented sequential feature selection strategies for projection selection in binary tomography and compared them to previously published methods. With experimental tests we showed that SFSR provides the best angle sets, especially in the case of few projections. The only random step is the starting angle-pair of the method whose effect can be weakened by restarting the method several times. Backward search methods are slow, and they do not provide better results than SFSR. However, the running time of this latter method increases with the size of the projection set, thus, for bigger sets, SBSR can be a reasonable alternative of SFSR.

In the future, we plan to examine feature selection based approaches in more general, for deeper understanding how they can be used for finding the most informative projection angles. We also intend to present our results using experimental tests on real data.

Acknowledgements. This research was supported by the project "Integrated program for training new generation of scientists in the fields of computer science", no EFOP-3.6.3-VEKOP-16-2017-0002. The project has been supported by the European Union and co-funded by the European Social Fund.The authors would like to thank László G. Varga for providing the reconstruction toolbox for the experimental tests.

References

1. Batenburg, K.J., Palenstijn, W.J., Balázs, P., Sijbers, J.: Dynamic angle selection in binary tomography. Comput. Vis. Image Underst. **117**(4), 306–318 (2013)
2. Dabravolski, A., Batenburg, K., Sijbers, J.: Dynamic angle selection in x-ray computed tomography. Nucl. Instrum. Methods Phys. Res. Sect. B: Beam Interact. Mater. Atoms **324**, 17–24 (2014)
3. Haque, M.A., Ahmad, M.O., Swamy, M.N.S., Hasan, M.K., Lee, S.Y.: Adaptive projection selection for computed tomography. IEEE Trans. Image Process. **22**(12), 5085–5095 (2013)
4. Herman, G.T.: Fundamentals of Computerized Tomography: Image Reconstruction from Projections, 2nd edn. Springer, Heidelberg (2009). https://doi.org/10.1007/978-1-84628-723-7
5. Herman, G.T., Kuba, A.: Discrete Tomography: Foundations, Algorithms, and Applications. Birkhäuser, Basel (1999). https://doi.org/10.1007/978-1-4612-1568-4
6. Herman, G.T., Kuba, A.: Advances in Discrete Tomography and Its Applications. Birkhäuser, Basel (2007). https://doi.org/10.1007/978-0-8176-4543-4
7. Lékó, G., Balázs, P., Varga, L.G.: Projection selection for binary tomographic reconstruction using global uncertainty. In: Campilho, A., Karray, F., ter Haar Romeny, B. (eds.) ICIAR 2018. LNCS, vol. 10882, pp. 3–10. Springer, Cham (2018). https://doi.org/10.1007/978-3-319-93000-8_1
8. Metropolis, N., Rosenbluth, A.W., Rosenbluth, M.N., Teller, A.H., Teller, E.: Equation of state calculations by fast computing machines. J. Chem. Phys. **21**(6), 1087–1092 (1953)
9. Molina, L.C., Belanche, L., Nebot, A.: Feature selection algorithms: a survey and experimental evaluation. In: 2002 Proceedings of 2002 IEEE International Conference on Data Mining, pp. 306–313 (2002)
10. Nagy, A., Kuba, A.: Reconstruction of binary matrices from fan-beam projections. Acta Cybernetica **17**(2), 359–385 (2005)
11. Pudil, P., Novovičová, J., Kittler, J.: Floating search methods in feature selection. Pattern Recognit. Lett. **15**(11), 1119–1125 (1994)

12. Varga, L., Balázs, P., Nagy, A.: Projection selection algorithms for discrete tomography. In: Blanc-Talon, J., Bone, D., Philips, W., Popescu, D., Scheunders, P. (eds.) ACIVS 2010. LNCS, vol. 6474, pp. 390–401. Springer, Heidelberg (2010). https://doi.org/10.1007/978-3-642-17688-3_37
13. Varga, L., Balázs, P., Nagy, A.: Direction-dependency of binary tomographic reconstruction algorithms. Graph. Models **73**(6), 365–375 (2011). Computational Modeling in Imaging Sciences

Variants of Simulated Annealing for Strip Constrained Binary Tomography

Judit Szűcs and Péter Balázs[✉]

Department of Image Processing and Computer Graphics, University of Szeged,
Árpád tér 2, Szeged 6720, Hungary
{jszucs,pbalazs}@inf.u-szeged.hu

Abstract. We consider the problem of reconstructing binary images
from their row and column sums with prescribed number of strips in each
row and column. In a previous paper we compared an exact deterministic
and an approximate stochastic method (Simulated Annealing – SA) to
solve the problem. We found that the latter one is much more suitable for
practical purposes. Since SA is sensitive to the choice of the initial state,
in this paper we present different strategies for choosing a starting image,
and thus we develop variants of the SA method for strip constrained
binary tomography. We evaluate the different approaches on images with
varying densities of object pixels.

Keywords: Binary tomography · Reconstruction · Nonogram ·
Simulated Annealing · Strip constraint

1 Introduction

Motivated by binary tomography and nonogram puzzles, in [2] we introduced
the problem of reconstructing binary images from their row and column sums
with prescribed number of strips in each row and column. We first formulated
the reconstruction as a Constraint Satisfaction Problem and solved it by an
integer linear programming approach. As an alternative, we presented also a
method based on Simulated Annealing (SA). After comparing the two methods,
it turned out that the SA-based approach is more suitable for practical issues,
even though it gives sometimes just approximate solutions. The effectiveness of
the SA method is influenced by several factors, among which, the initialization
strategy is one key issue. The aim of this paper is to develop variants of the SA
method for the abovementioned problem, and investigate their efficacy both in
running time and in reconstruction quality.

The paper is structured as follows. In Sect. 2 we introduce the binary reconstruction problem, the nonogram puzzles, and define the intermediate problem

This research was supported by the project "Integrated program for training new generation of scientists in the fields of computer science", no EFOP-3.6.3-VEKOP-16-
2017-0002. The project has been supported by the European Union and co-funded by
the European Social Fund.

© Springer Nature Switzerland AG 2019
R. P. Barneva et al. (Eds.): CompIMAGE 2018, LNCS 10986, pp. 82–92, 2019.
https://doi.org/10.1007/978-3-030-20805-9_8

of reconstructing binary matrices with fixed number of strips, from their row and column sums. In Sect. 3 we present variants of simulated annealing to solve the above problem. In Sect. 4 we present experimental results and provide an explanation of them. Finally, we summarize our work in Sect. 5.

2   Binary Tomography, Nonograms, and Strip Constrained Reconstruction

One of the basic problems of binary tomography [6] is to reconstruct a binary image from the horizontal and vertical projections. The image can be represented by a binary matrix, where 1 stands for the object (black) and 0 for the background (white) pixels, respectively. Furthermore, the *horizontal and vertical projection* of the image can be defined as the vector of the row and column sums, respectively, of the image matrix. Thus, formally the following problem is investigated.

Problem. BINARY TOMOGRAPHY (BT)
Input: Two non-negative integer vectors $H \in \mathbb{Z}^m$ and $V \in \mathbb{Z}^n$.
Output: A binary matrix of size $m \times n$, if it exists, with row sum vector H and column sum vector V.

A *switching component* in a binary matrix $A \in \{0,1\}^{m \times n}$ is a set of four positions $(i,j), (i',j), (i,j'), (i',j')$ $(1 \leq i, i' \leq m, 1 \leq j, j' \leq n)$ such that $a_{ij} = a_{i'j'}$ and $a_{i'j} = a_{ij'} = 1 - a_{ij}$. An *elementary switching* is when the 1s of a switching component are changed to 0s, and the 0s to 1s. Clearly, this operation does not affect the row and column sums. In his seminal work [9], Ryser made the following propositions.

Proposition 1. *Problem* BT *can be solved in* $\mathcal{O}(mn)$ *time.*

Proposition 2. *The presence of switching components is a sufficient and necessary condition for non-uniqueness of the solution.*

Proposition 3. *All the solutions of the same problem can be accessed from an arbitrary initial solution by applying a sequence of elementary switchings.*

As a consequence of Proposition 2 it is also clear, that uniqueness can be checked in polynomial-time. Problem BT has a natural connection to the logic puzzles called nonograms. To formally describe this problem, we introduce the notion of *strips* which are non-extendible (i.e. maximal) segments of black pixels of a row or column.

Definition 1. *Given a binary matrix A of size $m \times n$, a sequence of consecutive positions $(i, j_s), (i, j_{s+1}), \ldots, (i, j_{s+l-1})$ (where l is a positive integer, and $1 \leq j_s \leq n$) in the i-th row $(1 \leq i \leq m)$ form a strip if $a_{i,j_s} = 1, a_{i,j_{s+1}} = 1, \ldots, a_{i,j_{s+l-1}} = 1$, and $a_{i,j_s-1} = 0$ and $a_{i,j_s+l} = 0$ (if the latter two positions exist). The length of the strip is given by l. Strips of columns can be defined in an analogous way.*

The length of each strip in the rows of the matrix A can be encoded by an integer matrix LH of size $m \times n$, where lh_{ij} is the length of the j-th strip from the left, in the i-th row. Entries not used to indicate strips are set to 0. Similarly, a matrix LV of size $n \times m$ can describe the length of each strip in the columns of A. Now, the problem is given as follows.

Problem. NONOGRAM
Input: Two non-negative integer matrices LH of size $m \times n$ and LV of size $n \times m$.
Output: A binary matrix of size $m \times n$, if it exists, in each row and column having strips of length prescribed by LH and LV, respectively.

We know from [10] that both NONOGRAM as well as checking whether its solution is unique are NP-complete. Thus, NONOGRAM is much harder than BT, from both the viewpoints of existence and uniqueness. For further works on solvability and uniqueness of nonograms we refer to [1,3–5,8,11,13]. In [2], we defined the following intermediate problem.

Problem. STRIP CONSTRAINED BINARY TOMOGRAPHY (SCBT)
Input: Four non-negative integer vectors $H \in \mathbb{Z}^m$, $V \in \mathbb{Z}^n$, $SH \in \mathbb{Z}^m$, and $SV \in \mathbb{Z}^n$.
Output: A binary matrix of size $m \times n$, if it exists, with row sum vector H, column sum vector V, and in each row and column having the number of strips prescribed by SH and SV, respectively.

It was stated in [2] that this problem is also NP-complete in general and its solution is not always uniquely determined. This latter one is not surprising as the number of strips holds less information than the exact length of each strip, which is given in case of NONOGRAM. Figure 1 shows an example for non-uniqueness of SCBT. It is an open question whether deciding uniqueness is polynomially-solvable for SCBT. Of course, the existence of a switching component is necessary for non-uniqueness, but not always sufficient, as it can be seen, again, in Fig. 1. Based on this observation we cannot expect a result similar to Proposition 3.

Proposition 4. *For certain inputs, Problem* SCBT *can have several solutions, such that one cannot be transformed into the other by a sequence of elementary switchings.*

The three problems and their connections are presented in Fig. 2.

3 Variants of Simulated Annealing

Knowing that SCBT is NP-complete, in [2] we suggested simulated annealing (SA) [7] to solve the problem. Here we propose variants of this method using different initialization (and iteration) strategies. The general framework of the algorithm is given in Algorithm 1. The method starts from a randomly chosen initial solution (Line 1), with an initial temperature (Line 2). In each iteration,

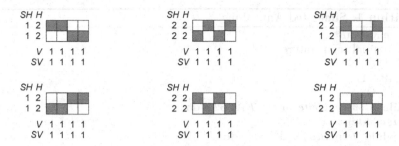

Fig. 1. Examples of uniqueness and non-uniqueness of the SCBT problem. The images of the left column cannot be distinguished by their H, V, SH, and SV vectors, thus, the solution in this case is non-unique. The same holds for the images in the middle column. Notice also that an elementary switching cannot transform one solution into the other. Images of the right column are uniquely determined by their vectors, even though they contain switching components

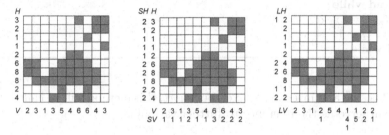

Fig. 2. Instances of the BT (left), SCBT (middle), and NONOGRAM (right) problems. Padding zero elements of the matrices LH and LV are not indicated

the current solution is slightly changed (Line 9). If the objective function value of the newly proposed solution is better than that of the current one, the actual solution will be replaced with the proposed one (Lines 10–11). Otherwise, the new proposal is accepted only with a given probability which is driven by the current temperature and the amount of increase of the objective function (Lines 12–13). The temperature is decreased in each iteration by parameter α (Line 17), and the maximal number of possibly rejected proposals on a fixed temperature is limited by β (Line 8). The method runs until the stopping criteria is not met.

The function we want to minimize is

$$f(\boldsymbol{x}) = ||H - H'||_2 + ||V - V'||_2 + ||SH - SH'||_2 + ||SV - SV'||_2 \, ,$$

where vectors H, V, SH, SV are given as input and H', V', SH', SV' are the corresponding vectors belonging to the current solution.

3.1 The Basic Method

Our basic method presented in [2] starts each time from a random binary image (each pixel is set to 1 with a 0.5 probability). Choosing a neighbor means ran-

Algorithm 1. Simulated Annealing

1: $s \leftarrow$ initial state
2: $T_1 \leftarrow$ initial temperature
3: $k \leftarrow 1$
4: $\alpha \in (0.5, 1)$
5: $\beta \in (0, 1)$
6: **while** ($stoppingCriteria == FALSE$) **do**
7:     $tempStay := 0$
8:     **while** ($tempStay < \beta \cdot f(s)$) **do**
9:         $actual := neighbor(s)$
10:        **if** ($f(actual) < f(s)$) **then**
11:            $s := actual$
12:        **else if** ($e^{\frac{f(s)-f(actual)}{T_k}} > rand(0,1)$) **then**
13:            $s := actual$
14:        **end if**
15:        $tempStay := tempStay + 1$
16:    **end while**
17:    $T_{k+1} := T_k \cdot \alpha$
18:    $k := k + 1$
19: **end while**

---

domly choosing and inverting a pixel. For short, this method will be called 'Basic' and it will serve as the reference to further variants.

3.2   Starting from Precalculated Number of Object Pixels

This approach exploits the fact that the sum of the row sums (alternatively, the sum of the column sums) equals the total number M of object pixels. Instead of starting out from completely random images, we choose M pixels form a uniform random distribution (without repetition) and set them to 1. The resulted image serves as the initial guess of SA. We call this method 'FixPixel'.

3.3   Initialization with Ryser's Algorithm

From, Proposition 1, we know that omitting the SH and SV vectors (thus, relaxing SCBT to BT) the H and V vectors can be satisfied (if a solution exists) in $\mathcal{O}(mn)$ time. Furthermore, Proposition 3 ensures that by elementary switchings, all the solutions of the BT problem can be reached. However, no efficient method is known to visit all of them, therefore checking all solutions of the BT whether they satisfy the vectors SH and SV seems not feasible. Nevertheless, starting from an arbitrary solution of BT, and applying randomly chosen elementary switchings to generate the new suggestions (the neighbor of the current state), we only have to focus on the $||SH - SH'||_2 + ||SV - SV'||_2$ term of the objective function as the remaining part is 0. We call this method 'RyserSA'.

4   Experimental Results

We conducted experiments on 50-50 binary images of sizes $3 \times 3, 4 \times 4, \ldots, 256 \times 256$, containing $0\%, 10\%, \ldots, 100\%$ randomly chosen object pixels. Thus, the test set contained a total of $50 \cdot 254 \cdot 11 = 139\,700$ images. Due to the stochastic nature of simulated annealing, each test was repeated 5 times and the average values of the results were calculated. For the numerical evaluation of the quality of the reconstructed images, we use

$$E(O, R) = \frac{\sum_{ij} |o_{ij} - r_{ij}|}{m \cdot n} \, ,$$

where O and R is the original and the reconstructed image, respectively and $m \times n$ is the size of the image.

The parameters of the SA algorithm has been set manually, in an empirical way. The stopping criteria of the algorithm is to reach 300 000 iterations or to perform 3 000 iterations without improving the solution. The initial temperature is set to $T_1 = 350$ and the cooling schedule is controlled by $\alpha = 0.99$. The SA algorithm may stay in identical temperature for some iteration, in our case this is defined by $\beta = 0.035$. The test was performed on a QuadCore Intel Core i7-4770 processor, 3800 MHz with 8 GB RAM. The algorithms were implemented in MATLAB.

In Fig. 3 we present the pixel error of the methods, Fig. 4 shows the average running time of the three approaches, finally, in Fig. 5 we report on the average final values of the objective function. In the figures, only the graphs of matrices with 0–50% object pixels are plotted. For 60–100% object pixel density we achieve very similar curves, owing to the symmetric nature of black and white pixels.

Considering the pixel error we deduce that there is no significant difference between the three approaches. The closer the image is to the uniform random the higher is the pixel error. Notice that, due to the binary nature of the problem, if the density of a matrix is fixed then for each misclassified object pixel there must exist a misclassified background pixel and vice versa. Therefore the maximum pixel error of a binary matrix A of size $m \times n$ is $2 \cdot \min\{\sum_{i,j} a_{ij}, mn - \sum_{i,j} a_{ij}\}$. This fact is also reflected in Fig. 3, in the relative position of the curves. Furthermore, we can see that in case of 50% density about 50% of the image pixels are misclassified, which is half of the theoretical bound. For 10% density the classification error can reach about 18 percent (very close to the theoretical bound). This is in accordance with the observation reported in [12], where the author generated 5000 random nonograms of size 30×30 with 50% object pixels, and found that 97.5% of the puzzles had a multiple solution. As we know that in SCBT we work with lesser amount of information than in NONOGRAM, we highly suspect that the results of Fig. 3 follow from the non-uniquely determined solutions of the SCBT instances solved.

Regarding the running times we can observe that in case of 'Basic' the running time excessively increases as the relative number of object pixels gets far

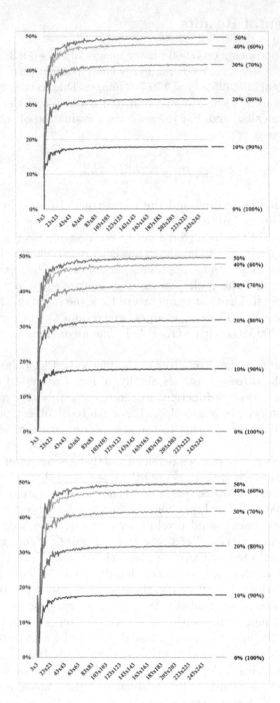

Fig. 3. Average pixel error (vertical axis) of the 'Basic', 'Fixpixel', and 'RyserSA' methods for different sized images (horizontal axis), from top to bottom, respectively

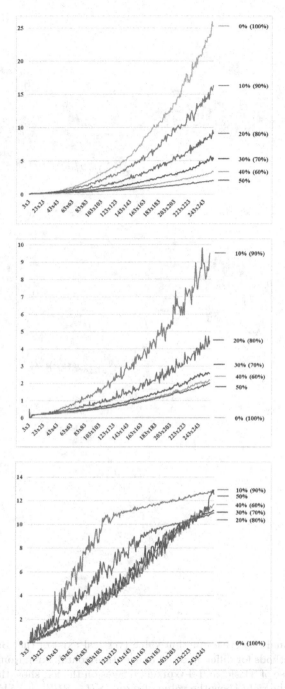

Fig. 4. Average running time in seconds (vertical axis) of the 'Basic', 'Fixpixel', and 'RyserSA' methods for different sized images (horizontal axis), from top to bottom, respectively

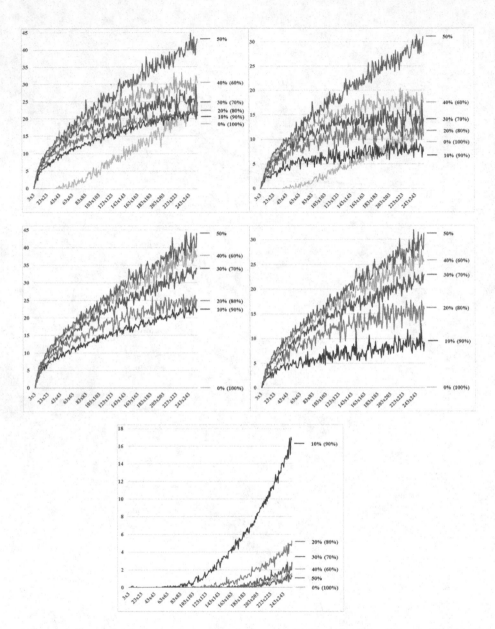

Fig. 5. Average final objective function value (vertical axis) of the 'Basic', 'Fixpixel', and 'RyserSA' methods for different sized images (horizontal axis), from top to bottom, respectively. In case of 'Basic' and 'Fixpixel', images on the left show the total function value, images on the right show the value of term $||SH - SH'||_2 + ||SV - SV'||_2$ of the objective function

from 50%. Since SA starts from a uniform random matrix, in these cases more inversions are needed to reach a matrix with the proper density. 'Fixpixel' does not suffer from this drawback, thus it terminates much faster (and of course, it finds the solution in one iteration when the matrix density is 0% or 100%). The running time of 'RyserSA' lies in between the two methods. It is slower than 'Fixpixel', although both approaches start with a matrix filled with exactly as many object pixels as the total sum of the horizontal (vertical) sums. However, finding a switching component in a matrix ('RyserSA') is a more costly operator than simply inverting one pixel ('Fixpixel'). Still, 'RyserSA' is faster than 'Basic', in average. The reason is that the former method often finds an optimal solution (with 0 objective function value) within less than 300 000 iterations, and then it stops, whereas the latter approach in many cases runs 300 000 iterations and terminates with a non-zero objective function value. For densities of 30% or more, the trend seems to be linear, as well as in the case of smaller matrices with smaller densities. However, for 10% and 20% matrix density we observe a drop in the slope of the graphs, at around size 120×120 and 180×180, respectively (the rest of the trend seems to remain linear, again). The drop is the consequence of the termination criteria of reaching 300 000 iterations. It takes effect only for matrices of bigger sizes and, in the same time, small (10–20%) densities. Otherwise it is very likely that we reach a zero value of the objective function and we can stop earlier. Letting the method run for at most 1 000 000 iterations, we found this phenomenon to disappear.

Concerning the final value of the objective function we see that 'Basic' and 'FixPixel' perform more or less similarly. Since $||H - H'||_2 + ||V - V'||_2$ is always zero during the 'RyserSA' algorithm, for better comparison we also presented the value of term $||SH - SH'||_2 + ||SV - SV'||_2$ for the 'Basic' and 'FixPixel' variants. From this, we deduce that Ryser outperforms the other two methods also from the viewpoint of 'strip error'. The graph belonging to 'RyserSA' once again underpins the earlier observation that matrices of bigger size and 10–20% percent of density are harder to reconstruct. In these cases we usually cannot reach 0 value within the maximal 300 000 iterations. One way to avoid this is to increase the maximal number of iterations permitted, which on the other hand, yields also an increased running time. Repeating the test by limiting the number of iterations in 1 000 000, this approach could reach a very small objective function value (always less than 3, and in most of the cases 0), for all the studied images.

5   Conclusion

In this paper, we studied variants of Simulated Annealing to solve the strip constrained binary tomography problem. We found that the 'FixPixel' method is faster than the one ('Basic') presented in [2]. The variant 'RyserSA', using Ryser's algorithm to identify the initial solution and elementary switchings to refine it, is faster than 'Basic' the and finds very often a perfect solution, especially in case of dense and/or small matrices. It needs a further study to understand why matrices of larger sizes and with smaller densities are harder to reconstruct.

We noticed that the average pixel error is very high in case of all three methods when the original image is compared to the reconstructed one. We suspect that this is a consequence of the high underdeterminedness of the problem which can be understood by a deeper analysis of the switching components of the image, one of our future plans.

Examining the survey of [12] we found that solving nonogram puzzles automatically can be very challenging even for images of size 30×30. In the future, we also intend to investigate whether solving SCBT can somehow facilitate finding a solution for NONOGRAM.

References

1. Artacho, F.J.A., Borwein, J.M., Tam, M.K.: Recent results on Douglas-Rachford methods for combinatorial optimization problems. J. Optim. Theory Appl. **163**(1), 1–30 (2014)
2. Balázs, P., Szűcs, J.: Reconstruction of binary images with fixed number of strips. In: Campilho, A., Karray, F., ter Haar Romeny, B. (eds.) ICIAR 2018. LNCS, vol. 10882, pp. 11–19. Springer, Cham (2018). https://doi.org/10.1007/978-3-319-93000-8_2
3. Batenburg, K.J., Kosters, W.A.: On the difficulty of nonograms. ICGA J. **35**(4), 195–205 (2012)
4. Batenburg, K.J., Kosters, W.A.: Solving nonograms by combining relaxations. Pattern Recognit. **42**(8), 1672–1683 (2009)
5. Berend, D., Pomeranz, D., Rabani, R., Raziel, B.: Nonograms: combinatorial questions and algorithms. Discrete Appl. Math. **169**, 30–42 (2014)
6. Herman, G.T., Kuba, A.: Advances in Discrete Tomography and Its Applications. Springer, Heidelberg (2008). https://doi.org/10.1007/978-0-8176-4543-4
7. Kirkpatrick, S., Gelatt, C.D., Vecchi, M.P., et al.: Optimization by simulated annealing. Science **220**(4598), 671–680 (1983)
8. Ortiz-García, E.G., Salcedo-Sanz, S., Leiva-Murillo, J.M., Pérez-Bellido, A.M., Portilla-Figueras, J.A.: Automated generation and visualization of picture-logic puzzles. Comput. Graphics **31**(5), 750–760 (2007)
9. Ryser, H.J.: Combinatorial properties of matrices of zeros and ones. Can. J. Math. **9**, 371–377 (1957)
10. Ueda, N., Nagao, T.: NP-completeness results for NONOGRAM via parsimonious reductions. preprint (1996)
11. Wang, W.L., Tang, M.H.: Simulated annealing approach to solve nonogram puzzles with multiple solutions. Procedia Comput. Sci. **36**, 541–548 (2014)
12. Wolter, J.: Survey of paint-by-numbers puzzle solvers (2013). http://webpbn.com/survey/index.html
13. Wu, I.C., et al.: An efficient approach to solving nonograms. IEEE Trans. Comput. Intell. AI Games **5**(3), 251–264 (2013)

Methods and Applications

Automatic Segmentation and Quantitative Analysis of Irradiated Zebrafish Embryos

Melinda Katona[1], Tünde Tőkés[2], Emília Rita Szabó[2], Szilvia Brunner[2],
Imre Zoltán Szabó[2], Róbert Polanek[2], Katalin Hideghéty[2],
and László G. Nyúl[1]([envelope])

[1] Department of Image Processing and Computer Graphics, University of Szeged,
Árpád tér 2, Szeged 6720, Hungary
{mkatona,nyul}@inf.u-szeged.hu
[2] ELI-HU Non-Profit Ltd., Dugonics tér 13, Szeged 6720, Hungary
{Tunde.Tokes,rita.szabo,Szilvia.Brunner,Zoltan.Szabo,robert.polanek,
Katalin.Hideghety}@eli-alps.hu

Abstract. Radiotherapy is one of the most common methods to treat
different cancer cells in clinical application despite having harmful effects
on healthy tissues. Radiobiological experiments are very important to
determine the irradiation-caused acute and chronic effects to define the
exact consequences of different irradiation sources. Photon irradiation
has been used on zebrafish embryos, a very new *in vivo* and appropriate
model system in radiobiology. After irradiation, dose-dependent morphological changes were observable in the embryos. These morphological
deteriorations were measured manually by biologist researchers during
three weeks, which was an extremely time demanding process (15 min
per image). The aim of this project was to automate this evaluating
process, to save time for researchers and to keep the consistence and
accuracy of the evaluation. Hence, an algorithm was developed and used
to detect the abnormal development of zebrafish embryos.

Keywords: Image segmentation · Quantitative analysis · Zebrafish ·
Gamma-irradiation · Morphology · Deterioration

1 Introduction

Ionizing radiation is successfully used in both adult and paediatric patients with
various primary and metastatic tumours [6,7]. Approximately 50% of all cancer
patients are subject to radiotherapy during the course of their illness with an
estimation that radiotherapy contributes to approximately 40% towards curative
treatment. Although photon beam therapy is frequently used in the locoregional
treatment of cancer, it has also detrimental effects, since radiotherapy induces
DNA damage and cell death in tumor cells, but can also induce carcinogene-
sis in the surrounding healthy tissue of the tumor. Ionizing radiation interacts

© Springer Nature Switzerland AG 2019
R. P. Barneva et al. (Eds.): CompIMAGE 2018, LNCS 10986, pp. 95–107, 2019.
https://doi.org/10.1007/978-3-030-20805-9_9

with matter by excitation and ionization of molecules, producing free radicals and subsequently reactive oxygen and nitrogen species which can attack cell membranes or break chemical bonds in biological molecules, leading to oxidative stress or DNA damage [5].

Zebrafish (*Danio rerio*) embryos have recently been introduced as a novel vertebrate research model for various human diseases and treatments [12]. Zebrafish are excellent model for experimental human cancer research, as they have many key genes involved in cell cycle, oncogenesis, tumor suppression, and DNA repair [8]. Embryo development is extremely rapid during the first few days post-fertilization while the embryos and larvae are transparent, giving the possibility to study the *in vivo* organ development [1]. These features make this animal model appropriate to investigate the effects of ionizing radiation on zebrafish development [3], and this model provides an interim step between the *in vitro* cell culture and rodent systems.

The advantage of using this vertebrate model is the biological endpoint assessment on large number of embryos, enabling high power statistical analysis. However, the more sophisticated morphological measurements—beyond the simple survival detection—are extremely time- and labor-intensive. The evaluating process for one study took several weeks for the biologists to complete. Only one image measurement took 15 min, and there were 175 photos (~2625 min, that is ~44 hours). Three biologists were working on this evaluating process to get valid results. Thus, automation of quantitative evaluation is highly desired and required. Furthermore, this will enable the whole sample analysis composed of several thousands of embryos in one experiment, and the dynamic assessment at defined timepoints.

Irradiation-caused DNA damage causes observable morphological changes in the zebrafish embryos, such as spinal curvature, shortening of the body length, yolk sac or pericardial edema, abnormality of the eyes (microphthalmia) or abnormal development of the head (microcephaly). The severity of these abnormalities are dose-dependent (see Fig. 1).

In the literature, there are many publications providing automatic methods for the work of biologist researchers. In some procedures, the aim is the detection of zebrafish. Wu et al. [14] used a hybrid active contour model to localize fish. The algorithm of Zhao et al. [16] is based on graph representation. They viewed a graph as a collection of histograms and the main process is similar to "bag-of-words" model. Other publications exist about tracking or detecting zebrafish on videos. Wang et al. [13] used a Gaussian mixture model to tracking multiple zebrafish. Pylatiuk et al. [10] detected heartbeat by digital motion analysis. Ishaq et al. [4] deal with the deformation of zebrafish tail for drug screening. This process is based on a redefined medial axis generation. However, our search did not reveal any system in the literature that supports the biological research by automatically extracting quantitative characteristics/morphological analysis.

In the present study, the various shape characteristics of zebrafish is obtained in order to give a quicker picture of the response of fish to irradiation. A procedure is presented that is capable of delimiting the area of the zebrafish, localizing

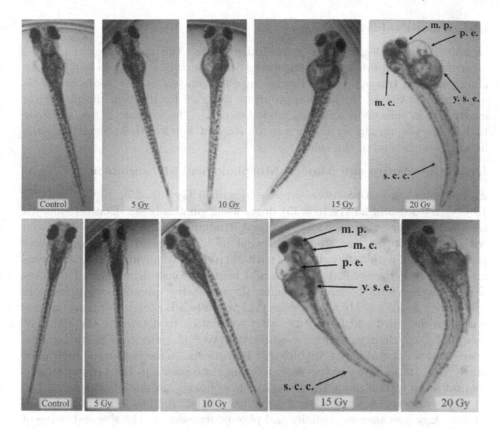

Fig. 1. Dose-dependent morphological changes after 3 days (top row) and 4 days (bottom row) of 0 Gy, 5 Gy, 10 Gy, 15 Gy, and 20 Gy photon irradiation. Significant morphological changes are observable regarding the microphthalmia (m.p.), pericardial edema (p.e.), yolk sac edema (y.s.e.), microcephaly (m.c.), spine cord curvature (s.c.c.).

the eye or the eyes, determining their diameter, the distance between the head and tail of the fish, and giving the position of the fish. The results are compared and contrasted with manually annotated data by biologists.

2 Materials and Methods

2.1 Biological Experimental Setup

The experimental protocol was approved by the Ethics Committee for the Protection of Animals in Scientific Research at the University of Szeged (XXXII./ 1838.2015) and followed the National Institutes of Health (Bethesda, MD) guidelines on the care and use of laboratory animals.

Image and Evaluation Dataset

In this study, biologists have measured manually the morphological changes after three and four days of irradiation to define numerically the dose-dependent changes, using ImageJ (Image Processing and Analysis in Java) Software. This application is one of the most appropriate program for different morphological evaluation in cells or in zebrafish model, too [11]. The software is free and easy to handle. The measured distance is the straight line length in pixels from the head tip to the end of the spine.

Irradiation Setup and Manual Morphological Measurement

24 hpf zebrafish embryos were irradiated with 5 Gy (n = 35), 10 Gy (n = 35), 15 Gy (n = 35) and 20 Gy (n = 35) doses using photon beam. Control embryos (n = 35) had the same procedure without irradiation. Embryos were irradiated with 6 MV photons, generated by a clinical linear accelerator. The embryos were placed in a well within 96-well plates with 200 μl embryo medium, the plates were inserted into a water filled phantom and homogeneously irradiated. The doses were delivered with horizontal beams. Representative photomicrographs were taken with AxioCam MRm at a Zeiss Axiovert 40 CFL (Zeiss, Germany) microscope on the third and fourth day after irradiation to determine the embryos' morphological changes and to measure the eye and spine cord perturbations. Some authors of this paper are biologist researchers. According to the their pilot study [12], these days are the most relevant time-points in the present experimental setup to determine the abnormal morphological deteriorations.

Embryos were observed without any manipulation in place in the microplates. Morphology was assessed visually and photo documented. The size and shape of the embryo, the spine and the eye were monitored continuously in the proportion of the living embryos.

During the manual measurement, researchers measured the two endpoints of the embryos (from the tip of the head to the end of the spine) as a parameter of the body shortening and the spinal curvature, and the diameter of the eyes, that refers to the abnormal eye development (microphthalmia). Numerical data regarding the two endpoints of the embryo and the size of the eye was measured in ImageJ (Fig. 2).

2.2   Image Processing Setup

Delimination of the Well ROI

The image processing task can be split into several subtasks. The wall of the well appears in the zebrafish images and in many cases, only a part of the well is visible. First, the ROI needs to be limited to the region where the fish is located. This is important as it makes it easier to filter the fish from the segmented false objects and reducing the original input image to the well area also reduces runtime. Hough transformation was used on the input grayscale images in order to locate wells for both types of recordings.

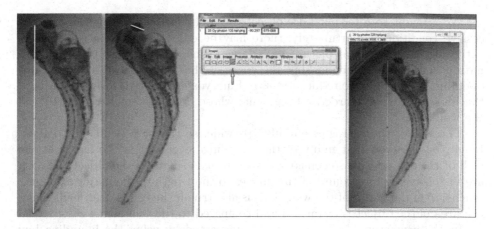

Fig. 2. Parameters measured manually by using the ImageJ Software. Straight yellow line segments represent the diameter of the eye and the distance between the two endpoints of the embryo as a parameter of the spinal curvature. (Color figure online)

Another procedure was used if a circular segment was not found in the picture. The disadvantage of this method is that it assumes that the well is completely visible in the picture. In the majority of the cases, Meniscus effect appears at the wall of the well. Illumination correction was applied to reduce this effect [9]. The wall can be considered as elongated or tubular structure in image, so the enhancement method from [2] article was used. The triangle method [15] was then used to binarize the image. The well is assumed to be located approximately in the center of the image, so first object point is taken by 45° degrees from the center and a circle is fitted to this data.

Zebrafish Segmentation and Feature Extraction

After localization of the well, the next task is segmentation of the fish. If the well can be delineated using Hough transformation, an illumination correction described in Sect. 2.2 has been used. A filter is used as a further preprocessing step when each output pixel contains the range value of the 3-by-3 neighborhood around the corresponding pixel in the image. A binary image with adaptive thresholding is produced after edge enhancement.

The resulting image may contain a number of false regions. This may be, for example, the shell of fish or a part of the well due to inaccurate localization. We divided the picture into four parts and calculated the average thickness of the components in each window. Then, we created a new well mask with this information, to reduce the number of false objects.

This may segment more objects, however, this is not critical to the characterization and morphological opening is used to remove the smaller, unnecessary parts. If there were more than two objects in the image, the two largest areas are kept for further processing.

We attempt to filter out false objects from the image by using a more concessive condition. Unfortunately, there may be cases where Meniscus effect is extremely strong in the picture and darker zones remain despite the illumination correction. After masking the edges of the well and the morphological opening, these areas are reduced in size. Embryos are relatively large objects in the images, so we discarded all segments whose area was smaller than 10% of the well area.

The wall of the well is essentially 1px wide, so this step is dilated to 10px. It can be observed that many of the recordings occur when the fish is at the wall of the pot, so we also consider the major axis length of the object. The fish are visible in the foreground of the images so the length of the major axis must reach 1/5 of the width of the well. This is also true if the fish is deformed. Then, the area of the object is examined and compared to the well area.

In the next step, the image size is constricted by using the bounding box of the object. We re-segmented this smaller area for better results. We used unsharp masking to enhance edges and adaptive thresholding for binarization. Only the largest segment is kept for the post-processing step. At least one eye of the fish is visible in the images, so the final filter step is to determine whether the object has an eye-like region.

For uniform handling and conditions, all images were rotated by 90°, when the height of the image is larger than the width. It is a basic task to determine which part of the object is the head and tail of the fish. The contour of the fish object can be determined (see Fig. 3 for illustration). Image boundaries that do not contain object point can mess up later averaging, so 1/16 of the picture was note used. The remaining image was then subdivided into two equal width regions. We calculated the distance between upper and lower contour point in every column. The head of the fish is larger object then the tail segment, so we compared average distance for the two parts.

Defining the head of a potential fish makes it easier to limit potential eyes. Hereinafter, the description deals with this part of the picture. This smaller section of the image is re-segmented at this stage with the aim of looking for

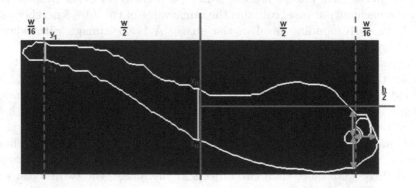

Fig. 3. Illustration of measures of head, tail and eye determination.

Algorithm 1. Eye scanning method

1: **function** EYEEXAMINATION(F, M, B) ▷ input grayscale image F, mean intensity of
    eye object M,   binary eye
    image B, the th_e threshold, th_o threshold
2:      $P_{x,y}$ ← closest horizontal perim point of well
3:      $C_{x,y}$ ← centroid of pre-segmented eye object
4:      dist = $| P_{x,y} - C_{x,y} |$
5:      F_{inc} ← increased F image size with dist value
                both in horizontal and vertical direction
6:      $F_{diff} = |F_{inc} - M|$
7:      F_{dist} ← Distance map of B
8:      F_{bin} ← []   ▷ empty binary image
9:      **for** i, j in all pixels **do**
10:         **if** F_{diff}(i,j) < th_e or F_{dist}(i, j) < 0.2 **then**
11:             $F_{bin}(i, j)$ ← 1
12:         **end if**
13:     **end for**
14:     Hough transformation in F_{bin} image
15:     **if** detected circles = 1 **then**
16:         H_{mask} ← mask of detected circle (dilated) mask
17:         **if** $H_{mask} \cap F_{bin}$ < th_o **then**
18:             Separate F_{bin} objects from each other along H_{mask}
19:         **end if**
20:     **else if** detected circles = 2 **then**
21:         continue
22:     **else**
23:         Keep two largest object
24:         H_{mask} ← mask of detected circle (dilated) mask
25:         Separate F_{bin} objects from each other along H_{mask}
26:     **end if**
27: **end function**

eye-like objects in the image. Te eyes appear as darker regions in the recordings and this information was used for the adaptive thresholding step. Objects were characterized by circumferences and distance from the contour of the head. If the object was not sufficiently circular and the distance was greater than a threshold, then it was eliminated. This gave a maximum of two possible eye regions.

If the fish is too close to the wall of the well, the eyes of the fish cannot be localized at this stage. Results that contain only one eye were re-tested. The pseudocode is shown in Algorithm 1.

In the last step of the method, the diameter of the eye and distance between the endpoints of the fish are calculated. The key stages of the procedure are summarized in Fig. 4.

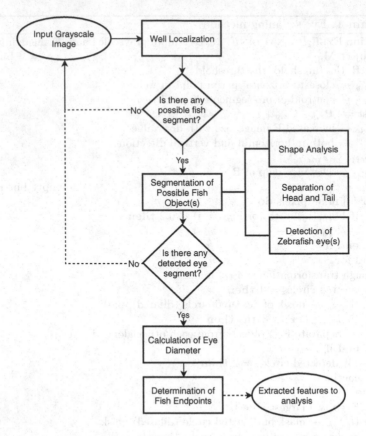

Fig. 4. Flowchart of the proposed algorithm.

3   Evaluation and Results

Data analysis was performed with a statistical software package (SigmaStat for Windows; Jandel Scientific, Erkrath, Germany). The differences between the manual and proposed groups were analysed with paired t-test. Mean (M) values and standard deviation (SD) are given in all reported Figures and Tables.

Figures 5 and 6 show that there is no significant difference between manual annotation and the values computed by the automatic algorithm. Table 1 presents the measured values. This means that the method can save a tremendous amount of time for biologist researchers while providing comparable results. The average execution time of about 5 s can be considered quite good. The runtime was higher for the well and fish segmentation due to the use of Hough transformation. Table 2 shows execution time of the stages of the algorithm and Fig. 7 illustrates segmentation results by the algorithm for some cases.

Five independent researchers have measured manually the morphological changes by the ImageJ Software from photo to photo, during 3 weeks. Notable deviation was found among the manual results, despite that the researchers have

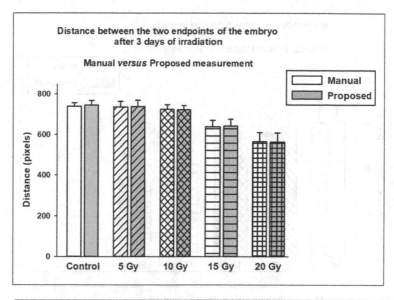

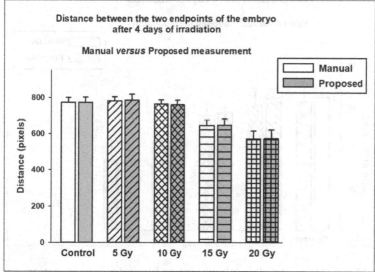

Fig. 5. Parameter of the length and spinal curvature after three and four days of irradiation.

discussed the exact method for the evaluations during the statistical analysis. The evaluation of one photo took ca. 15 min, so for two researchers to complete all the measurements, it would have taken at least 2 months human effort.

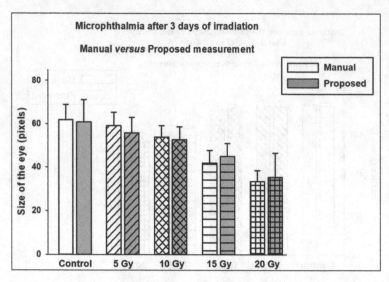

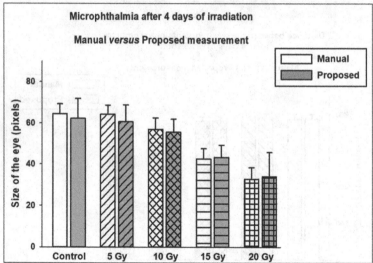

Fig. 6. Microphthalmia after three and four days of irradiation.

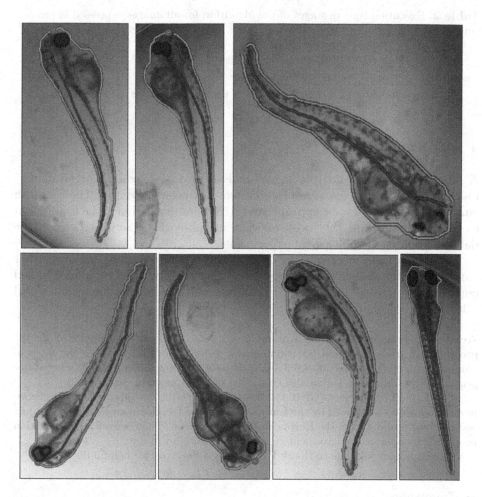

Fig. 7. Illustration of detected zebrafish embryos with their eye/eyes and endpoints.

Table 1. Results of manual and automatic measurements (mean ± standard deviation, in pixels).

		Head-to-tail distance		Eye diameter	
		3 days	4 days	3 days	4 days
Control	Manual	739.6 ± 16.9	774.3 ± 25.7	61.7 ± 7.1	64.5 ± 4.7
	Proposed	744.7 ± 22.9	773.4 ± 28.6	60.6 ± 10.3	62.2 ± 10.0
5 Gy	Manual	736.3 ± 27.0	782.6 ± 23.0	58.9 ± 6.2	63.6 ± 4.0
	Proposed	737.6 ± 31.3	785.8 ± 34.0	56.7 ± 6.3	60.9 ± 8.0
10 Gy	Manual	723.7 ± 24.1	764.8 ± 23.4	53.7 ± 5.3	56.9 ± 5.6
	Proposed	722.6 ± 21.1	760.1 ± 25.1	52.4 ± 6.0	55.5 ± 6.3
15 Gy	Manual	637.3 ± 32.6	645.9 ± 31.6	41.7 ± 5.8	42.5 ± 5.0
	Proposed	641.0 ± 34.0	647.8 ± 34.9	44.7 ± 6.0	45.0 ± 10.3
20 Gy	Manual	563.8 ± 45.5	572.2 ± 43.8	33.3 ± 5.0	32.8 ± 5.6
	Proposed	562.0 ± 46.6	573.6 ± 48.2	33.8 ± 8.6	34.1 ± 11.7

Table 2. Execution time of stages of the algorithm for all images expressed in seconds (mean values ± standard deviation).

	Well localization	Zebrafish detection	Feature extraction	All steps
Execution time	2.8 ± 0.54	2.06 ± 0.42	0.57 ± 0.48	4.92 ± 1.08

4   Conclusions

A reliable quantitative morphological analysis of dose-dependent organ malformations using an *in vivo* vertebrate system has been presented. The zebrafish embryo model proved to be appropriate for complex evaluation of the irradiation-caused damages, and the most relevant morphological parameters could be defined for later radiobiological experiments.

It is doubtlessly necessary to develop automatic evaluating programs that can perform the measurements very rapidly, accurately, more reproducibly and consequently, saving the time for researchers and resulting in more robust and reliable statistical analysis.

Acknowledgements. Melinda Katona and László G. Nyúl was supported by the project "Integrated program for training new generation of scientists in the fields of computer science", No. EFOP-3.6.3-VEKOP-16-2017-0002. The project has been supported by the European Union and co-funded by the European Social Fund.

The ELI-ALPS project (GINOP-2.3.6-15-2015-00001) is supported by the European Union and co-financed by the European Regional Development Fund. The project has received funding from the European Union's Horizon 2020 research and innovation programme under grant agreement No. 654148 Laserlab-Europe.

The authors would like to thank Dr. Andrew Cheesman for helpful discussions.

References

1. Bailey, J.M., Creamer, B.A., Hollingsworth, M.A.: What a fish can learn from a mouse: principles and strategies for modeling human cancer in mice. Zebrafish **6**(4), 329–337 (2009)
2. Frangi, A.F., Niessen, W.J., Vincken, K.L., Viergever, M.A.: Multiscale vessel enhancement filtering. In: Wells, W.M., Colchester, A., Delp, S. (eds.) MICCAI 1998. LNCS, vol. 1496, pp. 130–137. Springer, Heidelberg (1998). https://doi.org/10.1007/BFb0056195
3. Geiger, G.A., Fu, W., Kao, G.D.: Temozolomide-mediated radiosensitization of human glioma cells in a zebrafish embryonic system. Cancer Res. **68**(9), 3396–3404 (2008)
4. Ishaq, O., Negri, J., Bray, M.A., Pacureanu, A., Peterson, R.T., Wählby, C.: Automated quantification of zebrafish tail deformation for high-throughput drug screening. In: 2013 IEEE 10th International Symposium on Biomedical Imaging, pp. 902–905 (2013)

5. Jarvis, R., Knowles, J.: DNA damage in zebrafish larvae induced by exposure to low-dose rate γ-radiation: detection by the alkaline comet assay. Mutat. Res./Genet. Toxicol. Environ. Mutagen. **541**(1), 63–69 (2003)
6. Kalifa, C., Grill, J.: The therapy of infantile malignant brain tumors: current status? J. Neuro-Oncol. **75**(3), 279–285 (2005)
7. Larouche, V., Huang, A., Bartels, U., Bouffet, E.: Tumors of the central nervous system in the first year of life. Pediatr. Blood Cancer **49**(7), 1074–1082 (2007)
8. McAleer, M.F., et al.: Novel use of zebrafish as a vertebrate model to screen radiation protectors and sensitizers. Int. J. Radiat. Oncol. Biol. Phys. **61**(1), 10–13 (2005)
9. Narasimha-Iyer, H., et al.: Robust detection and classification of longitudinal changes in color retinal fundus images for monitoring diabetic retinopathy. IEEE Trans. Biomed. Eng. **53**(6), 1084–1098 (2006)
10. Pylatiuk, C., et al.: Automatic zebrafish heartbeat detection and analysis for zebrafish embryos. Zebrafish **11**(4), 379–383 (2014)
11. Smith, L.L., Beggs, A.H., Gupta, V.A.: Analysis of skeletal muscle defects in larval zebrafish by birefringence and touch-evoke escape response assays. J. Vis. Exp. **82**, 50925 (2013)
12. Szabó, E.R., et al.: L-Alpha glycerylphosphorylcholine as a potential radioprotective agent in zebrafish embryo model. Zebrafish **13**(6), 481–488 (2016)
13. Wang, X., Cheng, E., Burnett, I.S., Huang, Y., Wlodkowic, D.: Automatic multiple zebrafish larvae tracking in unconstrained microscopic video conditions. In: Scientific Reports, vol. 7 (2017)
14. Wu, T., Lu, J., Lu, Y., Liu, T., Yang, J.: Embryo zebrafish segmentation using an improved hybrid method. J. Microsc. **250**(1), 68–75 (2013)
15. Zack, G.W., Rogers, W.E., Latt, S.: Automatic measurement of sister chromatid exchange frequency. J. Histochem. Cytochem. **25**, 741–753 (1977)
16. Zhao, H., Zhou, J., Robles-Kelly, A., Lu, J., Yang, J.Y.: Automatic detection of defective zebrafish embryos via shape analysis. In: Digital Image Computing: Techniques and Applications, pp. 431–438 (2009)

Classification of Breast Lesions Using Quantitative Dynamic Contrast Enhanced-MRI

Mohan Jayatilake[1]([⊠]), Teresa Gonçalves[2], and Luís Rato[2]

[1] University of Peradeniya, Peradeniya, Sri Lanka
jayatiml@gmail.com
[2] Department of Informatics, University of Évora, Évora, Portugal
{tcg,lmr}@uevora.pt

Abstract. Imaging biomarkers are becoming important in both research and clinical studies. This study is focused on developing measures of tumour mean, fractal dimension, homogeneity, energy, skewness and kurtosis that reflect the values of the pharmacokinetic (PK) parameters within the breast tumours, evaluate those using clinical data, and investigate their feasibility as a biomarker to discriminate malign from benign breast lesions. In total, 75 patients with breast cancer underwent Dynamic Contrast Enhanced-Magnetic Resonance Imaging (DCE-MRI). Axial bilateral images with fat-saturation and full breast coverage were performed at 3T Siemens with a 3D gradient echo-based TWIST sequence. The whole tumour mean, fractal dimension, homogeneity, energy, skewness and kurtosis of K^{trans} and V_e values were calculated. Median of both the mean and the fractal dimension of K^{trans} and V_e for benign and malignant tumour show significant discrimination. Further, the median of skewness and kurtosis of V_e significantly vary between benign and malignant cases. In conclusion, the mean and the fractal dimension of both K^{trans} and V_e and skewness and kurtosis of V_e for typical breast cancer, computed from PK parametric maps, show potential as a biomarker for breast tumour diagnosis either as a benign or malignant.

Keywords: Magnetic resonance imaging · Breast cancer · Texture

1 Introduction

Breast cancer is the highest cause of cancer death and the most common cancer in women [1]. Therefore, early and precise detection of breast cancer would help decrease mortality rates of breast cancer patients and improve chances of successful treatment [3]. Even though mammography is the most widespread imaging modality for breast cancer screening and early detection, both the sensitivity and specificity of screening mammography is not satisfactory, especially with dense breast tissues or multiple foci in fibroglandular [22]. Further, mammography has given false positive readings leading to unnecessary biopsies as

© Springer Nature Switzerland AG 2019
R. P. Barneva et al. (Eds.): CompIMAGE 2018, LNCS 10986, pp. 108–119, 2019.
https://doi.org/10.1007/978-3-030-20805-9_10

well as false negative readings leading to fail diagnosis of malignant lesions [8]. Therefore, a number of imaging techniques have been experimented to enhance breast cancer detection using different imaging modalities.

The DCE-MRI has shown a higher sensitivity in detecting breast cancers as well as has a great potential for screening high-risk women, staging newly diagnosed breast cancers, and assessing therapy effects [23], not available with mammography or with ultrasound. DCE-MRI is a non-invasive technique to study in vivo microvascular characteristics such as blood volume, blood flow and endothelial permeability in breast lesions [9,15,20]. DCE-MRI, in which the passage of a contrast agent through a mammary tissue is monitored after a bolus injection, has emerged as a valuable clinical tool to diagnose breast tumours.

Great research efforts have been made to interpret the images more precisely and efficiently in last few decades using morphological features of tumour such as, volume, shape, and boundary speculation, and the quantitative analysis of the tumour kinetic features extracted from the DCE-MR images have been used to develop and test automated detection systems of breast MR images [8,22]. Imaging biomarkers, sensitive to the effects of diagnosis, are becoming increasingly important in both research and clinical studies. Using the pharmacokinetic (PK) standard model (SM), the contrast uptake curve per voxel as measured by DCE-MRI can be summarized with a small number of descriptive parameters [19,25,26]. The most promising diagnostic markers are measures of the exchange effects: K^{trans}, (contrast agent extravasation rate from blood plasma to extravascular extracellular space) and V_e (volume fraction of extravascular extracellular space) [11,12,16,19,25]. However, traditionally, the parameter values used for discrimination of benign and malignant breast lesions are tumour ROI-averaged, lacking information in parameter heterogeneity [2,14,28]. Analysis of pixel parameter values is required to quantify PK parameter heterogeneity, which remains a significant challenge [13,14].

The gray-level co-occurrence matrix (GLCM), which is a popular algorithm for texture analysis [2,10] has shown potential in the application of tumour differentiation and treatment response prediction [28,29]. It is found that the tumour response group in limb sarcoma had a high feature of image coherence in pre-treatment DCE-MRI K^{trans} maps [2,4,17,18]. However, the texture analysis of DCE-MRI pharmacokinetic maps has hardly been used yet in breast cancers for investigating the potential of features to quantify DCE-MRI data, as well as, a treatment response.

Hence, in this study, using breast DCE-MRI data from a pre-biopsy population, we sought to explore the utility of higher order moments, fractal dimension and GLCM-based texture features of homogeneity and energy in 3D from K^{trans} and V_e parametric maps and their spatial locations within the breast tumours and evaluate those using clinical investigating their feasibility as a biomarker for discriminating malignant from benign breast lesions.

2   Theory

In this section we present the theoretical basis for the estimation of higher order moments (skewness and kurtosis), fractal dimension and GLCM-based texture analysis (energy and homogeneity) of DCE-MRI quantitative PK parameters (K^{trans} and V_e).

2.1   Skewness and Kurtosis

The skewness (3rd moment) and kurtosis (4th moment) are measures of asymmetry and normalized form of the central moment of the PK parameter values K^{trans} and V_e for the whole tumour ROI, respectively. If the skewness is negative, the PK parametric values are spread out more to the left of the mean than to the right; if skewness is positive, the PK parametric values are spread out more to the right. [13]. Kurtosis indicates the degree of peakedness of the values; it is based on the size of the tail of the PK value distribution.

The skewness and kurtosis for whole tumour ROI can be determined using Eq. (1). Here, pi and i represent the PK parameters of K^{trans} and V_e values in ith pixel and number of pixels within the tumour ROI, respectively; p and f(pi) characterize the mean of the PK value and the probability of the PK parameter falling within a specific value given by the range of this variable's density, respectively.

$$n^{th}\ moment = \sum_i (p_i - p)^n . f(p_i) \qquad (1)$$

2.2   Energy and Homogeneity

Energy and heterogeneity are two statistical texture features. These features are based on the normalized GLCM; for a 2D PK parametric map f, the co-occurrence matrix $M_{f,\delta}(k, l)$ represents the joint probability occurrence of pixel pairs (with a defined spatial relationship) having gray level values k and l , for a given spatial offset $\delta = (\delta x, \delta y)$ between the pair [10,29]. The $M_{f,\delta}(k, l)$ is defined by Eq. (2)

$$M_{f,\delta}(k, l) = \begin{cases} \sum_{x=1}^{n} \sum_{y=1}^{n} 1 & \text{if } f(x, y) = k \text{ and } f(x + \delta x, y + \delta y) = l \\ \sum_{x=1}^{n} \sum_{y=1}^{n} 0 & \text{otherwise} \end{cases} \qquad (2)$$

The co-occurrence matrix $M_{f,\delta}(k, l)$ has dimension $n \times n$, where n is the number of gray levels in the f. The GLCM accounts for the spatial inter-dependency or co-occurrence of two pixels at specific relative positions. Co-occurrence matrices are calculated for the directions of 0°, 45°, 90° and 135⁰. The GLCM matrices are computed for the 4 directions corresponding to offsets of 0°, 45°, 90°, and 135°, and the average matrix over all offsets can be used [4,17]. In this study, we used the M 2D formulation with 8-connexity, computed with 8 different offsets. On the basis of this matrix, we derived the second-order statistical features of energy and homogeneity [10] for each image slice. The energy and homogeneity averages over all slices were calculated.

Energy. Energy is defined as the measure of the extent of pixel pair repetitions in matrix M and can be estimated using Eq. (3). When pixels are very similar, the energy value will be large.

$$\text{Energy} = \sum_{x=1}^{n} \sum_{l=1}^{n} M_{f,\delta}(k,l) \tag{3}$$

Homogeneity. Homogeneity is the statistical measure of the similarity of pixels in matrix M and can be estimated using Eq. (4). A diagonal gray level co-occurrence matrix gives homogeneity of 1. It becomes large if local textures only have minimal changes.

$$\text{Homogeneity} = \sum_{x=1}^{n} \sum_{l=1}^{n} \frac{M_{f,\delta}(k,l)}{1+|k-l|} \tag{4}$$

2.3   Fractal Dimension

In this study, we used the blanket method described developed by Peleg et al. [21] to evaluate the fractal dimension of the 2D surface of PK parameter values within the whole tumour ROI [10,17]. The Blanket method estimates the area of a surface by considering all points in the three dimensional space at distance from the surface on both sides and constituting a blanket of thickness 2. This volume is then divided by 2 to estimate the area [2,21]. The covering blanket consists of upper blanket surface u_ϵ and lower blanket surface $b_\epsilon psilon$. Initially when $\epsilon - 0$, both upper and lower blanket surfaces are given by the same gray level function $g(i,j)$ for pixel (i,j) i.e., $g(i,j) = u_\epsilon(i,j) = b_\epsilon(i,j)$. For $\epsilon = 1,2,3,\ldots$, blanket surfaces are defined by Eqs. (5) and (6), respectively.

$$u_\epsilon(i,j) = \max\{u_\epsilon - 1(i,j) + 1\} \text{ with } |(m,n) - (i,j) \leq 1| \tag{5}$$

$$b_\epsilon(i,j) = \max\{b_\epsilon - 1(i,j) + 1\} \text{ with } |(m,n) - (i,j) \leq 1| \tag{6}$$

where the image points (m,n) with distance less than one from (i,j) were considered to be the four immediate neighbours of (i,j). Then the volume between the blanket, $V(\epsilon)$ is calculated as sum of the differences (Eq. (7)) [6].

$$V(\epsilon) = \sum_{i,j} u_\epsilon(i,j) - b_\epsilon(i,j) \tag{7}$$

Therefore, the surface area, $A(\epsilon)$ of the blanket is computed by Eq. (8).

$$A(\epsilon) = \frac{V(\epsilon) - V(\epsilon - 1)}{2\epsilon} \tag{8}$$

Since $V(\epsilon)$ depends on small scale features, $V(\epsilon - 1)$ is subtracted to isolate those features that change from scale $\epsilon - 1$ to scale ϵ. This isolation from the effects of smaller scale features is necessary for non-fractal objects. For pure fractal objects both $V(\epsilon) - V(\epsilon - 1)/2\epsilon$ and $V(\epsilon)/2\epsilon$ are identical since property changes do not depend on scale. However, the above Eq. (8) gives reasonable measures for both fractal and non-fractal surfaces. Eq. (9) presents Mandelbrot's defined fractal surface area [5,6].

$$A(\epsilon) = F\epsilon^{2-D} \tag{9}$$

where F is a constant and D is the fractal dimension of the surface. When the $\log(A(\epsilon))$ is plotted against $\log(\epsilon)$ a straight line is obtained with a slope equals to $2 - D$ which gives an estimations of fractal dimension.

$$\log(A(\epsilon)) = \log(F) + (2 - D)\log(\epsilon) \tag{10}$$

3   Methods

3.1   Data Acquisition

Seventy five (75) women diagnosed with suspicious breast lesions underwent DCE-MRI scans. Axial bilateral DCE-MRI images with fat-saturation and full breast coverage were acquired from each subject with 3T Siemens system using 3D gradient echo-based TWIST sequence, 10° flip angle, 2.9/6.2 ms TE/TR, a parallel imaging acceleration factor of two, 30–34 cm FOV, 320 × 320 matrix size, and 1.4 mm slice thickness. The total DCE-MRI acquisition time was 10 min for 32–34 image volume sets 18–20 s temporal resolution. Gadolinium contrast agent (Prohance©) IV injection (0.1 mmol/kg at 2 ml/s) was carried out following acquisitions of two baseline image volumes. Parametric maps for PK parameters, K^{trans} and V_e, were generated under the standard model.

The first step for quantifying the tumour heterogeneity is to identify regions of interest (ROI) in these parametric maps. tumour ROIs were drawn by experienced radiologists based on post-contrast DCE images and whole tumour ROI mean parameter value was calculated by weighted (by pixel number) average of slice ROI values. MATLAB Simulink image processing software was used for the data analysis.

3.2   Estimation of Mean Parametric Values of K^{trans} and V_e

Parametric maps for the PK parameters K^{trans} and V_e were generated under the Standard Model. For quantitative data analysis, region of interest (ROI)s on multiple image slices were drawn encompassing tumour on post-contrast DCE images. tumour ROI and pixel (within the ROI) DCE-MRI time-course data were then analyzed to extract K^{trans} and V_e pixel values. Then, the whole tumour ROI mean of K^{trans} and V_e pixel values were computed by weighted (by pixel number) average of slice ROI values using all pixel values within the multi-slice ROIs encompassing the tumour. The histograms of K^{trans} and V_e were plotted with the mean values.

3.3   Fractal Dimension Analysis

The whole tumour higher order moments (skewness and kurtosis) and fractal dimension of K^{trans} and V_e values were calculated within the whole tumour ROI using the Eqs. (1) and (10) for each image slice covering the entire tumour. The fractal dimension was estimated after linear fitting of $\log A(\epsilon)$ vs. $\log \epsilon$ (see Eq. (10)).

3.4   Heterogeneity and Energy Analysis

Image texture analysis was performed on parametric maps of K^{trans} and V_e at all 2D tumour slice within the 3D ROI. The normalized GLCM was calculated for each 2D slice, and based on the GLCM obtained, the two feature measures of energy and homogeneity were computed (Eqs. (3) and (4)).

4   Results and Analysis

Each subject participated in a DCE-MRI acquisition following the clinical mammography and/or MRI screening but prior to the biopsy procedure and the pathology analysis. All subjects had MRI contrast-enhanced lesions radiologically classified as BIRADS (Breast Imaging Reporting and Data System) three (B-3, probably benign), four (B-4, suspicious abnormality) or five (B-5, highly suggestive of malignancy).

The magnitude of K^{trans} and V_e pixel values were analyzed within the 59 benign and 30 malignant tumours in 3D ROIs. The overlaid K^{trans} and V_e maps on coronal views of the right breast of a benign and a malignant lesion are presented in Figs. 1 and 2 respectively. The minimal values of K^{trans} and V_e were set to 0.001 (min^{-1}); as shown in Fig. 1(A) and (B), pixel values of K^{trans} in the benign lesion were considerably lower than that of the malignant lesions. The K^{trans} maps shown in Fig. 1(B) reveal clear hot spots on the malignant lesion. Although hot spot have K^{trans} values greater than 0.25 min^{-1} some are as small as 2 mm in diameter (see Fig. 1(B)). Among all 30 malignant tumours in the population, the large area of tumour regions has K^{trans} values greater than 0.10 min^{-1}, but the K^{trans} pixel values of benign lesions are lower than 0.2 min^{-1}.

The DCE pharmacokinetic images of V_e coronal slices of a benign and malignant lesion after contrast injection are illustrated in Fig. 2(A) and (B) respectively. As shown in Fig. 2, pixel values of V_e in the benign lesion are significantly higher than that of the malignant lesion. The overlaid V_e maps reveal hot spots on the posterior edge of the both benign and malignant lesion. The hot spot of benign lesion has V_e values of 0.5 or greater, but the V_e of the malignant lesion has significantly lower (values below 0.25). In general, among all tumours in the population, majority of V_e pixel values are greater than 0.4 in benign but smaller than 0.2 in malignant.

Table 1 summarizes and compares the average, median and standard deviation of mean, skewness, kurtosis, fractal dimension, homogeneity and energy

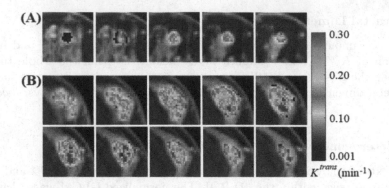

Fig. 1. K^{trans} parametric maps generated by the standard model. A coronal, fat–suppressed breast DCE-MR image with benign (A) and malignant lesion (B).

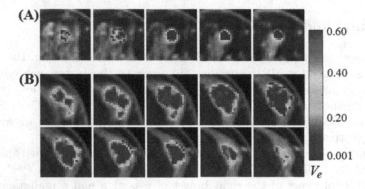

Fig. 2. V_e parametric maps generated by the standard model. A coronal, fat–suppressed breast DCE-MR image with benign (A) and malignant lesion (B).

K^{trans} between the malignant and benign breast tumours. Table 2 shows the same measures for V_e.

As shown, mean K^{trans} value is higher in malignant than in benign (0.09 vs 0.05, respectively; $p < 0.01$), whereas mean V_e is lower in malignant than in benign (0.23 vs 0.44, respectively; $p < 0.01$). Similarly, median of mean K^{trans} value is high in malignant but median of mean V_e is low.

Further, the average fractal dimension of benign is higher than of malignant for K^{trans} (3.50 vs 2.85, respectively; $p < 0.01$) and for V_e (3.13 vs 2.54, respectively; $p < 0.01$) and the same happens for the median fractal dimension (K^{trans} shows 2.95 vs 2.85, respectively; $p < 0.01$ and V_e shows 3.09 vs 2.88, respectively; $p < 0.01$). However, average homogeneity and energy of K^{trans} of between benign and malignant are marginally altered ($p > 0.01$) similarly that of V_e are also slightly varying ($p > 0.01$). Similarly, median homogeneity of both V_e and K^{trans} of between benign and malignant are also somewhat varying.

Nonetheless, skewness and kurtosis of V_e between benign and malignant and are significantly varying (skewness of V_e 0.35 vs 2.29 respectively; $p < 0.01$)

Table 1. K^{trans} statistical measures values of benign and malignant breast tumours. The units of K^{trans} values are in min^{-1}

Statistical measures	Benign			Malignant			p-value
	Avg	Median	SD	Avg	Median	SD	
Mean	0.05	0.06	0.04	0.09	0.12	0.16	0.0068
Skewness	1.10	1.17	0.98	1.23	1.64	0.53	0.7360
Kurtosis	5.04	4.07	0.29	5.22	8.65	1.41	0.5650
Fractal dim	3.50	2.96	0.29	2.85	2.85	0.58	0.0010
Homogeneity	0.16	0.08	0.06	0.04	0.01	0.08	0.0970
Energy	0.03	0.02	0.03	0.02	0.00	0.02	0.0390

Table 2. v_E statistical measures values of benign and malignant breast tumours.

Statistical measures	Benign			Malignant			p-value
	Avg	Median	SD	Avg	Median	SD	
Mean	0.44	0.55	0.02	0.23	0.37	0.11	0.0010
Skewness	0.35	0.03	0.52	2.29	2.00	1.12	0.0001
Kurtosis	2.48	1.62	1.30	8.94	6.39	1.75	0.0002
Fractal dim	3.13	3.09	0.26	2.54	2.88	0.33	0.0030
Homogeneity	0.19	0.08	0.02	0.05	0.01	0.03	0.0380
Energy	0.03	0.02	0.00	0.02	0.00	0.01	0.0460

and (Kurtosis of V_e 2.48 vs 8.94 respectively; $p < 0.01$) and V_e of malignant is higher than that of benign. However, average of skewness of K^{trans} between benign and malignant are not significantly varying ($p0.01$). Nevertheless, median of both skewness and kurtosis of V_e between benign and malignant are again significantly varying (median of skewness of V_e 0.03 vs 2.00 respectively) and (median Kurtosis of V_e 1.62 vs 6.39 respectively) and V_e of malignant is higher than that of benign. But, average of skewness and kurtosis of K^{trans} between benign and malignant are not significantly varying ($p > 0.01$), however, median of skewness of K^{trans} between benign and malignant are considerably varying.

Figure 3 shows box plots of the whole tumour skewness, kurtosis, fractal dimension, energy and homogeneity of K^{trans} and V_e measures for the malignant (light blue) and benign (dark blue) groups. The horizontal red line on each box indicates the median value.

According to the box plots, the average of both the mean of K^{trans} and V_e (Fig. 3A) and the average of fractal dimension of the both K^{trans} and V_e (Fig. 3D) indicate a significant variation for tumour discrimination. Further, the average of skewness and kurtosis of V_e (Fig. 3B and 3C) also show significant differences. However, both K^{trans} and V_e values of homogeneity and energy distributions (Fig. 3E and 3F) for benign and malignant are not discriminant.

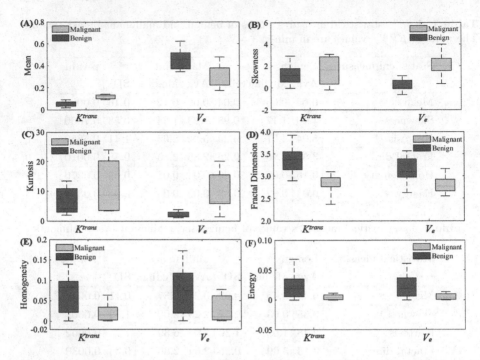

Fig. 3. The box plot distribution of mean (A), skewness (B), kurtosis (C), fractal dimension (D), homogeneity (E) and energy (F) of K^{trans} and V_e for the tumour ROI. (Color figure online)

Still looking at the box-plots the measure that seem to have the biggest discriminant power is skewness V_e (Fig. 3B) since the box-plots for benign and malignant show a bigger distance. As a minor exercise we used a Machine Learning technique to check the features' discriminant power over the problem; specifically, we fed the full data to a Decision Tree algorithm using the Weka framework with default parameters [27]. It gave rise to a tree of depth one that can be translated to the following rule:

> *if* skewness-$V_e \leq 1.112121$ *then* benign *else* malignant

This simple rule supports the idea that the proposed features do have a discriminant value over the problem. Moreover, the skewness-V_e alone is enough to differentiate between benign and malignant tumours. Using a 10-fold cross validation procedure, this rules only misclassified one instance over the total of 75 subjects.

5   Discussion, Conclusions and Future Work

The major goal of this study was to estimate the capability of texture features derived from different quantitative DCE-MRI maps for early prediction of neoadjuvant chemotherapy of breast cancer patients. The PK parametric maps of K^{trans} and V_e generated by SM from the DCE-MRI data in this study revealed that they were heterogeneous between benign and malignant breast tumour ROIs.

According to this study, the mean K^{trans} values varied between between 0.14 min-1 and 0.09 min-1 for malignant tumour ROIs, which are comparable with other studies [24]. However, the range of mean K^{trans} values for malignant breast tumours reported by Li et al. (0.14 min^{-1} to 0.17 min^{-1}) [16] is slightly higher than that of our study. Nonetheless, there is no pronounced difference between benign and malignant breast tumours with respect to either of the PK parameters because K^{trans} and V_e values exhibit an overlap for benign and malignant tumours [2]. In addition, it was suggested in the literature that V_e values derived from SM are not a reliable biomarker of the extra vascular extra cellular space [11,12]. Furthermore, K^{trans} and V_e values returned by SM are acceptable when the underlying assumptions of this model hold approximately.

Therefore, conventional distributional statistics describing the parametric values obtained from DCE-MRI modelling alone are not adequate to separate breast tumours as benign and malignant. This study incorporates skewness, kurtosis, fractal dimension, energy and homogeneity in addition to PK parametric maps to describe texture heterogeneity over the spatial location within tumour ROIs and a significant difference between benign and malignant breast tumours was evident in the box plots obtained (for fractal dimension of K^{trans} and V_e, homogeneity of K^{trans} and V_e of skewness and kurtosis) and the results are compliant with the pathological reports as well.

Both PK parameters indicate higher values of fractal dimension for benign breast tumours when compared to malignant tumours. Hence, it can be concluded that fractal dimension shows a potential to discriminate benign and malignant breast tumours. Similarly, Chan and Tuszynski [7] stated that the fractal dimension showed great potential of predicting tumour malignancy and could be used to assist in the diagnosis of breast tumours. In contrast to Blanket method used in this study, box counting was employed by Chan and Tuszynski.

This study shows that mean, fractal dimension of DCE-MRI quantitative PK parameters and skewness and kurtosis of V_e are likely to be more useful than those of the semi-quantitative metrics for early prediction of breast cancer neoadjuvant chemotherapy response, showing the benefit of performing PK modeling of the DCE time-course data. This study's major limitation is small size of the sample, and thus, it is important to validate this initial findings with a larger patient cohort in the future.

Although it clearly needs to be validated with larger patient populations, this non-invasive 3D imaging feature extraction approach has the potential to become an important clinical tool in the emerging era of precision medicine to classify tumours in the early stages of treatment.

In conclusion, this study has investigated the capability of mean and fractal dimension, of DCE-MRI quantitative PK parameters and skewness and kurtosis of V_e for the typical breast cancer, computed from pharmacokinetic parametric maps and show potential as a biomarker for diagnosis breast tumour either as a benign or malignant.

As future work we aim at making a similar study for the malignant tumour severity scale and apply, if necessary, Machine Learning techniques to enhance its prediction.

Acknowledgement. The research reported in this publication was supported by the gLINK Erasmus Mundus project.

References

1. Breast Cancer Statistics. http://www.wcrf.org/int/cancer-facts-figures/data-specific-cancers/breast-cancer-statistics. Accessed 30 Apr 2017
2. Alic, L., van Vliet, M., van Dijke, C., Eggermont, A., Veenland, J., Niessen, W.: Heterogeneity in DCE-MRI parametric maps: a biomarker for treatment response. Phys. Med. Biol. **56**(6), 1601–1616 (2011)
3. Andreea, G., Pegza, R., Lascu, L., Bondari, S., Stoica, Z., Bondari, A.: The role of imaging techniques in diagnosis of breast cancer. Curr. Health Sci. J. **37**(2), 55–61 (2011)
4. Asselin, M.C., O'Connor, J., Boellaard, R., Thacker, N., Jackson, A.: Quantifying heterogeneity in human tumours using MRI and PET. Eur. J. Cancer **48**(4), 447–455 (2012)
5. Baish, J., Jain, R.: Fractals and cancer. Cancer Res. **60**(14), 3683–3688 (2000)
6. Bianciardi, G., Pontenani, F.: Fractals and pathology. J. Biostat. Biomet. Appl. **1**(1), 104 (2015)
7. Chan, A., Tuszynski, J.: Automatic prediction of tumour malignancy in breast cancer with fractal dimension. Roy. Soc. Open Sci. **3**(12), 160558 (2016)
8. Fuller, S., Lee, I., Elmore, G.: Breast cancer screening: an evidence-based update. Med. Clin. North Am. **99**(3), 451–468 (2015)
9. Fusco, R., Sansone, M., Filice, S.: Pattern recognition approaches for breast cancer DCE-MRI classification: a systematic review. J. Med. Biol. Eng. **36**(4), 449–459 (2016)
10. Haralick, R., Shanmugam, K., Dinstein, I.: Texture features for image classification. IEEE Trans. Syst. Man Cybern. **3**(6), 610–621 (1973)
11. Huang, W., et al.: Variations of dynamic contrast-enhanced magnetic resonance imaging in evaluation of breast cancer therapy response: a multicenter data analysis challenge. Transl. Oncol. **7**(1), 153–166 (2014)
12. Huang, W., Li, X., Morris, E.: The magnetic resonance shutter speed discriminates vascular properties of malignant and benign breast tumors in vivo. Proc. Nat. Acad. Sci. USA **105**(46), 17943–17948 (2008)
13. Just, N.: Improving tumour heterogeneity MRI assessment with histograms. Br. J. Cancer **111**(12), 2205–2213 (2014)
14. Karahaliou, A., Vassiou, K., Arikidis, N., Skiadopoulos, S., Kanavou, T., Costaridou, L.: Assessing heterogeneity of lesion enhancement kinetics in dynamic contrast-enhanced MRI for breast cancer diagnosis. Br. J. Radiol. **83**(988), 296–309 (2010)
15. Lang, V., Berbaum, S., Lutgendorf, K.: Large-core breast biopsy: abnormal salivary cortisol profiles associated with uncertainty of diagnosis. Radiology **250**(3), 631–637 (2009)

16. Li, X., et al.: Dynamic NMR effects in breast cancer dynamic-contrast-enhanced MRI. Proc. Nat. Acad. Sci. USA **105**(46), 17937–17942 (2008)
17. Materka, A., Strzelecki, M.: Texture analysis methods - a review. COST B11 report, Technical University of Lodz. Brussels (1998)
18. Nagy, J., Chang, S., Shih, S., Dvorak, A., Dvorak, H.: Heterogeneity of the tumor vasculature. Semin. Thromb. Hemost. **36**(3), 321–331 (2010)
19. O'Connor, J., Tofts, P., Miles, K., Parkes, L., Thompson, G., Jackson, A.: Dynamic contrast-enhanced imaging techniques: CT and MRI. Br. J. Radiol. **84**(2), S112–S120 (2011)
20. Padhani, R.: Dynamic contrast-enhanced MRI in clinical oncology: current status and future directions. J. Magn. Reson. Imaging **16**(4), 407–422 (2002)
21. Peleg, S., Naor, J., Hartley, R., Avnir, D.: Multiple resolution texture analysis and classification. IEEE Trans. Pattern Anal. Mach. Intell. **6**(4), 518–523 (1984)
22. Prasad, S., Houserkova, D.: The role of various modalities in breast imaging. Biomed. Pap. Med. Fac. Univ. Palacky Olomouc Czech Repub. **151**(2), 209–218 (2007)
23. Salem, S., Kamal, M., Mansour, M., Salah, A., Wessam, R.: Breast imaging in the young: the role of magnetic resonance imaging in breast cancer screening, diagnosis and follow-up. J. Thorac. Dis. **5**(1), S9–S18 (2013)
24. Schabel, M., Morrell, G., Oh, K., Walczak, C., Barlow, R., Neumayer, L.: Pharmacokinetic mapping for lesion classification in dynamic breast MRI. J. Magn. Reson. Imaging **31**(6), 1371–1378 (2010)
25. Tofts, P.: Modeling tracer kinetics in dynamic GD-DTPA MR imaging. J. Magn. Reson. Imaging **7**(1), 91–101 (1997)
26. Tofts, P., Brix, G., Buckley, D.: Estimating kinetic parameters from dynamic contrast-enhanced T1-weighted MRI of a diffusable tracer: standardized quantities and symbols. J. Magn. Reson. Imaging **10**(3), 223–232 (1999)
27. Witten, I., Frank, E., Hall, M., Chris, J.: Data Mining: Practical Machine Learning Tools and Techniques, 2nd edn. Morgan Kaufmann Publishers, San Francisco (2016)
28. Yang, X., Knopp, M.: Quantifying tumor vascular heterogeneity with dynamic contrast-enhanced magnetic resonance imaging. Rev. J. Biomed. Biotechnol. **2011**, 12 (2011). Article id 732848
29. Zhang, X., Cui, J., Wang, W., Lin, C.: A study for texture feature extraction of high-resolution satellite images based on a direction measure and gray level co-occurrence matrix fusion algorithm. Sensors **17**(7), 1474 (2017)

Recognizing Emotions
with EmotionalDAN

Ivona Tautkute[1,2,3]([✉]), Tomasz Trzciński[1,2,3], and Adam Bielski[1,2,3]

[1] Polish-Japanese Academy of Information Technology, Warsaw, Poland
s16352@pjwstk.edu.pl
[2] Warsaw University of Technology, Warsaw, Poland
{t.trzcinski,pro}@ii.pw.edu.pl
[3] Tooploox, Wrocław, Poland

Abstract. Classification of human emotions remains an important and challenging task for many computer vision algorithms, especially in the era of humanoid robots which coexist with humans in their everyday life. Currently proposed methods for emotion recognition solve this task using multi-layered convolutional networks that do not explicitly infer any facial features in the classification phase. In this work, we postulate a fundamentally different approach to solve emotion recognition task that relies on incorporating facial landmarks as a part of the classification loss function. To that end, we extend a recently proposed Deep Alignment Network (DAN), that achieves state-of-the-art results in the recent facial landmark recognition challenge, with a term related to facial features. Thanks to this simple modification, our model called EmotionalDAN is able to outperform state-of-the-art emotion classification methods on two challenging benchmark dataset by up to 5%.

Keywords: Machine learning · Emotion recognition ·
Facial expression recognition

1 Introduction

Since autonomous AI systems, such as anthropomorphic robots, start to rapidly enter our lives, their ability to understand social and emotional context of many everyday situations becomes increasingly important. One key element that allows the machines to infer this context is their ability to correctly identify human emotions, such as happiness or sorrow. This is a highly challenging task, as people express their emotions in a multitude of ways, depending on their personal characteristics, *e.g.* people with an introvert character tend to be more secretive about their emotions, while extroverts show them more openly. Although some simplifications can be applied, for instance reducing the space of recognized emotions or directly applying Facial Action Coding System (FACS) [3], there is an intrinsic difficulty embedded in the problem of human emotion classification.

© Springer Nature Switzerland AG 2019
R. P. Barneva et al. (Eds.): CompIMAGE 2018, LNCS 10986, pp. 120–128, 2019.
https://doi.org/10.1007/978-3-030-20805-9_11

While many Facial Expression Recognition (FER) systems already exist [1,5,7,8,13,14,18], the problem is far from being solved, in particular for expressions that are easily confusable when judged without context (e.g. *fear* and *surprise*). While correlation between facial landmarks location and expressed emotion is an evident one, not many methods focus on relationship between facial landmark localization and emotion classification. We therefore propose to use a state-of-the-art facial landmark detection model – Deep Alignment Network (DAN) [9] – and extend it by adding a surrogate term that aims to correctly classify emotions to the neural network loss function. This simple modification allows our method, dubbed EmotionalDAN, to exploit the location of facial landmarks and incorporate this information into the classification process. By training both terms jointly, we obtain state-of-the-art results on two challenging datasets for facial emotion recognition: CK+ [11] and ISED [4].

The remainder of this work is organized in the following manner. In Sect. 2 we discuss related work in facial expression recognition. In Sect. 3 we present our approach and introduce EmotionalDAN model. In Sect. 4 we present the datasets used for evaluation, explain in detail how our experiments are performed and present the results compared against baselines. Section 5 illustrates real life application of our proposed model. Finally, Sect. 6 concludes the paper.

2 Related Work

In this section we present a brief overview of methods that showed state-of-the-art results in emotion recognition. We focus on Deep Learning based methods as they have proven to be more successful at emotion prediction than hand-crafted features [1,7,10]. Most of the currently available methods that address this problem use some variation of a deep neural network with convolutional layers.

With their broad spectrum of applications to various computer vision tasks, convolutional neural networks (CNN) have also been successful at recognizing emotions. For instance [10] propose to use a standard architecture of a CNN with two convolutional, two subsamping and one fully connected layer. Before being processed, the image is spatially normalized with a pre-processing step. Their model achieves state-of-the-art accuracy on CK+ [11] database of 97.81%. Some modified versions of this approach also include different numbers of layers (e.g. five convolutional layers).

A number of methods is inspired by Inception model [17] that achieves state-of-the-art object classification results on the ImageNet dataset [2]. Inception layers provide an approximation of sparse networks hence are often applied to emotion recognition problem [5]. Ranging from simple transfer learning approaches where Inception-V3 model pretrained on ImageNet [2] is used with custom softmax classification layer [18] to custom architectures with Inception layers [13]. In another example [14] propose a deep neural network architecture consisting of two convolutional layers each followed by max pooling and then four Inception layers.

Another method called EmotionNet [1] and its extension EmotionNet2 [8] builds up on the ultra-deep ResNet architecture [6] and improves the accuracy by using face detection algorithm that reduces the variance caused by a background noise.

Although all the above methods rely on the state-of-the-art deep learning architectures, they draw their inspiration mostly from the analogical models that are successfully used for object classification tasks. We believe that as a result these approaches do not exploit intrinsic characteristics of how humans express emotions, *i.e.* by modifying their face expression through moving the landmark features of their faces.

Moreover, vast majority of published methods is evaluated within the same database that the model was trained for with no cross-database comparison. While such accuracy results might be impressive they often lack the ability to generalize to different shooting conditions (lightning, angles, image quality) or subjects of different ethnic backgrounds.

3   EmotionalDAN

Our approach builds up on the Deep Alignment Network architecture [9], initially proposed for robust face alignment. The main advantage of DAN over the competing face alignment methods comes from an iterative process of adjusting the locations of facial landmarks. The iterations are incorporated into the neural network architecture, as the information about the landmark locations detected in the previous stage (layer) are transferred to the next stages through the use of facial landmark heatmaps. As a result and contrary to the competing methods, DAN can therefore handle entire face images instead of patches which leads to a significant reduction in head pose variance and improves its performance on a landmark recognition task. DAN ranked 3rd in a recent face landmark recognition challenge Menpo [19].

Originally, DAN was inspired by the Cascade Shape Regression framework and similarly it starts with initial estimate of face shape which is refined after following iterations. In DAN, each iteration is represented with a single stage of deep neural network. During each stage (iteration) features are extracted from entire image instead of local images patches (in contrast to CSR).

Training is composed of consecutive stages where single stage consists of feed-forward neural network and connection layers generating input for next stage. Each stage takes three types of inputs: input image aligned with the canonical shape, features image generated from dense layer of the previous stage and landmarks heatmap. Therefore output at each DAN stage is defined as:

$$S_t = T_t^{-1}(S_{t-1}) + \Delta S_t, \tag{1}$$

where ΔS_t is the landmarks output at stage t and T_t is the transform that is used to warp the input image to canonical pose.

In this work, we hypothesize that DAN's ability to handle images with large variation and provide robust information about facial landmarks transfers well to the task of emotion recognition. To that end, we extend the network learning task with an additional goal of estimating expressed facial emotions. We incarnate this idea by modifying the loss function with a surrogate term that addresses specifically emotion recognition task and we minimize both landmark location and emotion recognition terms jointly. The resulting loss function $\mathcal{L}$ can be therefore expressed as:

$$\mathcal{L} = \alpha \cdot \frac{\| S_t - S^* \|}{d} - \beta \cdot E^* \cdot log(E_t), \qquad (2)$$

where S_t is the transformed output of predicted facial landmarks at stage t, E is the softmax output for emotion prediction. S^* is the vector of ground truth landmark locations, d is the distance between the pupils of ground truth that serves as a normalization scalar and E^* is the ground truth for emotion labels. We weigh the influence of the terms with α and β coefficients and after an initial set of experiments we set their values to $\alpha = 0.4$ and $\beta = 0.6$.

We present the final version of our network in the Table 1. It was originally inspired by network used in ImageNet ILSVRC competition (2014) [16] and contains four convolutional layer pairs followed by pooling layers. Top layers of the network consist of one common fully connected layer and two separate fully connected layers for landmark and emotion features.

Table 1. Structure of the feed-forward part of EmotionalDAN network stage with multiple outputs. Dimensions of the last fully connected layer before emotion classification depend on the number of emotion classes used in training.

Name	Input shape	Output shape	Kernel
conv1a	$224 \times 224 \times 1$	$224 \times 224 \times 64$	$3 \times 3, 1, 1$
conv1b	$224 \times 224 \times 64$	$224 \times 224 \times 64$	$3 \times 3, 64, 1$
pool1	$224 \times 224 \times 64$	$112 \times 112 \times 64$	$2 \times 2, 1, 2$
conv2a	$112 \times 112 \times 64$	$112 \times 112 \times 128$	$3 \times 3, 64, 1$
conv2b	$112 \times 112 \times 128$	$112 \times 112 \times 128$	$3 \times 3, 128, 1$
pool2	$112 \times 112 \times 128$	$56 \times 56 \times 128$	$2 \times 2, 1, 2$
conv3a	$56 \times 56 \times 128$	$56 \times 56 \times 256$	$3 \times 3, 128, 1$
conv3b	$56 \times 56 \times 256$	$56 \times 56 \times 256$	$3 \times 3, 256, 1$
pool3	$56 \times 56 \times 256$	$28 \times 28 \times 256$	$2 \times 2, 1, 2$
conv4a	$28 \times 28 \times 256$	$28 \times 28 \times 512$	$3 \times 3, 256, 1$
conv4b	$28 \times 28 \times 512$	$28 \times 28 \times 512$	$3 \times 3, 512, 1$
pool4	$28 \times 28 \times 512$	$14 \times 14 \times 512$	$2 \times 2, 1, 2$
fc1	$14 \times 14 \times 512$	$1 \times 1 \times 256$	-
fc2_landmark	$1 \times 1 \times 256$	$1 \times 1 \times 136$	-
fc2_emotion	$1 \times 1 \times 256$	$1 \times 1 \times \{3,7\}$	-

Fig. 1. Mapping of EmotionDAN predictions to original images from evaluated test sets. The top row shows examples of correct predictions while the bottom one illustrates classification errors. Most of the errors happen when ambiguous emotions are expressed.

4   Experiments

In this section we perform quantitative evaluation of our model against published baselines as well as present an overview of datasets used for training and testing.

4.1   Datasets

We include datasets that are made available to the public (upon request) and present a high variety of subjects' ethnicity. All compared models are trained on AffectNet [15] and evaluated cross-database on remaining test sets.

AffectNet [15] is by far the largest available database for facial expression. It contains more than 1,000,000 facial images from the Internet collected by querying major search engines with emotion related keywords. About half of the retrieved images were manually annotated for the presence of seven main facial expressions.

CK+ [11] includes both posed and non-posed (spontaneous) expressions. 123 subjects are photographed in 6 prototypic emotions. For our analysis we only include images with validated emotion labels.

JAFFE [12] The database contains 213 images of 7 facial expressions (6 basic facial expressions + 1 neutral) posed by 10 Japanese female models. Each image has been rated on 6 emotion adjectives by 60 Japanese subjects.

ISED [4] Indian Spontaneous Expression Database. Near frontal face video was recorded for 50 participants while watching emotional video clips. The novel experiment design induced spontaneous emotions among the participants and simultaneously gathered their self ratings of experienced emotion. For evaluation individual frames from recorded videos are used.

4.2 Datasets Preparation and Training

To allow for fair comparison we follow an unified approach for all datasets and methods.

While some datasets come with ground-truth information about bounding boxes of present faces (AffectNet), most test sets do not contain such information. Face regions often account only for small part of the image with a lot of unnecessary background (ISED). To address this issue, we extracted regions of interest with face detection algorithm Multi-task CNN [20]. For <2% of test images where algorithm failed to recognize a face, full images were used. All test images were resized to 224 × 224 and normalized by standard deviation.

Training procedures are independent for different number of emotion classes. For simplified emotions we perform a mapping of original ground truth labels where *fear, sadness, disgust* and *anger* are mapped to *negative* emotion, *happiness* and *contempt* to *positive* emotion and *neutral* class is kept without change. In this case we do not include images labeled with *surprise* as this emotion might have both positive and negative connotations.

Similarly to [9], training of EmotionalDAN is performed sequentially - first stage is trained until validation error stops improving. Afterwards, second stage is added and trained.

Table 2. Cross-database accuracy results compared for different model architectures and seven emotion categories. All models are trained on AffectNet database. Face detection is applied as a preprocessing step on all test sets for all methods.

	CK+	JAFFE	ISED
CNN (2)	0.628	0.484	0.516
CNN (5)	0.728	**0.502**	0.593
Inception-V3	0.304	0.268	0.479
EmotionNet 2	0.204	0.249	0.21
EmotionalDAN	**0.736**	0.465	**0.62**

4.3 Results

Tables 2 and 3 show the results of the evaluation of our EmotionalDAN method and the competing approaches. Although the accuracy varies between the tested datasets, our approach outperforms the competitors by a large factor of up to 5% on two out of three benchmark datasets, namely on CK+ and ISED. The performance of our method is inferior to convolutional neural networks on

Fig. 2. Our emotion recognition model in passenger detection system for autonomous cars. Emotion recognition is performed on detected facial regions.

Table 3. Cross-database accuracy results compared for different model architectures and three emotion categories - positive, negative and neutral.

	CK+	JAFFE	ISED
CNN (2)	0.819	0.525	0.814
CNN (5)	0.92	**0.765**	0.867
Inception-V3	0.582	0.536	0.673
EmotionNet 2	0.478	0.497	0.587
EmotionalDAN	**0.921**	0.634	**0.896**

the JAFFE dataset, although the accuracy values obtained on this dataset are generally lower than the competitors. We believe that this may be the result of a more challenging image acquisition conditions. Furthermore, our results show that convolutional neural networks achieve competitive results when compared with other methods despite their simplistic architecture.

Qualitative results are presented in Fig. 1 and show examples of correct and incorrect predictions for each testset.

5   Application

We implement our emotion recognition model as a part of the in-car analytics system to be deployed in autonomous cars. Figure 2 shows the results obtained by the camera installed inside a car. As autonomous car operation can potentially be influenced by emotions of the passengers (*e.g.* fear of speed expressed on passenger's face could signal the need for speed reduction), this is an excellent playground for our method to show its full potential. Although alternative applications are possible, we believe that this use case showcases the capabilities of our method and can serve as an interesting input to the driving system, typically focused on the exterior views from outside the car.

6   Conclusion

In this paper, we overview a work-in-progress method for emotion recognition that allows to exploit facial landmarks. Although the results computed on the JAFFE dataset show that there is still place for improvement, we believe that this approach has a strong potential to outperform currently proposed methods. In future work, we will therefore focus on improving our method by using attention mechanism on facial landmarks and experiment with additional loss function terms. We also plan to investigate other applications of our method, *e.g.* in the context of autistic children with incapabilities related to emotion recognition.

References

1. Benitez-Quiroz, C.F., Srinivasan, R., Martinez, A.M.: Emotionet: an accurate, real-time algorithm for the automatic annotation of a million facial expressions in the wild. In CVPR (2016)
2. Deng, J., Dong, W., Socher, R., Li, L.J., Li, K., Fei-Fei, L.: ImageNet: a large-scale hierarchical image database. In: CVPR 2009 (2009)
3. Ekman, P., Friesen, W.: Facial Action Coding System: Investigator's Guide. Consulting Psychologists Press, Washington, DC (1978)
4. Happy, S.L., Patnaik, P., Routray, A., Guha, R.: The Indian spontaneous expression database for emotion recognition. IEEE Trans. Affect. Comput. **8**, 131–142 (2017)
5. Hasani, B., Mahoor, M.: Facial expression recognition using enhanced deep 3D convolutional neural networks. In: IEEE Conference on Computer Vision and Pattern Recognition Workshops (2017)
6. He, K., Zhang, X., Ren, S., Sun, J.: Deep residual learning for image recognition. CoRR abs/1512.03385 (2015)
7. Kahou, S., Michalski, V., Konda, K.: Recurrent neural networks for emotion recognition in video. In: Proceedings of the ACM on International Conference on Multimodal Interaction (2015)
8. Kennedy, B., Balint, A.: Emotionnet2. https://github.com/co60ca/EmotionNet
9. Kowalski, M., Naruniec, J., Trzcinski, T.: Deep alignment network: a convolutional neural network for robust face alignment. In: CVPRW (2017)
10. Lopes, A.T., de Aguiar, E., Oliveira-Santos, T.: A facial expression recognition system using convolutional networks. In: SIBGRAPI (2015)
11. Lucey, P., Cohn, J.F., Kanade, T., Saragih, J., Ambadar, Z., Matthews, I.: The extended cohn-kanade dataset (CK+): a complete dataset for action unit and emotion-specified expression. In: CVPRW (2010)
12. Lyons, M.J., Akamatsu, S., Kamachi, M., Gyoba, J.: The Japanese female facial expressions database. http://www.kasrl.org/jaffe.html
13. Mollahosseini, A., Chan, D., Mahoor, M.H.: Going deeper in facial expression recognition using deep neural networks. In: 2016 IEEE Winter Conference on Applications of Computer Vision (WACV) (2016)
14. Mollahosseini, A., Chan, D., Mahoor, M.H.: Going deeper in facial expression recognition using deep neural networks. In: IEEE Winter Conference on Applications of Computer Vision (WACV) (2016)

15. Mollahosseini, A., Hasani, B., Mahoor, M.H.: Affectnet: a database for facial expression, valence, and arousal computing in the wild. IEEE Trans. Affect. Comput. (2017)
16. Simonyan, K., Zisserman, A.: Very deep convolutional networks for large-scale image recognition. Comput. Res. Repository (2014)
17. Szegedy, C., et al.: Going deeper with convolutions. In: CVPR (2015)
18. Xia, X.L., Xu, C., Nan, B.: Facial expression recognition based on tensorflow platform. In: ITM Web of Conferences (2017)
19. Zafeiriou, S., Trigeorgis, G., Chrysos, G., Deng, J., Shen, J.: The menpo facial landmark localisation challenge: a step towards the solution. In: 2017 IEEE Conference on Computer Vision and Pattern Recognition Workshops (CVPRW) (2017)
20. Zhang, K., Zhang, Z., Li, Z., Qiao, Y.: Joint face detection and alignment using multitask cascaded convolutional networks. IEEE Sig. Process. Lett. **23**, 1499–1503 (2016)

Clustering Functional MRI Patterns
with Fuzzy and Competitive Algorithms

Alberto Arturo Vergani$^{(\boxtimes)}$, Samuele Martinelli, and Elisabetta Binaghi

University of Insubria, Varese, Italy
{aavergani,smartinelli,elisabetta.binaghi}@uninsubria.it

Abstract. We used model-free methods to explore the brain's functional properties adopting a partitioning procedure based on cross-clustering. We selected Fuzzy C-Means (FCM) and Neural Gas (NG) algorithms to find spatial patterns with temporal features and temporal patterns with spatial features. We applied these algorithms to a shared fMRI repository of face recognition tasks. We matched the classes found and our results of functional connectivity analysis with partitioning of BOLD signal signatures. We compared the outcomes using the just acquired model-based knowledge as likely ground truth, confirming the role of Fusiform Brain Regions. In general, partitioning results show a better spatial clustering than temporal clustering for both algorithms. In the case of temporal clustering, FCM outperforms Neural Gas. The relevance of brain sub-regions related to face recognition were correctly distinguished by the algorithms and the results are in agreement with the current neuroscientific literature.

Keywords: fMRI · Partitive clustering · Fuzzy C-means algorithm · Neural Gas algorithm

1 Introduction

In functional Magnetic Resonance Imaging (fMRI) there are two kinds of approaches to data analysis: model-based methods and model-free methods. The main difference between the methodologies is that the first one needs *a priori* knowledge about the functional data structures, whereas the second one does not need any assumptions related the images to be investigated. The main model-based approach to fMRI data is the Statistical Parametric Maps (SPMs) approach introduced by Friston [3]. The main model-free models are the Analysis of Independent Components (ICA) or the Analysis of Principal Components (PCA) (for an overview see [11]). In addition, there are other model-free techniques to explore fMRI data properties that allow to classify functional patterns, such as the clustering algorithms, that are a class of computational models used to find the *natural groupings* of input features [13]. Several kinds of separation methodologies based on different theoretical framework are proposed in the literature [6]. Generally, clustering is divided in crisp or soft partitioning:

© Springer Nature Switzerland AG 2019
R. P. Barneva et al. (Eds.): CompIMAGE 2018, LNCS 10986, pp. 129–144, 2019.
https://doi.org/10.1007/978-3-030-20805-9_12

crisp classes have unshared elements (e.g., k-Means Algorithm), whereas soft classes have elements that could be shared with more then one class (e.g., fuzzy sets based algorithms [1]). The soft properties in clustering have a wide meaning that encompasses not only the data multi-membership feature, but also (in computational learning theory) the competitive learning approach that is used by unsupervised algorithms to adapt themselves on the data to be clustered (e.g. self-organizing maps). Using this double meaning of the *soft clustering category*, we selected **Fuzzy C-Means (FCM)** and **Neural Gas (NG)** algorithms, where the first one is a soft algorithm in terms of multi-class properties and the second one is a soft algorithm in terms of competitive learning rule [16].

Clustering techniques applied to fMRI time series data are an interesting approaches to explore brain functional properties [9,10,14]. Partitioning works grouping image voxels together based on how much they are alike in relation to some measure (distances, correlation, etc.), that probes how their intensity profiles in time are similar. More in details, let n denote the number of scans in a fMRI experiment, and let K be the number of voxels in each volume: the dynamics of each voxel $\mu \in \{1, ..., K\}$, are the signal values $\{\mathbf{x}^{\mu}(1), ..., \mathbf{x}^{\mu}(n)\}$ that can be modeled as a vector $\mathbf{x}^{\mu}(i) \in \Re^{n}$ in the n-dimensional (Euclidean) feature space of possible time series. Each of the these points is partitioned into clusters based on the similarity of their intensity profile in time. Therefore, the principal approach to fMRI clustering is to cluster spatial features (i.e., brain regions) that have similar temporal patterns (i.e., the brain functional signatures). In other words, the procedure to cluster functional images has the goal to find common functional structures in different Region of Interest (ROIs).

In this work, we also aim to find functional structures in temporal features that have similar spatial patterns: we named these objects as "Times of Interest" (TOIs), that in computational terms mean to cluster the experimental blocks related to each brain volume. The assumption is that the exploration of TOIs allows to find properties related to the peculiarity of each block of the experimental design (e.g., imagine a block design structured as TASK-REST stimuli alternations; the TOIs clustering could allows finding spatial structures that are similar to TASK or REST blocks, whereas the classic ROIs clustering allows finding in different brain regions temporal structures that are similar). We named this global procedure **cross-clustering** that want as it finds spatial patterns in the temporal features (TOIs) and temporal patterns in the spatial features (ROIs). The postclustering procedure we applied performs a statistical evaluation of the obtained clusters. We used parametric and nonparametric tests to study whether the classes are statistically different with the aim to investigate the numerical properties that distinguished the clustering outcomes. Furthermore, we compared the classes computed by the algorithms using Jaccard similarity index. Also, we compared the functional connectivity of the fMRI scans within various subjects in order to find useful information to be associated with adopted clustering techniques. In the next section, we present the dataset we selected to be clustered, the computational methodologies we used, and the results we obtained. We conclude with a discussion and possible future works.

2   Materials and Methods

2.1   Data

We selected the dataset proposed by Wakeman and Henson [15] available in **openfmri** repository (https://openfmri.org/dataset/ds000117). This dataset contains face recognition task paradigms applied to 16 healthy and young subjects. The study of Wakeman and Henson showed functional peculiarity along the fusiform regions in the brain temporal and occipital parts. Keeping in mind these features, we clustered the subjects paying special attention on the clustering outcomes related to eight fusiform cortexes using Harvard-Oxford labels. According to these labels, they are ROIs 73:74 L/R Temporal Fusiform Cx Anterior Divisions, ROIs 75:76 L/R Temporal Fusiform Cx Posterior Divisions, ROIs 77:78 L/R Temporo-Occipital Fusiform Cx, and ROIs 79:80 L/R Occipital Fusiform Cx. Before to cluster the images, we performed preprocessing with FSL standard tools [7]: such as spatial and temporal filtering, motion correction, standard registration (with MNI152 reference), and time-series extraction as per the meaning of Harvard-Oxford Atlas using 96 lateralized labels.

2.2   Clustering Algorithms

We adopted two soft clustering algorithms to process the fRMI data: **Fuzzy C-Means (FCM)** and **Neural Gas (NG)**. We used as an input features of both Regions of Interest (ROIs) and Times of Interest (TOIs). We validated the optimal clustering using Davies-Bouldin index [2] and we compared the various clustering outcomes using the Jaccard similarity measure. We investigated the statistical difference of the clusters computed with parametric (One-way Analysis of Variance – ANOVA-1) and non-parametric method (Kruskall-Wallis) using the p-value as a decision criterion. Furthermore, we computed the brain functional connectivity with the Pearson Linear Correlation Coefficient across the ROIs: we wanted to analyse the overall dynamics of the subjects in relation to the task-oriented study, i.e., the face recognition paradigm, in order to obtain similar results about the brain face processing as the ones in the literature specialized in experimental neuroscience (see [5]).

Fuzzy C-Means. Fuzzy C-means is a clustering method that allows to each element of a dataset to be a part of more than one cluster with a respective degree of membership [1]. The algorithm is based on the optimization of the following objective function:

$$J_m = \sum_{i=1}^{D} \sum_{j=1}^{C} \mu_{ij}^m ||X_i - A_j||^2 \qquad (1)$$

For the $||...||^2$ we chose a distance, D is the number of the data points, C is the number of the clusters, m is the partition exponent controlling the fuzzy overlap between clusters that determines how fuzzy the boundaries between the clusters are ($m > 1$; in the computational set-up we adopted $m = 2$). X_i are the points, A_j are the centroids of the clusters and μ_{ij} is the degree of membership of X_i in the jth cluster (i.e., for a given cluster j, $\sum_{i=1}^{N} \mu_{ij} = 1$). FCM works randomly initializing the membership values μ_{ij} and then calculating the cluster centers. It repeats the updating of μ_{ij} until the objective function J_m reaches the minimum value. FCM is a useful clustering algorithm that allows to handle the *softness* of datasets. In many cases is necessary to take into account the possibility that data-points could be within more then one class, for example when they represent complex objects without a crisp natural shape (e.g., in the case of fMRI functional partitioning); so, the use of FCM could be an appropriate choice for the task-based paradigm, when periodically the brain functionally varies due to the stimulation of the rapidly changing experimental blocks.

Neural Gas. Neural Gas (NG) algorithm for clustering analysis is a vector-quantization approach inspired by the Self Organizing Map [12]. The method converges quickly to low error rate, and also has lower distortion value than the Kohonen's feature map. It uses the gradient descent method as optimization solver. NG utilized a neighborhood-ranking of the reference vectors $\mathbf{w}_i$ for the given data vector $\mathbf{x}$. The learning model is determined by the formula:

$$\mathbf{w}_i(t+1) = \mathbf{w}_i(t) + \epsilon(t) \exp\{-k_i(\mathbf{x}, \frac{\mathbf{w}_i}{\lambda}\}(\mathbf{x}(t) - \mathbf{w}_i(t)) \tag{2}$$

Here $k_i = 0, ..., N - 1$ are the rank indexes describing the ranking of the neighbourhood of the reference vectors $\mathbf{w}_i$ to the data vector $\mathbf{x}$ in a decreasing order; N is the cardinality of the neural network units that update their synapses for each iteration; the step-size variable $\epsilon \in [0, 1]$ tunes the ranges of modification. Referred to Kohonen algorithm, NG has the advantage that it does not need a prespecified network and it produces a topologically-preserving maps. Prototype classification is based on distance. It updates the prototypes and assigns the data to the prototype closest to it. When the number of maximum iterations is reached, the algorithm terminates; otherwise, it goes through the next iteration.

3   Results

In this section, we describe the obtained results, which are illustrated in Figs. 1, 2, 3, 4, 5, 6, 7, 8, 9, 10, 11, 12, 13 and 14. We discuss the results in the Sect. 4.

Figure 1 shows the empirical distributions of the overall Correlation Coefficients (CC) of every subject and the global correlation matrix represented as a mean of the correlation matrices of each subject.

Figure 2 shows, first, the best Davies-Bouldin Indexes (DBI) computed for clusters ranging from 2 to 20 for both FCM and NG algorithms applied on both ROIs and Time Points. Figure 3 illustrates spatial semantics of FCM and NG in the case of 2-classes computed as the statistical mode of the subjects (i.e., if a region frequently appears in a cluster i, than it belongs to the cluster i in the representation). Table 1 gives details about he the best DBI configurations for the dataset.

Figures 4 and 5 display the results of the non-parametric (Kruskal-Wallis) and parametric (ANOVA 1-way) statistical tests applied to the optimal FCM and NG algorithms in both the spatial and the temporal configuration. The figures demonstrate that in the spatial configurations of both FCM and NG, the p-value was always less then 0.05. Hence, we can reject the hypothesis that all clusters have all the same means. In contrast, the p-value computed in the temporal configuration clustering for either FCM or NG, is not always less then 0.05, as the worst behaviour is in the case of NG algorithm.

In the Figs. 6 and 7, the results are almost the ones in Figs. 4 and 5.

In general, spatial clustering (i.e., ROIs partitioning) is always statistically significant (p-value less then 0.05) for both NG and FCM in the optimal case as well as in the case of 2-classes. Temporal clustering (i.e., TOIs partitioning) has lesser p-value, but it is not always significant; according to the non-parametric test, it is significant only in the case of FCM, where p-value is around 0.05.

Figure 8 shows the comparison of the Regions of Interests (ROIs) clustering of 2-classes using Jaccard matrix. The comparison is between subjects in case when applying NG and FCM algorithms. Under the matrices, the distributions of the Jaccard distance values are shown. In general, the distributions of the similarity of the subjects are uniform, expect when using the FCM algorithm. The explanation of this fact is not related to the quality of the clustering itself, but is rather rooted in the initialization procedure of the algorithms we used.

Figure 9 shows the comparison of the Times of Interest (TOIs) clustering with 2-classes using Jaccard matrix. The comparison is between subjects in case of NG and FCM. Under the matrices, the distributions of the Jaccard distance values are shown. In general, the similarity distributions between subjects are uniform (for NG) and middle-centred (for FCM). The main result is that none of the outcomes seems to be in agreement between clustering algorithms. Instead, it is interesting to note that the empirical distributions of the indexes vary widely from almost unimodal to multi-modal distributions.

Figure 10 shows the Jaccard's distance of the NG and FCM results using 2-classes. The ROIs clustering configuration exhibits almost uniform distribution of the values, while the TOIs clustering configuration exhibits unimodal (gaussian-like) distribution.

In sum, Figs. 8, 9 and 10 demonstrate that when clustering algorithms perform the computations in a different way, it is hard to compare the results. This does not mean that the clustering methods miscalculated the data, but rather that the initialization procedures used by the algorithms lead to assigning different classes to the same pattern found among the subjects.

Figures 11, 12, 13 and 14 shows the results related to one-subject analysis. We selected specifically the FCM 2-clusters for the Subject 12 because it has good performance in spatial and temporal configurations according to both the parametric and the non-parametric tests. Figure 11 shows the graph-based topological representation that gives an idea about the parcellation. In the top-left part of Fig. 12 there are details about the relation between ROIs and clusters: in particular, following the horizontal lines, it is notable that the Fusiform regions (ROI from 73 to 80) are splitted half and half in the Cluster 1 and the Cluster 2; this peculiarity is due to the different BOLD signal amplitude that allows to discriminate the membership to clusters, as indicated in the centre plot of Fig. 12. The difficulty to distinguish temporal pattern along the time points is evident in the right plot of Fig. 12, where there is no clear data structure that explains the two partitions, though the statistical tests for temporal clusters have always a p-value less then (or around) 0.05 for the Subject 12. Specially, Figs. 13 and 14 show the brain voxels parcellation of Subject 12 clustered with FCM using the optimal configuration. The algorithms computed 14 clusters that grouped differently all brain portions. Figure 14 shows the Fusiform regions superimposed to the brain parcellation in Fig. 13: the eight Fusiform cortexes belong to different clusters according to their BOLD values: i.e., L/R Temporo-Occipital Fusiform Cx and L/R Occipital Fusiform Cx have greater BOLD values than the L/R Temporal Fusiform Cx Anterior and Posterior Divisions. Clusters 2, 6 and 8 contain the Fusiform ROIs with greater activations, Cluster 3, 13, 14 contain the ones with the less activations.

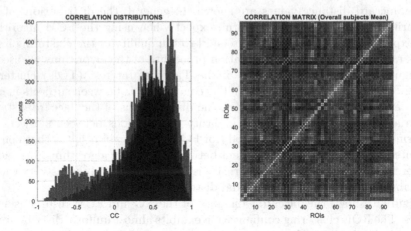

Fig. 1. The figure shows the information related to the correlation coefficients. The left plot is the empirical distribution of the all correlation coefficients (CC) computed for every subject. The right plot is the mean correlation matrix computed for all subjects' correlations

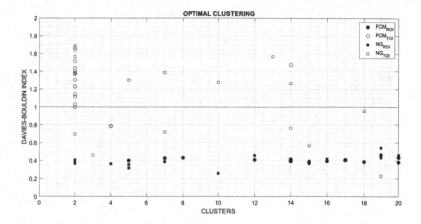

Fig. 2. The figure shows the plot of the optimal clusters *versus* the lesser Davies-Bouldin index for clustering with FCM and NG algorithms, that differentiated by the Regions of Interest (ROIs) configuration and the Time Of Interest (TOIs) configuration. Globally, the partitioning of ROIs with both FCM and NG had lower Davies-Bouldin index values then the partitioning of TOIs.

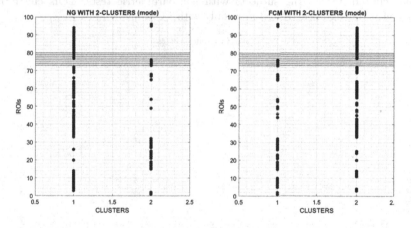

Fig. 3. The figure shows the more frequent ROIs partitioning in the special case of clustering with 2 groups for NG and FCM for all the subjects; the horizontal line from ROIs 73 to 80 are the ones related to the eight Fusiform regions, i.e., they are ROIs 73:74 L/R Temporal Fusiform Cx Anterior Divisions, ROIs 75:76 L/R Temporal Fusiform Cx Posterior Divisions, ROIs 77:78 L/R Temporo-Occipital Fusiform Cx and ROIs 79:80 L/R Occipital Fusiform Cx.

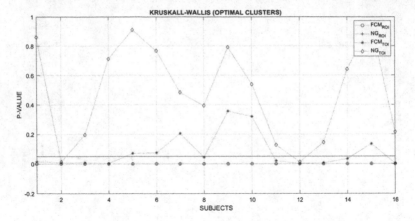

Fig. 4. The figure shows the results of non-parametric tests (Kruskall-Wallis) for the clusters obtained with FCM and NG algorithms for the ROIs (Regions of Interest) and TOIs (Times of Interest) inputs in case of the optimal configurations. The black line is the significance level 0.05. The values under the black line allow to reject the null hypothesis of the test. ROIs clustering with both FCM and NG have statistically different clusters for all the subjects with non-parametric tests. TOIs clustering is globally near the significative criterion only with FCM algorithms.

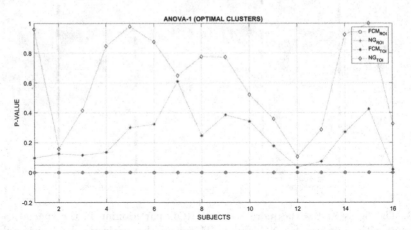

Fig. 5. The figure shows the results of the parametric test (ANOVA-1) for the clusters obtained with FCM and NG algorithms for the ROIs (Regions of Interest) and TOIs (Times of Interest) in the case of the optimal clusters configurations. The black line is the significance level 0.05. The results were similar to Fig. 4, but with a higher p-value for the TOIs clustering with FCM algorithm.

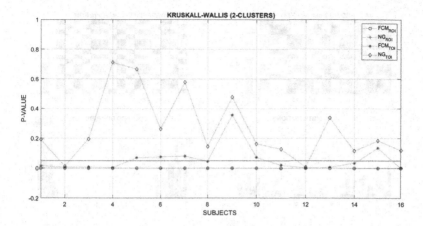

Fig. 6. The figure shows the results of the non parametric test (Kruskall-Wallis) for the clusters obtained with FCM and NG algorithms for the ROIs (Regions of Interest) and TOIs (Times of Interest) configurations in the special case of 2-clusters partitioning. The black line is the significance level 0.05. The results were similar to Figs. 4 and 5, but with lower p-value for the TOIs clustering with FCM algorithm.

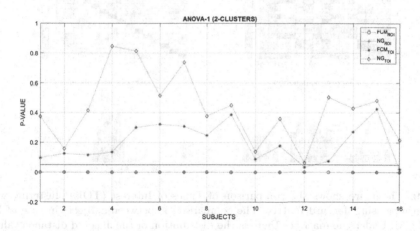

Fig. 7. The figure shows the results of the parametric (one-way ANOVA) for the clusters obtained with FCM and NG algorithms for the ROIs (Regions of Interest) and TOIs (Times of Interest) in the case of 2-clusters partitioning. The black line is the significance level 0.05. The results were similar to Fig. 6, but with a higher p-value for the TOIs clustering with FCM algorithm.

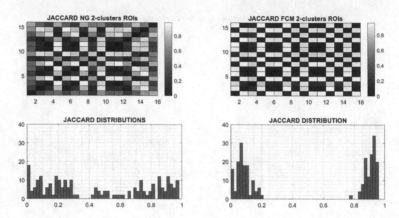

Fig. 8. The figure shows the comparison of Regions of Interests (ROIs) clustering of two groups using Jaccard matrix. The comparison is between subjects in case of applying NG and FCM algorithms. Under the matrices there is the distribution of the Jaccard distance values. In general, the similarity distribution between the subjects is uniform and without big differences, expect when using the FCM algorithm.

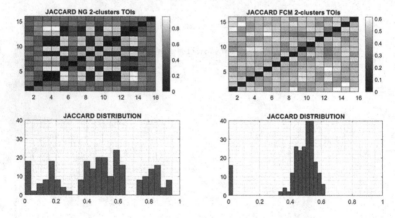

Fig. 9. The figure shows the comparison of Times of Interest (TOIs) clustering with two groups using Jaccard matrix. The comparison is between subjects in case of NG and FCM. Under the matrices there is the distribution of the Jaccard distance values. In general, the similarity distribution between the subjects is uniform (for NG) and middle-centered (for FCM).

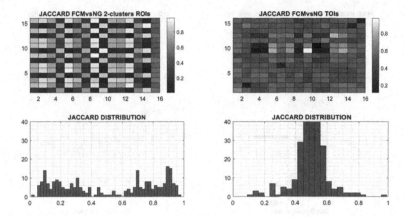

Fig. 10. The figure shows the Jaccard Matrices in both the cases of two classes clustering with Regions of Interest (ROIs) and Times of Interest (TOIs). The comparison is between subjects in cases of NG and FCM. Under the matrices there is the distribution of the Jaccard distance values. In general, the similarity distribution between subjects is weakly bimodal for the ROIs clustering (bottom left) and middle-centred for the TOIs clustering (bottom right).

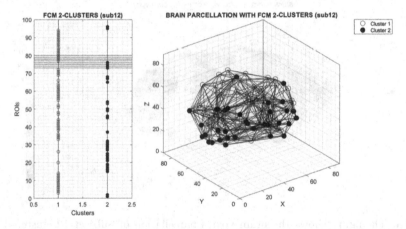

Fig. 11. The figure shows the brain parcellation based on a graph model and the Regions of Interest (ROIs) organization partitioned with two clusters. In the left plot the horizontal line indicates the Fusiform Cortexes (ROIs 73:80) and their clusters. In the right image the nodes are the 96 centroids according to Harvard-Oxford atlas. In general, the inferior regions were clustered in the Class 2 and the superior regions were clustered in the Class 1. The figure is referred specifically to the Regions of Interest (ROIs) of Subject 12 clustered with FCM.

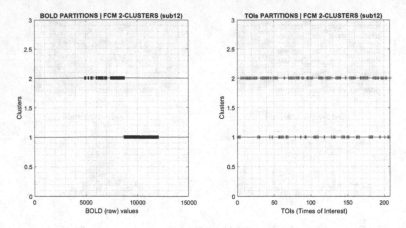

Fig. 12. The figure shows the BOLD values partitioning among the two clusters and the Times of Interests (TOIs) partition among the two clusters. In the left plot, clusters exhibit the BOLD amplitude and in the right plot the clusters seem to exhibit spatio-temporal patterns. The figure refers specifically to Subject 12 clustered with FCM.

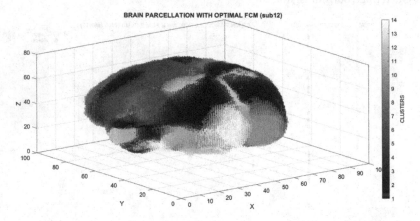

Fig. 13. The figure shows the brain voxels parcellation of Subject 12 clustered with FCM using the optimal configuration (with the lesser Davies-Bouldin index). There are 14 clusters that covered all brain voxels (cfr. Fig. 14 for more details).

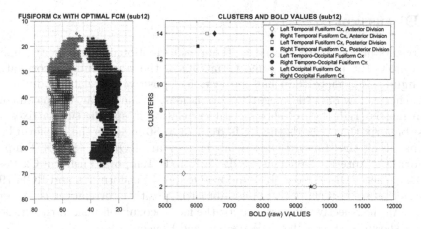

Fig. 14. The left plot shows the substructures of the Fusiform regions (the legend is the same of the right plot). In the right plot there are the eight Fusiform regions distributed to different clusters according to their BOLD values: L/R Temporo-Occipital Fusiform Cx and L/R Occipital Fusiform Cx have greater BOLD values than the L/R Temporal Fusiform Cx Anterior and Posterior Divisions. Precisely, clusters 2, 6 and 8 contain the Fusiform ROIs with greater activations, whereas clusters 3, 13, 14 the ones with lesser activations.

Table 1. The table describes the Davies-Bouldin (DB) index computation for each subject differentiated for clustering (FCM or NG) and inputs (ROIs or TOIs). The values presented are the lesser DB associated with the corresponding number of clusters.

Sub	DB	FCM_{ROI}	DB	NG_{ROI}	DB	FCM_{TOI}	DB	NG_{TOI}
1	0.47	19	0.46	12	1.37	2	0.95	18
2	0.40	5	0.37	15	1.23	2	1.38	2
3	0.39	18	0.42	16	1.23	2	0.69	2
4	0.41	14	0.41	2	1.14	2	1.57	2
5	0.40	14	0.46	20	1.44	2	1.30	5
6	0.41	17	0.37	2	1.64	2	1.39	7
7	0.40	14	0.32	5	1.47	14	0.46	3
8	0.43	20	0.39	15	1.52	2	1.28	10
9	0.40	16	0.36	5	1.00	2	0.76	14
10	0.43	7	0.26	10	0.78	4	0.57	15
11	0.43	8	0.38	2	1.40	2	1.69	2
12	0.39	14	0.36	4	1.11	2	0.78	4
13	0.41	17	0.43	19	1.03	2	0.72	7
14	0.38	15	0.39	7	1.38	2	1.27	14
15	0.38	20	0.45	19	1.67	2	1.57	13
16	0.41	12	0.54	19	1.30	2	0.23	19

4   Discussion

The results in Fig. 1 are related to the global functional connectivity analysis that reflects the presence of some variability in the single subject correlations (left figure), i.e., more than half subjects had positive correlations during the task, whereas few ones had negative correlations. In particular, the mean correlation matrix (right figure) shows great correlation in specific submatrixes, e.g. the submatrix that regards the ROIs from 73 to 80 includes the Fusiform brain regions (using the Harvard-Oxford labels, they are ROIs 73:74 L/R Temporal Fusiform Cx Anterior Divisions, ROIs 75:76 L/R Temporal Fusiform Cx Posterior Divisions, ROIs 77:78 L/R Temporo-Occipital Fusiform Cx and ROIs 79:80 L/R Occipital Fusiform Cx). This submatrix positive correlation is in agreement with the selective importance for the face recognition task of the Fusiform regions shown in the results of Wakeman and Henson [15].

The results presented in Figs. 4, 5, 6 and 7 reveal the important evidence that optimal clustering and 2-group clustering are both statistically different for the spatial configuration in the case of both FCM and NG for both the parametric and non-parametric test. Knowing that the two spatial clusters are sufficient to be statistically different is helpful for the comparison of the optimal clustering outcomes between subjects, that in our case leads a different number of clusters for subjects (see. Table 1). The use of 2-clusters (or a fixed-clusters) classifications allows to easy compare subjects for post-clustering analysis. Furthermore, spatial clustering has in general good properties, but temporal clustering does not have the same quality, due to difficulty to find statistically different clusters, albeit FCM outperformed NG, but not always with p-value less than 0.05, as better results were achieved for 2-clusters setting.

The results presented in Figs. 8 , 9 and 10 are regarding to the variability observed in the clustering results. Jaccard similarity matrices highlight huge differences within and between clustering algorithms. This fact could be explained with the random initialization labels; then, although the clustering reached the optimal configurations, it could be the case that the i label is not assigned to the i pattern in all the subjects. In other words, the same pattern in different subjects could be labelled sometimes with label i or with label j.

Figures 11 and 12 present the results in the special case of the clustering computed for the Subject 12. It had the best behaviour for both the parametric and the non-parametric tests. The figures show the topological graph-based parcellation of FCM clustering in 2-group, where many inferior regions were clustered in the Class 1, whereas many superior regions were clustered in Class 2. The two spatial clusters differed two BOLD signal macro-levels, but the two temporal clusters do not have easily distinguishable differences, although they have in fact statistical differences probed by the non-parametric test.

Subject 12 was also studied with a voxel-based parcellation that has found 14 clusters with FCM in the case of ROIs clustering. Precisely, considerations about results in the Figs. 13 and 14 refer to the Fusiform regions classification. The eight regions involved in the Fusiform bilateral portions were correctly distinguished in zones with more activation that the others. This clustering evidences detailed the role of brain substructures particularly related to the Face Recognition task, confirming the specialized nature for the Fusiform cortexes, according, for example, to the results of Wakeman and Henson [15] that have shared the data we processed, and also the main related works (cfr. the seminal paper by Kanwisher [8], or the recent findings by Ghuman [4] and Grill-Spector [5]).

5 Conclusion and Future Works

In this paper we adopted a cross-clustering approach to fMRI data with the aim to cluster both spatial and temporal patterns, given that the main information related to brain activity, in the case of task-based paradigm, stems from both the anatomical regions with their BOLD temporal signatures and the ON/OFF blocks during an experiment in which they exhibit brain spatial response. More specifically, we processed fMRI images from a repository of images for face recognition. The selected images depict with 16 healthy subjects that did a Face Recognition Task. We investigated spatial (ROIs - Regions Of Interest) and temporal (TOIs - Times Of Interest) features, using Fuzzy C-Means (FCM) and Neural Gas (NG) algorithms to find similar and structured patterns. We validated the optimal clustering using the Davies-Bouldin index and we compared the different subjects outcomes using with Jaccard measure. We used parametrical and non-parametrical statistical tests to evaluate whether the differences between the classes are significant throughout clusters, using the p-value as a decision criterion. Also, we employed the functional connectivity analysis to explore the brain BOLD co-relations activities. This procedure is useful to understand the ROIs clustering meaning as it associates with the functional properties referred as task-based paradigm. The results showed that, in general, ROIs clustering was performed easier than TOIs clustering by either of the algorithms. However, in the case of TOIs clustering, which is more complex then the spatial one, Fuzzy C-Means method outperformed the Neural Gas Method, based on the statistical significance test.

This study has some limitations. The first one is the random assignment of starting clusters for each of the algorithms. The second limitation is the absence fo known block paradigm that matches the TOIs clustering. This is a theoretical limitation, because it depends on the amount of information available in a repository. The first limitation is more important because it sheds light why when two clusters are used the algorithm marks the same pattern with different labels (see Jaccard matrix). The results indicates that even if there is a correct classification of statistically different clusters, there isn't an easy way to compare the same class with objects from different datasets. In other words, there is no clustering consistency in terms of labels names for the subjects. This peculiarity could be overcome using a linguist procedure based on a formal description able to combine the labels of similar patterns. As future task, we plan to develop a translation procedure able to merge under one name different labels that are associated to similar patterns. Furthermore, we will investigate the cross-clustering more in detail. In this study, we clustered ROIs and TOIs and we tested the classes properties *uncoupled*. Using other statistical tests, e.g., the two-way ANOVA or Friedman test, we can evaluate whether the *coupled − classes* are significantly different, i.e., we plan to test whether the clusters of ROIs combined with the clusters of TOIs have elements that are significantly different. This procedure would allow to find spatial patterns that are associated statistically with temporal patterns and *viceversa*. Combining the clustering results is a more precise exploration of the brain during task-paradigm, where the main features are both spatial dynamics (the regional signatures) and temporal dynamics (the ON-OFF blocks paradigm).

References

1. Bezdek, J.C., Ehrlich, R., Full, W.: FCM: the fuzzy c-means clustering algorithm. Comput. Geosci. **10**(2–3), 191–203 (1984)
2. Davies, D.L., Bouldin, D.W.: A cluster separation measure. IEEE Trans. Pattern Anal. Mach. Intell. **2**, 224–227 (1979)
3. Friston, K.J., et al.: Functional and effective connectivity in neuroimaging: a synthesis. Hum. Brain Mapp. **2**(1–2), 56–78 (1994)
4. Ghuman, A.S., et al.: Dynamic encoding of face information in the human fusiform gyrus. Nat. Commun. **5**, 5672 (2014)
5. Grill-Spector, K., Weiner, K.S.: The functional architecture of the ventral temporal cortex and its role in categorization. Nat. Rev. Neurosci. **15**(8), 536 (2014)
6. Jain, A.K.: Data clustering: 50 years beyond k-means. Pattern Recogn. Lett. **31**(8), 651–666 (2010)
7. Jenkinson, M., Beckmann, C.F., Behrens, T.E., Woolrich, M.W., Smith, S.M.: FSL. Neuroimage **62**(2), 782–790 (2012)
8. Kanwisher, N., McDermott, J., Chun, M.M.: The fusiform face area: a module in human extrastriate cortex specialized for face perception. J. Neurosci. **17**(11), 4302–4311 (1997)
9. Lee, M.H., et al.: Clustering of resting state networks. PloS One **7**(7), e40370 (2012)
10. Liao, T.W.: Clustering of time series data survey. Pattern Recogn. **38**(11), 1857–1874 (2005)
11. Lindquist, M.A., et al.: The statistical analysis of fMRI data. Stat. Sci. **23**(4), 439–464 (2008)
12. Martinetz, T., Schulten, K., et al.: "Neural-gas" network learns topologies (1991)
13. Duda, R.O., Hart, P.E., Stork, D.G.: Pattern Classification, 2nd edn. Wiley, Hoboken (2001)
14. Vergani, A.A., Martinelli, S., Binaghi, E.: Cluster analysis of functional neuroimages using data reduction and competitive learning algorithms. In: Tavares, J.M.R.S., Natal Jorge, R.M. (eds.) ECCOMAS 2017. LNCVB, vol. 27, pp. 62–71. Springer, Cham (2018). https://doi.org/10.1007/978-3-319-68195-5_7
15. Wakeman, D.G., Henson, R.N.: A multi-subject, multi-modal human neuroimaging dataset. Sci. Data **2**, 150001 (2015)
16. Wismüller, A., Meyer-Bäse, A., Lange, O., Auer, D., Reiser, M.F., Sumners, D.: Model-free functional MRI analysis based on unsupervised clustering. J. Biomed. Inform. **37**(1), 10–18 (2004)

Applicability of Deep Learned vs Traditional Features for Depth Based Classification

Fabio Bracci[✉], Mo Li, Ingo Kossyk, and Zoltan-Csaba Marton

Institute of Robotics and Mechatronics, German Aerospace Center (DLR),
Weßling, Germany
{fabio.bracci,mo.li,zoltan.marton}@dlr.de, fabio.bracci@freenet.de,
inkoss74@gmail.com

Abstract. In robotic applications, highly specific objects such as industrial parts, for example, often need to be recognized. In these cases methods can't rely on the online availability of large labeled training data sets or pre-trained models. This is especially true for depth data, thus making it challenging for deep learning (DL) approaches. Therefore, this work analyzes the performance of various traditional (global or part-based) and DL features on a restricted depth data set, depending on the tasks complexity. While the sample size is small, we can conclude that pre-trained DL descriptors are the most descriptive, but not by a statistically significant margin and therefore part-based descriptors are still a viable option for small, but difficult 3D data sets.

Keywords: 3D shape descriptor · Point cloud descriptor ·
Deep learning features · Object recognition · Scene analysis

1 Introduction - Research Question

Most robotics applications involve some degree of perception of the environment. The availability of inexpensive imaging sensors delivering depth data is the reason for robotic vision to take a major role in such applications. This in turn mandates processing techniques for 3D data. One of the required capabilities is the 3D object classification. Given some image measurement taken by the robotic unit, a question arises, what kind of objects and items can be detected in the measured 3D data.

This is often done through the concept of point clouds, a collection of points representing a surface, in this case of an object. Objects can be differentiated by their geometric properties, which are encoded by means of several descriptors. In the past two decades a number of handcrafted descriptors have been studied in the literature. Recently from the field of Neural Networks the so called Deep Learning techniques gained momentum, some of which are able to learn descriptors suitable for the same purpose.

© Springer Nature Switzerland AG 2019
R. P. Barneva et al. (Eds.): CompIMAGE 2018, LNCS 10986, pp. 145–159, 2019.
https://doi.org/10.1007/978-3-030-20805-9_13

| bird | fish | non flying insect | flying insect | biped | quadru- ped | apart- ment | sky- scraper | bottle | mug |

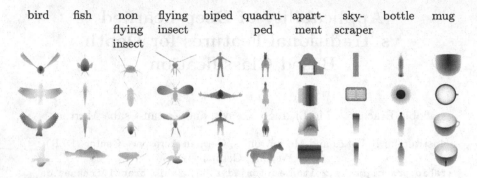

Fig. 1. Sample object views. The rows in the table are from top to bottom: front view, top view, rear inclined view, right inclined view. The objects are taken form the SHREC 2010 object database.

We want to investigate the descriptiveness of traditional point-based features as well as of pre-trained or trained (on a specific data set) deep learned features for 3D object recognition, depending on the shape complexity. Considering the growing popularity of Deep Neural Networks (DNN), we want to evaluate if the feature sets extracted from a DNN are always the best choice for describing a 3D object shape. We also want to investigate how the considered features perform when the shape differences are at the coarse level and when they are at a fine grain level.

A general problem for DNNs is the huge quantity of data needed for the training phase. This impedes the deployment of DNNs in robotics as large 3D data sets are scarce (there are few public data sets available with a medium-small number of objects) and within robotic setups to collect large samplings is usually not possible. Therefore, we want to perform this analysis in a context of limited data, as often it is the case in robotics applications.

2   Method

In our approach we consider view-based object classification. That is, given a 2.5D surface representation of an object view, we want to infer its class by finding the most similar surface in a collection of known ones. Those surfaces can come from real world observations as well as synthetic sources. The shape of the objects is encoded through traditional descriptors (VFH [14], CVFH [2] and OUR-VFH [1]) and deep learned ones (CaffeNet pre-trained features [5], VAE learned features [6] and DLR-VAE learned features [7]). The considered features are resumed in Table 1.

Traditional 3D Descriptors

The Viewpoint Feature Histogram (VFH [14]) is an evolution of the Fast Point Feature Histogram (FPFH [13]) which keeps scale invariance and adds viewpoint

Table 1. Feature types overview.

	handcrafted features	part-based	pre-trained	fully trained	supervised training
VFH	✓				
CVFH	✓	✓			
OUR-CVFH	✓	✓			
CaffeNet			✓		
VAE				✓	
DLR-VAE				✓	✓

variance. The VFH encodes a surface patch by means of a histogram of pan, tilt, yaw and surface normal angle relative to a given viewpoint vector. The VFH describes the whole object with a normalized histogram of 263 (45, 45, 45, 128) bins (45 bins for pan, tilt and yaw angles, 128 bins for the surface normals angles with the viewpoint vector) and qualifies itself as a global descriptor.

The Clustered Viewpoint Feature Histogram (CVFH [2]) is based on object parts, the so called stable regions. Those regions are obtained by applying on the point cloud a region growing algorithm with a maximum point distance and normal angle difference, as well as a minimum point number to accept the region. The stable regions are meant to represent the object and are robust against occlusions and missing parts and an example of such regions is shown in Fig. 2. The CVFH describes each region by extending the VFH vector with an unnormalized histogram of 45 bins, the Shape Distribution Component (SDC), computed by accumulating the quadratic point distances to the region centroid. For hypothesis verification, the Camera Roll Histogram (CRH) is added, a 90-bins histogram of the relative angles between the region normals and the camera view-up vector. This last histogram is useful for pose estimation problems. For our purposes, we regard the CVFH descriptor as a set of extended VFH descriptors, one for each part with 308 (45, 45, 45, 45, 128) bins and with the total descriptor size depending on the number of parts.

The Oriented, Unique and Repeatable Clustered Viewpoint Feature Histogram descriptor (OUR-VFH [1]) is an evolution of the CVFH descriptor, where the CRH component is removed and the normal angles histogram is halved as the normals always point to the hemisphere where the viewing point lies. The authors propose Semi-Global Unique Reference Frames (SGURF), a method to compute a reference frame for every patch. With this reference frame they subdivide the region's points in octants, and for each they compute a 13-bins histogram of the distances to the centroid which gives a total histogram size of 104 bins. The final descriptor consists of 303 (45 * 3, 13 * 8, 64) bins.

Both CVFH and OUR-VFH rely on the stable regions which represent parts of the analyzed objects and this qualifies them as part-based descriptors. All these methods were developed for fully 3D point clouds.

Deep Learned Descriptors

DNNs enjoy a growing popularity but require large amounts of training data and depth information requires more complex approaches [9,19], or involves transforming it into RGB images [17,19]. For example, in [17] transfer learning was attempted, where an RGB-based Places-CNN was fine-tuned with depth data using a proposed HHA embedding. On depth data this approach was found less effective than training from scratch.

We consider three kinds of DNNs, a pre-trained one and two fully trained ones, which synthesize global descriptors. The use of a pre-trained Convolutional Neural Network (CNN) to extract features is well known. For example, in [11] such features are benchmarked and deep learning models are publicly accessible since the high performances shown in the ImageNet Large Scale Visual Recognition Challenge [12], for instance, the networks studied in [5] and in [16].

The first DL descriptors are synthesized with the well known CaffeNet pre-trained network presented in [5]. There fully-connected Neural Networks are trained on RGB images subdivided in 1000 classes coming from ImageNet [8]. To one side CNN's synthesize representations which are increasingly abstract with the layer depth, to the other side the deeper layers tune the abstraction to the training problem. The challenge is to find the layer with an abstract representation which generalizes to a different problem, like the depth images which are mono-dimensional and untextured. We extract the features produced at the fc6 layer, since it was shown that it is the best level of abstraction on depth data in the CaffeNet pre-trained network as shown in [18]. Because of the limited amount of training data, no fine-tuning is possible for this network.

The second kind of DL descriptors are fully trained and come from the Variational Auto Encoder (VAE) [6]. We trained this net on our unlabeled images data set and we extracted the features from the learned latent representation.

The last kind of DL descriptors is fully trained as well and come from a new flavor of VAE, the DLR-VAE [7]. Here the training is similar to the VAE's one, where the DLR-VAE considers also class labels and is therefore a supervised learner.

The last two DNNs need a smaller amount of data compared to CaffeNet, and the DLR-VAE is semi-supervised and better able than the original VAE to learn from small data sets, as shown in [7]. In our study, the training data is very limited and therefore challenging for both of the VAE methods. These limitations might lead to an advantage for the hand-crafted descriptors.

Descriptors and Metrics

This work focusses on a simple nearest neighbor classifier (1NN) because we want to focus on the descriptiveness of the features instead of on the tuning of various classification techniques from the vast machine learning field. The nearest neighbor classifier compares the feature vectors based on a given metric. 1NN prefers data which is cleanly clustered into classes in the feature space and is sensitive to class overlap, therefore it reveals feature weaknesses.

Fig. 2. Example of stable regions in CVFH and OUR-CVFH. Each color encodes a different stable region. (Color figure online)

The VFH features in [14] are compared with a simple Euclidean distance. In [2] the CVFH are compared with a histogram metric defined as the sum of bin intersections divided by sum of bin unions. With this metric they retrieve the nearest ten candidates and find geometrically the best match by Iterative Closest Points (ICP [3]) alignment and inliers count. This last stage is known as hypothesis verification.

The OUR-CVFH features are compared in a similar way to the CVFH: the candidates number is raised to fourteen and the hypothesis verification is done with inliers and outliers count. Both approaches are not suitable to our 1NN classification scheme because of the hypothesis verification stage; for each surface patch both approaches represent the geometry with a set of multidimensional features (VFH histograms) instead of a single multidimensional feature (a single VFH histogram).

Generally the Euclidean metric is applied on DNN features, while different metrics are recommended for the traditional descriptors. In order to compare properly all the features we consider a set of metrics, namely the L1, L2, Hellinger and the χ^2 distance. However, CVFH and OUR-CVFH are based on the segmentation in stable regions which are mapped to a set of descriptors and cannot be compared trivially, hence a scoring scheme is needed. The average vector, minimum distance and weighted confidence voting were considered; we report only the best performing, which in our setup is the weighted voting with a Gaussian distance scoring. For the DL descriptors, only the L1 and L2 distances were considered, Since the Hellinger and the χ^2 distances are meant for histograms and distributions we considered instead the cosine distance, which is the distance used by the DLR-VAE and the VAE learners.

3   Experimental Setup

The descriptiveness of the studied features is evaluated by measuring the retrieval accuracy on a subset of objects taken from the SHREC 2010 database - the Shape Retrieval Contest of Range Scans [10]. The subset consists of 10 objects taken from each of 11 object classes and for every object we take four selected views (front, top, top-rear and top-left) for a total of 440 labeled depth images. This setup comes from [4]; some examples of surfaces are shown in Fig. 1.

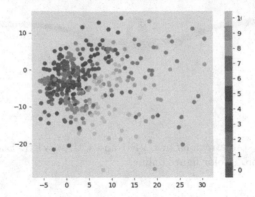

Fig. 3. DLR-VAE 2D latent space visualization. The eleven classes are encoded by different colors. (Color figure online)

For simplicity we evaluate the considered features with a simple 1NN classifier while more advanced classifiers than 1NN are better able to reach high accuracies. This would happen at the cost of shifting the focus from feature quality to classifier quality. We choose 1NN in order to highlight the shape descriptiveness of the considered features as explained in Subsect. 2.

Each pair of surfaces is compared with the metrics explained in Sect. 2. We perform a leave-one-out cross-validation and we collect the classification confusion matrices as well as the average accuracies. This procedure is applied to the whole set of 440 surfaces from 11 classes as well as to two subsets: distinct objects {Biped, Bird, Quadruped, Fish, Mug} where objects are distinguishable at a coarse level through few details and similar objects {Apartment House, Flying Insect, Non Flying Insect, Single House, Skyscraper} where objects are distinguishable at a fine grained level with larger amount of details. In this second subset we have semantically related classes. The goal here is to highlight differences in the feature descriptiveness for such cases. Each of those subsets is made of 5 classes for which ten instances with the before mentioned views are considered. The 11 classes set is the union of the distinct objects set with the similar objects set and the class Bottle.

The methods are implemented with the commonly available Point Cloud Library [15]. For both the VAE and DLR-VAE learners we used the whole 440 surfaces. This is a small training data set for learning methods in general and for DNNs in particular, as such methods may overfit or fail to reach their maximal learning potential. Because of the data scarcity for robotic applications this is a relevant setup.

4   Results

We performed the 1NN classification for all the considered features and we collected the outcomes. Figure 5 shows the confusion matrices for the 1NN classification of the considered features for all classes with the metric giving the best accuracy. Figure 6 shows the same for the distinct classes and Fig. 7 for the similar classes. An overview of the best classification accuracies is given in Fig. 4 and the results for the classification of the three objects sets are listed in Tables 2, 3 and 4. The 1NN classification was performed based on the 100 dimensional latent space learned by the DLR-VAE and the learned 2D latent space representation is shown in Fig. 3. Finally, a 2D projection of the CaffeNet features and the VFH features of the 440 patches is shown in Fig. 8.

On average, the classification of the similar objects shows a lower accuracy for all the used feature-metric pair, than the classification of the distinct objects. The classification accuracies of all the objects are in between the accuracies of the classification of the similar objects and distinct objects groups, except in the case of VAE features. The spread among the accuracies also varies with the classification problem: it is the smallest on the distinct classes, the largest on all classes and almost as large as on all classes on the similar classes. The CaffeNet features with L2 metric show the best 1NN classification accuracy, closely followed by CVFH features with L1 metric and OUR-CVFH features with the χ^2 metric. The VFH features with the L1 metric, the VAE and DLR-VAE features with the cosine metric follow with an accuracy gap on the all classes problem and are almost indistinguishable from each other.

The inspection of the confusion matrices reveals some specific features. In the similar objects case, all the global methods confuse Apartment House for Single House, Flying Insect for Non Flying Insect and vice versa, with the degree of confusion varying with the total accuracy. The VAE based methods tend to confuse a single Non Flying Insect and a Flying Insect for Apartment House and Skyscraper. For the part-based features Flying Insect is mistaken for Apartment House and Single House for Non Flying Insect. The VAE features confuse Skyscraper and Single House for Non Flying Insect.

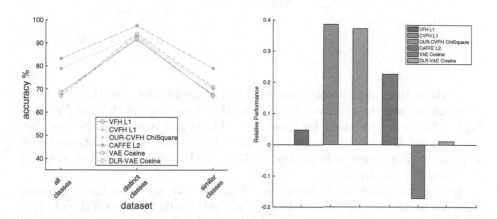

Fig. 4. Classification results. Left: classification results. The vertical axis shows the classification accuracy, the horizontal axis shows the classification problem. Right: Relative accuracy plot. The horizontal axis represents the different combination of feature and metric, the vertical one represents the accuracy on the complete data relative to the two data sets. See the main text for details.

Table 2. Classification accuracy percentages on all classes. Features' best performance is marked in bold, second best in italics.

	VFH	CVFH	OUR-CVFH	CaffeNet	VAE	DLR-VAE
L1	**68.64%**	**78.86%**	77.73%	*82.95%*	52.05%	58.64%
L2	59.82%	74.09%	*78.18%*	**83.18%**	*57.73%*	*60.00%*
χ^2	66.82%	*78.41%*	**78.86%**	-	-	-
Hellinger	*67.05%*	76.36%	**78.86%**	-	-	-
Cosine	-	-	-	-	**67.04%**	**67.27%**

Table 3. Classification accuracy percentages on similar classes. Features' best performance is marked in bold, second best in italics.

	VFH	CVFH	OUR-CVFH	CaffeNet	VAE	DLR-VAE
L1	**67.5%**	*70.0%*	69.0%	**79.0%**	60.5%	52.0%
L2	58.5%	*70.0%*	69.0%	**79.0%**	*62.5%*	*59.5%*
χ^2	*67.0%*	**71.5%**	70.5%	-	-	-
Hellinger	*67.0%*	69.0%	*69.5%*	-	-	-
Cosine	-	-	-	-	**71.0%**	**67.0%**

Table 4. Classification accuracy percentages on distinct classes. Features' best performance is marked in bold, second best in italics.

	VFH	CVFH	OUR-CVFH	CaffeNet	VAE	DLR-VAE
L1	**91.5%**	**93.0%**	**93.0%**	**98.5%**	89.5%	82.5%
L2	86.0%	91.0%	90.0%	*97.5%*	*90.5%*	*90.0%*
χ^2	*90.5%*	*92.5%*	**93.0%**	-	-	-
Hellinger	90.0%	92.0%	*92.5%*	-	-	-
Cosine	-	-	-	-	**94.0%**	**92.5%**

In the distinct objects case the overall accuracies are higher and the scatter in the confusion matrices is lower. With global descriptors except the CaffeNet ones Biped objects are confused for Quadruped objects and, including the CaffeNet features, the Quadruped objects for Biped objects and Bird objects and Fish objects for Quadruped objects. For both the VAE features, Biped objects are confused for Fish objects.

In the classification problem for all classes, we see that the confusions observed in the two subsets translate to the total classification, with the addition of some cross set confusion, where objects from the distinct classes are confused for objects of the similar classes, and vice versa. We observe that both the part based features confuse Bird and Biped objects for Non Flying Insects objects as well as Bottle objects for Mug, Quadruped, Apartment House, Single House and

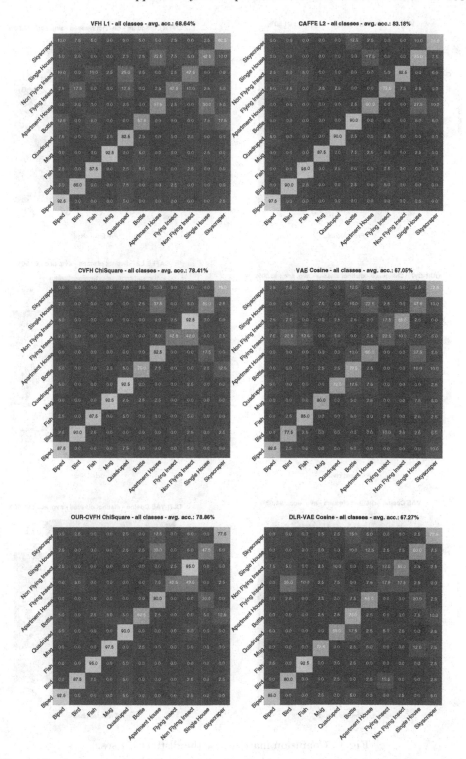

Fig. 5. Confusion matrices for all classes. On the vertical axis the labels of the queried class, on the horizontal axis the labels of the predicted class.

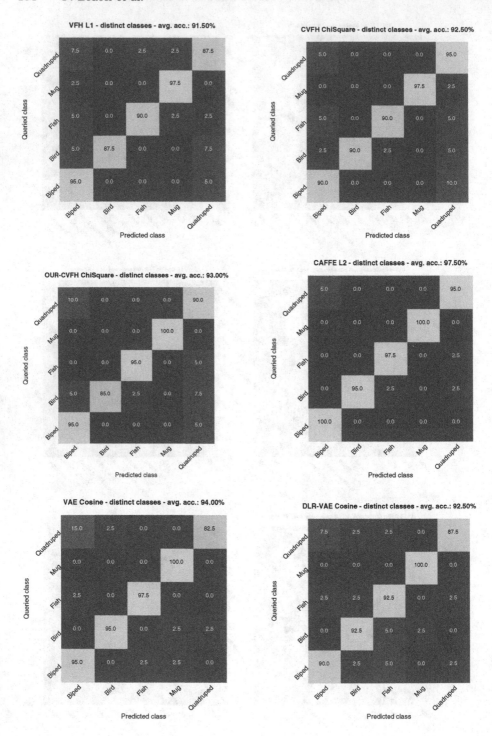

Fig. 6. Confusion matrices for the distinct classes.

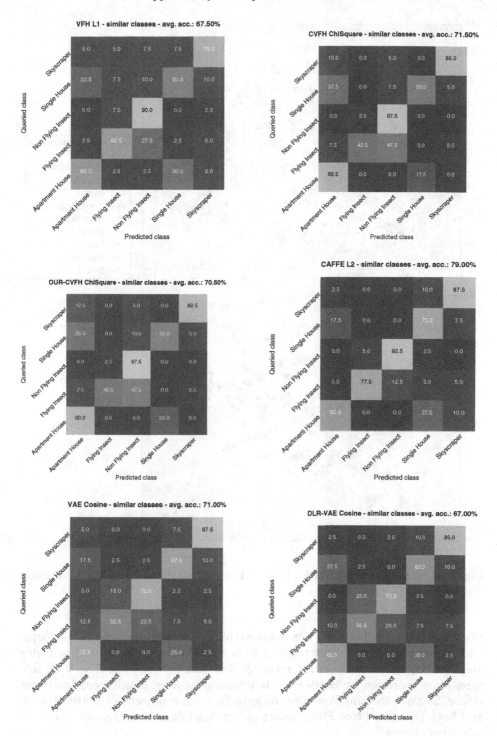

Fig. 7. Confusion matrices for the similar classes.

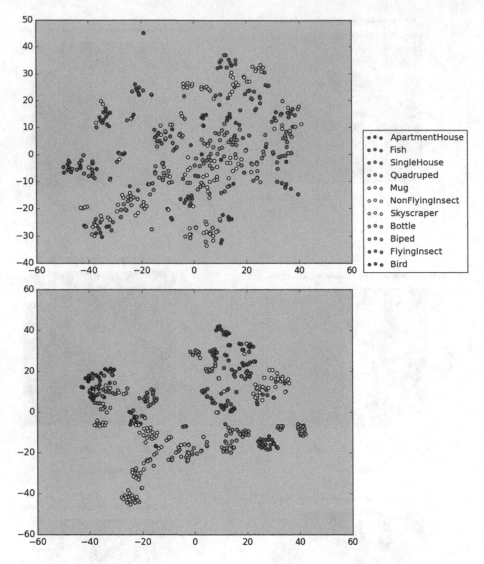

Fig. 8. 2D projection using t-SNE of the VFH features (top) and the CaffeNet features (bottom).

Skyscraper objects. The CaffeNet features confuse Bottle objects for Single House and Skyscraper objects, Skyscraper objects for Bottle objects, as well as Flying and Non Flying Insect objects for Biped, Bird and Fish objects. The VAE features show confusion for Bottle objects mistaken for Mug, Quadruped, Apartment House, Single House and Skyscraper objects, Skyscraper objects for Bottle objects, and both Flying and Non Flying Insect objects mistaken for objects of almost all the other classes.

We also estimate the stability of these performances by relating the accuracy for all objects with the ones for distinct objects and for the similar objects. We estimate the following score: $(acc_{all} - acc_{similar}) / (acc_{distinct} - acc_{similar})$. The obtained ratios are shown in Fig. 4.

Finally we analyzed the Jeffreys intervals for the best accuracies reported in Table 2 according to [7]. The 95% credible interval for the best performing CaffeNet features with L2 metric is [79.5% 86.5%], for the next best performing CVFH features with L1 metric and the OUR-CVFH features with χ^2 metric is [74.8% 82.5%], while for the following VFH features with L1 metric is [64.2% 0.72.8%]. The first two intervals are not disjoint while the last two are disjoint, therefore the accuracy difference between the CaffeNet features and the CVFH and OUR-CVFH features is statistically not significant while the accuracy difference between the second best performing features and the third best VFH features is statistically significant.

5   Conclusions

This study focuses on a 3D object classification scenario with limited data, which is a plausible scenario in robotics applications. The classification of 3D data, whether it being point clouds or other sparse and volumetric data, is a subject of current research and yet to be fully solved.

First of all, we see that the performance of the CaffeNet features is best and the VAE features is worst. The 2D projection of the feature data with the t-SNE method as shown in Fig. 8 qualitatively indicates that the CaffeNet features group into separated clusters, while the lower quality VFH ones result in a more scattered distribution with many overlapping regions between different classes.

Second, we notice that the similar objects are more difficult to discriminate than distinct objects, as expected. Also we note that semantically similar objects here imply a certain degree of geometrical similarity, which in turn implies similarity between the final features. This way, semantic ambiguity among classes translates into low feature discriminability.

Third, as expected the part based methods performances are very correlated, as CVFH and OUR-CVFH are both based on the same concept of stable regions.

Further, in this study the CaffeNet features perform best for discriminating the considered objects, and the second best features by a small accuracy difference are the part-based methods. We also showed how the accuracy difference on all objects classification between the CaffeNet features and the part-based features is not statistically significant. This comparable performance obtained using part-based descriptors and a large (pre-trained) CNN holds for depth data, where comparatively less information is encoded than in RGB data. Depth images are usually smoother and have less high-frequency information.

Moreover, the VAE descriptors perform comparably to the DLR-VAE descriptors. We believe that unsupervised pre-training and data augmentation might help building a more robust embedding, where the DLR-VAE's supervised training might provide an improvement for classification tasks.

On one hand, the CaffeNet features are likely to benefit from the extensive pre-training and work better than the VAE and DLR-VAE methods trained on this limited surfaces set. This might be improved by a larger (unlabeled) pre-training data set, as the minimal training requirements for both VAE methods need to be assessed. On the other hand, despite the clear disadvantage constituted by such a limited training data set, both the VAE methods perform similarly to each other and to the VFH descriptor.

Finally, the bar plot in Fig. 4 shows that when more similar objects are added to the classification problem, in terms of discriminative power the degradation for the part based method is the least, the CaffeNet features are second best and the global methods are the worst, with the performance dropping near or below the accuracy of the similar objects classification. All in all for limited data scenarios the use of part-based descriptors remains an option to consider.

In the future we plan to investigate more complex part based approaches where part relationships are encoded, as well as the use of DNN features within the part-based methods. Also other classifiers like k-Nearest-Neighbors (kNN) could be investigated, where for this specific classifier we don't intuitively expect to see different trends in the accuracies, rather only higher values.

References

1. Aldoma, A., Tombari, F., Rusu, R.B., Vincze, M.: OUR-CVFH – oriented, unique and repeatable clustered viewpoint feature histogram for object recognition and 6DOF pose estimation. In: Pinz, A., Pock, T., Bischof, H., Leberl, F. (eds.) DAGM/OAGM 2012. LNCS, vol. 7476, pp. 113–122. Springer, Heidelberg (2012). https://doi.org/10.1007/978-3-642-32717-9_12
2. Aldoma, A., et al.: CAD-model recognition and 6DOF pose estimation using 3D cues. In: 2011 IEEE International Conference on Computer Vision Workshops (ICCV Workshops), pp. 585–592. IEEE, November 2011. http://dx.doi.org/10.1109/iccvw.2011.6130296
3. Besl, P.J., McKay, N.D.: A method for registration of 3-D shapes. IEEE Trans. Pattern Anal. Mach. Intell. **14**(2), 239–256 (1992). http://dx.doi.org/10.1109/34.121791
4. Bracci, F., Hillenbrand, U., Marton, Z.-C., Wilkinson, M.H.F.: On the use of the tree structure of depth levels for comparing 3D object views. In: Felsberg, M., Heyden, A., Krüger, N. (eds.) CAIP 2017. LNCS, vol. 10424, pp. 251–263. Springer, Cham (2017). https://doi.org/10.1007/978-3-319-64689-3_21
5. Jia, Y., et al.: Caffe: convolutional architecture for fast feature embedding. In: Proceedings of the 22nd ACM International Conference on Multimedia, MM 2014, pp. 675–678. ACM, New York (2014). http://doi.acm.org/10.1145/2647868.2654889
6. Kingma, D.P.: Variational inference & deep learning: A new synthesis. Intelligent Sensory Information Systems (IVI, FNWI) (2017). http://dare.uva.nl/personal/pure/en/publications/variational-inference-deep-learning(8e55e07f-e4be-458f-a929-2f9bc2d169e8).html
7. Kossyk, I., Marton, Z.S.: Discriminative regularization of the latent manifold of variational auto-encoders for semi-supervised recognition. Online (2017). https://tinyurl.com/y8p3tjle

8. Krizhevsky, A., Sutskever, I., Hinton, G.E.: Imagenet classification with deep convolutional neural networks. In: Advances in Neural Information Processing Systems, vol. 25 (2012). http://citeseerx.ist.psu.edu/viewdoc/summary?doi=10.1.1.299.205

9. Masci, J., Rodolà, E., Boscaini, D., Bronstein, M.M., Li, H.: Geometric deep learning. In: SIGGRAPH ASIA 2016 Courses, SA 2016. ACM, New York (2016). http://dx.doi.org/10.1145/2988458.2988485

10. Pratikakis, I., et al.: SHREC 2010 - Shape Retrieval Contest of Range Scans. http://citeseerx.ist.psu.edu/viewdoc/summary?doi=10.1.1.361.8068

11. Razavian, A.S., Azizpour, H., Sullivan, J., Carlsson, S.: CNN Features off-the-shelf: an astounding baseline for recognition, May 2014. http://arxiv.org/abs/1403.6382

12. Russakovsky, O., et al.: ImageNet large scale visual recognition challenge. Int. J. Comput. Vis. **115**, 211–252 (2015). Springer, US. http://dx.doi.org/10.1007/s11263-015-0816-y

13. Rusu, R.B., Blodow, N., Beetz, M.: Fast point feature histograms (FPFH) for 3D registration. In: The IEEE International Conference on Robotics and Automation (ICRA), Kobe, Japan (2009). http://files.rbrusu.com/publications/Rusu09ICRA.pdf

14. Rusu, R.B., Bradski, G., Thibaux, R., Hsu, J.: Fast 3D recognition and pose using the viewpoint feature histogram. In: 2010 IEEE/RSJ International Conference on Intelligent Robots and Systems (IROS), pp. 2155–2162. IEEE, October 2010. http://dx.doi.org/10.1109/iros.2010.5651280

15. Rusu, R.B., Cousins, S.: 3D is here: point cloud library (PCL). In: 2011 IEEE International Conference on Robotics and Automation, pp. 1–4. IEEE, May 2011. http://dx.doi.org/10.1109/icra.2011.5980567

16. Simonyan, K., Zisserman, A.: Very Deep Convolutional Networks for Large-Scale Image Recognition, April 2015. http://arxiv.org/abs/1409.1556v5.pdf

17. Song, X., Herranz, L., Jiang, S.: Depth CNNs for RGB-D scene recognition: learning from scratch better than transferring from RGB-CNNs. ArXiv e-prints, January 2018. http://arxiv.org/abs/1801.06797

18. Ullrich, M., Ali, H., Durner, M., Marton, Z.C., Triebel, R.: Selecting CNN features for online learning of 3D objects. In: 2017 IEEE/RSJ International Conference on Intelligent Robots and Systems (IROS), pp. 5086–5091. IEEE, September 2017. http://dx.doi.org/10.1109/iros.2017.8206393

19. Zaki, H.F.M., Shafait, F., Mian, A.: Convolutional hypercube pyramid for accurate RGB-D object category and instance recognition. In: 2016 IEEE International Conference on Robotics and Automation (ICRA), pp. 1685–1692. IEEE, May 2016. http://dx.doi.org/10.1109/icra.2016.7487310

Effect of Image View for Mammogram Mass Classification – An Extreme Learning Based Approach

Sk. Md. Obaidullah[✉], Sajib Ahmed, and Teresa Gonçalves

Department of Informatics, University of Évora, Evora, Portugal
sk.obaidullah@gmail.com, jack6148@gmail.com, tcg@uevora.pt

Abstract. Mammogram images are broadly categorized into two types: carniocaudal (CC) view and mediolateral oblique (MLO) view. In this paper, we study the effect of different image views for mammogram mass classification. For the experiments, we consider a dataset of 328 CC view images and 334 MLO view images (almost equal ratio) from a publicly available film mammogram image dataset [3]. First, features are extracted using a novel radon-wavelet based image descriptor. Then an extreme learning machine (ELM) based classification technique is applied and the performance of five different ELM kernels are compared: sigmoidal, sine, triangular basis, hard limiter and radial basis function. Performances are reported in terms of three important statistical measures namely, sensitivity or true positive rate (TPR), specificity or false negative rate (SPC) and recognition accuracy (ACC). Our experimental outcome for the present setup is two-fold: (i) CC view performs better then MLO for mammogram mass classification, (ii) hard limiter is the best ELM kernel for this problem.

Keywords: Breast cancer · Mammogram mass classification · Image view · Image descriptors · Extreme learning

1 Introduction

Breast cancer (BC) is one of the top cancer among women irrespective of the geographic location across the world. As per the report by the World Health Organization (WHO), BC is impacting over 1.5 million women each year from the developed and developing countries causing the highest number of death among women. In one of their latest reports [20], in the year 2015 more than 500,000 women died from breast cancer which is about 15% of all cancer death among women. In the developing countries breast cancer is increasing very rapidly due to several social-economic factors like higher life expectancy, increased urbanization and adoption of the so called modern lifestyles. It is said that "prevention is better than cure", so some risk reduction may be achieved with prevention but these strategies fail to eliminate the decease completely, since many times the

© Springer Nature Switzerland AG 2019
R. P. Barneva et al. (Eds.): CompIMAGE 2018, LNCS 10986, pp. 160–172, 2019.
https://doi.org/10.1007/978-3-030-20805-9_14

detection is done at a very late stage, particularly in low and middle-income countries. It is indeed clear that, if breast cancer is early detected, then it is one of the most treatable cancer types, therefore, to improve breast cancer outcome in terms of survival, early detection remains the mainspring of breast cancer control.

There are several modalities for BC imaging like X-Ray, MRI, Ultrasound, etc. Among all, X-Ray imaging which is also know as mammography, is the one of the easiest and low-cost techniques and is followed widely as a tool for primary diagnosis. Mammogram images are mainly of two types based on the processing modalities: (i) Screen Film Mammography (SFM) and (ii) Full Field Digital Mammography (FFDM). In case of SFM, films are used to capture the images and later they are scanned and stored into the computer; in case of FFDM, images are directly stored in the digital computer, so the additional scanning step is avoided. Some advantages of FFDM over SFM are better image quality and lesser storage requirement but, in terms of the ability to detect suspicious lesions in the breast, a recent literature [22, 26] study reveals that, both the SFM and FFDM, have almost equal ability. In this paper we deal with the SFM images which are available through the BCDR-F03 dataset [2, 3], one of the latest breast imaging film mammography datasets.

CAD System – An Overview. In recent years many computational approaches have been proposed for interpretation of medical images; these methods are known as Computer Aided Diagnostic methods or, in short, CAD [17]. Diagnostics through different imaging techniques like X-Ray, MRI or Ultrasound generates a huge amount of information that the radiologists or medical professionals need to analyse in a very short period of time. It is here that the advantage of a CAD system comes: it can play the role of an intelligent support system for the medical professional by providing a scope of double checking their predicted results thus reducing false positive cases. Another advantage is cost: for the developing countries there is a shortage of medical professionals, so providing more than one medical personnel for the double checking task is like day-dream; here, the CAD system can replace the need for another professional by supporting the radiologists' observation, That's why developing CAD systems is in demand.

The general framework for a traditional CAD system consists of three major parts: (i) image pre-processing which includes several tasks like ROI extraction and contrast enhancement; (ii) feature extraction and, finally, (iii) classification. Recently, deep learning based approaches are also reported in literature; these approaches replace the extraction of hand-crafted features by combining step (ii) and (iii) into a single stage. In literature we found several works where image descriptors are combined with clinical information for better classification accuracy [17]. The present work focuses on an image descriptor based classification of masses from mammogram images using an extreme learning (EL) based approach; no clinical information is considered.

A Quick Review. Constantinidis *et al.* [5] and Belkasim *et al.* [4] considered the Zernike moment based descriptor to classify masses; texture based classification of calcification and masses using Haralick features [11] was reported by different authors [7,8,25,28,29]. Haralick texture features were employed in other areas of medical imaging also [16] and a comparison of texture features and a deep learning approach is reported in [21]. Wavelet [10,24] and curvelet [9] analysis based feature descriptors are also used by different authors and a combination of intensity and texture descriptors was explored by Ramos *et al.* [23]. Histograms of oriented gradient (HOG) based features were employed along with the clinical information for mammogram image classification by Moura and Guevara [17] and Arevalo *et al.* [3] used a convolution neural network to separate malignant and benign masses without using any clinical information and reported the effectiveness of a deep learning based approach over the traditional hand-crafted one. In all the above mentioned works the focus was mainly on classification of malignant and benign masses in a straight forward manner; different machine learning based approaches are used to train different hand-crafted features; sometimes clinical information is also added as features.

In this paper, we report the effect of image view for mammogram mass classification. We explore the possibility of applying an extreme learning based approach for the present application. Not only that, we have compared the performance of different kernels of EL to find the best performer. The block diagram of the proposed method is shown in Fig. 1. First film mammogram dataset is considered and images are separated based their views; during pre-processing ROIs are extracted and their contrast is enhanced; next a feature vector is followed by classification using EL; finally, a performance comparison of different ELM kernels is made.

The rest of the paper is organized as follows: the contributions are outlined in Sect. 2 where we discuss the proposed feature extraction methodology and the ELM based classification approach; experimental details are reported in Sect. 3, which include dataset description, experimental setup and results with a comparative study. Finally we conclude the paper in Sect. 4.

2 Contribution Outline

In this paper we study the effect of image view for mammogram classification. A novel image descriptor based on radon-wavelet is used to extract features from the ROI images [18]. Further we classify images through the features using extreme learning machine. In addition to that, the performance of different ELM kernels is compared and the best performer for the present problem is chosen.

2.1 Design of Image Descriptors

Radon-wavelet is a novel image descriptor [18] used to extract features from ROI images. Next sub-section introduces it.

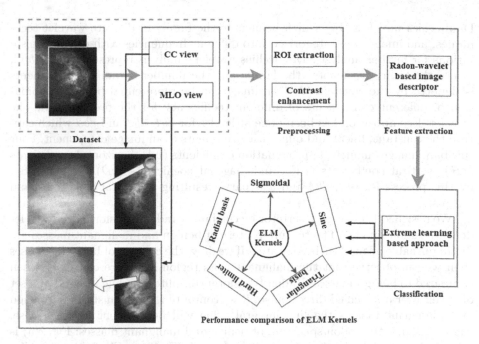

Fig. 1. Block diagram of the proposed method.

Radon Transform. Radon transform is an integral transform that consists of a set of projections of a pattern at different angles [6]. It is a mapping of a function $f(x, y)$ to another function $fR(x, y)$ which is defined on the 2-Dimensional space of lines in the plane. Now the value at a particular line is computed as the line integral of the function over that line for a pre-defined set of angles. To say alternatively, the radon transform of a pattern $f(x, y)$ for a pre-defined set of angles can be considered as follows: it is the projection of all non-zero points and the projection output is the sum of the non-zero points for the image pattern in each direction (angle between 0 to π). Finally, a matrix is formed; matrix elements are related to the integral of $f(x, y)$ over a line $Lin(\rho, \theta)$ defined by $\rho = x \cos \theta + y \sin \theta$ and can formally be expressed as

$$fR(\rho, \theta) = \int_{-\infty}^{\infty} \int_{-\infty}^{\infty} f(x, y) \delta(x \cos \theta + y \sin \theta - \rho) dx dy$$

where $\delta(.)$ is the Dirac delta function, $\delta(x) = 1$, if $x = 0$ and 0 otherwise. Also, $\theta \in [0, \pi]$ and $\rho \in [-\infty, \infty]$. For the radon transform, Lin_i is in normal form (ρ_i, θ_i).

Wavelet Analysis. The time-frequency response of a signal is represented through wavelet transform (for the present work, the signal is an image); wavelets are used for multi-resolution analysis and their advantages include computational ease with minimum resource and time requirements. In this work, we use

Daubechies wavelets [15], which belongs to the family of discrete wavelet techniques, and images are categorized into different frequencies with different resolutions for further analysis. Daubechies wavelet family is represented as 'dbN', where the term 'db' denotes the family and the number of vanishing moments is denoted by the constant 'N'. An image can be represented by the combination of different components of different coefficients; for the present work, the wavelet decomposition has been done at level 1 for $db1$, $db2$ and $db3$ which capture the constant, linear and quadratic coefficients of an image component. Four sub-band images namely, approximation coefficients (cA), horizontal coefficients (cH), vertical coefficients (cV), and diagonal coefficients (cD) are generated by this process for $db1$, $db2$ and $db3$ parts, resulting in a total of 12 sub-band images.

We designed the image descriptor by combining radon transform over wavelet decomposition images. The texture pattern of benign and malignant masses are distinguishable around their edge area. If we draw the contour of both the masses then we can observe that the malignant mass region has more convexity when compared to benign masses. Radon transform computes the line integral of a set of pixels over a specified direction so, if we compute radon transform on benign and malignant masses the line integral value will be different for each case. Figure 2 shows the radon spectrum of benign and malignant masses: Fig. 2(a) is a benign mass and its radon spectrum is shown in Fig. 2(c); Fig. 2(b) is a malignant mass and its radon spectrum is shown in Fig. 2(d). To extract more local information, we chose wavelet decomposition since different directional approximation can be found through this. Finally, from each of the sub-band images, i.e. on cA, cH, cV and cD, we computed the radon spectrum and statistical values were computed for those radon-wavelet spectrum and used to construct the feature vector.

Feature Vector. In what follows, we discuss the construction of the feature vector using the above mentioned method:

- Wavelet decomposition at level 1 was done on ROI images using Daubechies method for $db1$, $db2$ and $db3$. In this way 04 sub-band images for each coefficient results into a total of 12 sub-band generated.
- Radon transform is applied on the original ROI image and on each of the 12 sub-band images generated on the previous step, totaling 13 radon spectrum.
- For each of the 13 radon spectrum, features values namely: mean, standard deviation and maximum radon coefficient were computed; Altogether this step generates 52 features (04×13). Additionally 04 statistical features from the original gray-scale image are also computed, so overall feature dimension is 56.

2.2 Extreme Learning Machine

Extreme learning machine is a generalized version of the artificial neural network which is applied in different application areas, such as OCR (MNIST and

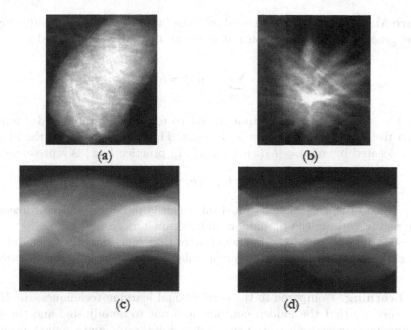

Fig. 2. ROI extracted from mammogram images and their radon spectrum: (a) benign mass, (b) malignant mass, (c) radon spectrum for (a), (d) radon spectrum for (b).

other datasets), 3D shape classification, speech recognition, traffic sign recognition (GTSRB dataset) and biological data classification [1,19]. Inspired from aforementioned applications and considering ELM's generality, we propose to study ELM with all possible activation functions for mammogram mass classification based on image views. For ELM, human intervention for tuning the number of hidden layers and nodes is small [12–14,27], thus providing an efficient and unified learning framework by generalizing a single-hidden layer feed forward neural networks (SLFNs).

In general, ELM can be used to solve various classification or regression problems with a very fast and random learning model. Unlike a conventional neural network, ELM is independent of tuning multiple hidden layers. The tuning is done using a mathematical formula for each hidden layer. An ideally optimal value is found by varying the weights of the hidden nodes. Basically there are two tunable parameters: (i) the regularization and (ii) the number of hidden nodes. By default, the number of output neurons is equal to the number of classes. The number of hidden nodes (neurons) can be increased or decreased. The tuning of the regularization co-efficient is optional (range is from 0.1 to 10). The learning of the ELM involves two key steps: (i) feature mapping and (ii) ELM learning.

Feature Mapping. The ELM transforms the input data into the hidden layer. For the generalized SLFN, the output function of ELM is represented as

$$f(x) = \sum_{i=1}^{L} \beta_i h_i(x) = h(x)\beta$$

where $\beta = [\beta_1.....\beta_L]^T$, is the output weight vector between the L-noded hidden layer to the output layer with $m \geq 1$ nodes. The output vector of the hidden layer is denoted by: $h(x) = [h_1(x).....h_L(x)]$. In practice $h_i(x)$ is represented by

$$h_i(x) = G(a_i, b_i, x), a_i \in R^d, b_i \in R$$

where, $G(a,b,x)$ is a continuous function which is piecewise and non linear in nature and (a_i, b_i) are the i_{th} hidden node parameters.

In our study, we used the following activation functions: (i) sigmoidal, (ii) sine function, (iii) hard limiter, (iv) triangular basis, (v) radial basis function.

ELM Learning. Compared to the conventional learning techniques, the ELM theory specifies that the hidden neurons need not to be adjusted and the goal is to simultaneously reach to the smallest training error and smallest norm of output weights. The ELM satisfies the universal approximation [13,27], which means $Lim_{L\to\infty} \parallel \sum_{i=1}^{L} \beta_i h_i(x) - f(x) = 0 \parallel$. This holds with probability 1 for proper output weights β.

Further, ELM has the classification capability, which means that if SLFNs can be approximated for any target function $f(x)$ by means of parameter tuning of hidden neurons, then SLFNs with random hidden layer mapping $h(x)$ can separate arbitrary disjoint regions.

3 Experiments

This section presents the dataset and its pre-processing, the evaluation setup and results obtained.

3.1 Dataset and Pre-processing

A benchmark film mammography dataset known as BCDR-F03 [2,3] from the Breast Cancer Digital Repository, a wide-ranging public repository composed of Breast Cancer patients' cases from Portugal [17], was used in our experiment. BCDR-F03 is one of the latest benchmarked film mammography dataset which consists of 668 film mammogram images. Out of these 668 image there are 736 biopsy proven masses containing 426 benign masses and 310 malignant masses from 344 patients. Thus, in many cases, a single image contains more than one mass. For the present work, we have considered one mass per image having a total of 668 masses; out of these, 662 images were considered for classification after removal of few extremely low resolution images. The samples provided are available in two different views namely carniocaudal (CC) and mediolateral oblique (MLO) view. In our data we have 328 CC views and 334 MLO views (almost equal ratio for fair comparison). Figure 3 shows different mammogram views with the lesions marked.

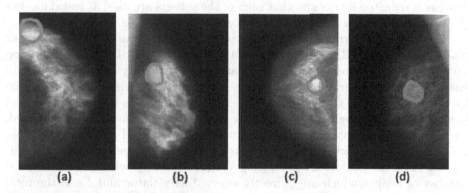

Fig. 3. Different mammogram views: (a) LCC, (b) LO, (c) RCC, (d) RO. The green boundary is the ROI. (Color figure online)

During pre-processing we have carried out (i) ROI extraction and (ii) contrast enhancement. Based on the information provided by the radiologist the ROIs were extracted; along with the BCDR-F03 dataset an annotated file with the ROI coordinate information is provided which helped us to extract ROIs automatically. Further, these ROIs were categorized into two class folders namely benign and malignant. Next, ROIs contrast enhancement was performed since original film mammograms are of very low contrast due to several factors (poor lighting condition, orientation, etc.); contrast is enhanced by subtracting the mean of the intensities in the image to each pixel. Figure 4 shows one original ROI and its contrast enhanced version.

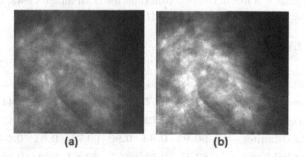

Fig. 4. Contrast enhancement: (a) original low contrast ROI, (b) contrast enhanced image.

3.2   Evaluation Protocol and System Information

During experimentation we followed k-fold cross validation. Initially all ROIs are divided into k subsets; out of k subsets one subset is used for testing the model and the remaining $k-1$ subsets are used for training purposes. The same process is repeated k times so that each of the subsets are used as test data. For the present work, the value of k was chosen heuristically to be 5.

The system performance was measured using three parameters: sensitivity or true positive rate (TPR), specificity or false negative rate (SPC) and recognition accuracy (ACC). Sensitivity is the measure of probability that ELM says an image belongs to a particular class which is actually true. Sensitivity is expressed by the equation: $Sensitivity = T_P/(T_P + F_N)$, where T_P is the total number of images correctly classified and F_N is the total number of image falsely rejected. On the other hand, specificity is the probability that ELM says an image dose not belong to a particular class and in reality it does not belongs. Sensitivity is expressed by the equation: $Specificity = T_N/(T_N + F_P)$, where T_N is the total number of images which are correctly rejected as violator and F_P is the total number of images from different class which are considered for the present class. Finally, Accuracy is defined as: $Accuracy = (T_P + T_N)/(T_P + T_N + F_P + F_N)$.

Regarding the system resources, all experiments were carried out using MAT-LAB 2017b software in a system with 2.8 GHz CPU, 8 GB RAM, 4 GB NVIDIA GPU.

3.3   Results and Analysis

The primary objective of this work was to find the performance of different image views for mammogram mass classification. Extreme learning machine along with five different kernels (sigmoidal, sine, triangular basis, hard limiter and radial basis) were used as classifiers. Table 1 shows the performance of ELM for benign and malignant mass separation on both CC and MLO view images.

Table 1. Performance of five activation functions for both image views; ACC (accuracy in %), TPR (true positive rate), and SPC (true negative rate).

ELM kernel type	CC view			MLO view		
	ACC	TPR	SPC	ACC	TPR	SPC
Sigmoidal	87.88	0.81	0.85	60.68	0.54	0.42
Sine	58.27	0.57	0.45	58.18	0.55	0.44
Triangular basis	79.60	0.72	0.70	61.09	0.53	0.42
Hard limiter	**90.95**	**0.84**	**0.90**	60.74	**0.61**	**0.54**
Radial basis	82.97	0.72	0.57	**62.82**	0.58	0.49

Our experimental outcome is two-fold:

1. for mammogram mass separation, CC view performs better than MLO view irrespective of the ELM kernel type. The highest CC view accuracy of 90.95% was found using hard limiter kernel; using the same kernel the MLO view shows an accuracy of 60.74%. For MLO view the highest accuracy of 62.82% was found using radial basis kernel. The highest sensitivity and specificity scores for CC and MLO views were using hard limiter kernel and the values obtained 0.84, 0.90 and 0.61, 0.54 respectively.
2. For the ELM classifier, the hard limiter kernel is the best performer among all for CC view images; For MLO view, the hard limiter kernel perform best for sensitivity and specificity measures and radial basis kernel perform best for accuracy measure.

Another factor is the convergence time for ELM. For the present work we considered the number of hidden neurons ranging from 1 to 500. Figure 5 shows the optimal result. For CC view, the convergence time of radial basis is the lowest and sine is the highest; on the other hand, for MLO view, radial basis is the fastest kernel and triangular basis is the slowest one. The hard limiter kernel, which shows the best efficiency among all (as discussed in the previous paragraph), takes 173 and 319 neurons to converge for CC and MLO views respectively.

Comparative Study. Moura *et al.* [17] reported histogram oriented gradient based work for mammogram mass classification on BCDR-F01 dataset which is a subset of the dataset we worked presently. By combining image descriptor and clinical information together they found an average AUC of 0.787. Very recently

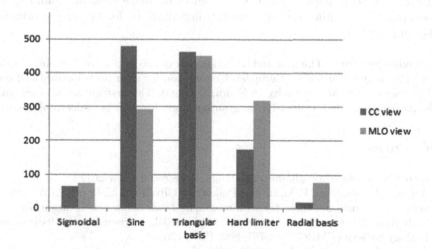

Fig. 5. Number of hidden neurons to find the optimum result in terms of accuracy for each of the five activation functions.

Arevalo *et al.* [2,3] reported an convolution neural network based work on BCDR-F03 dataset where they found AUC of 0.822. But these works are not comparable with present work in true sense due to following reasons: (i) In present work our objective is not only mammogram mass classification rather we explored the performance of different image views on mammogram mass classification, so, the experimental framework is different from the existing works. (ii) The original BCDR-F03 dataset contains For a fair comparison we have taken almost 1:1 ratio of both type of mammogram view images. (iii) The experimental framework are not always same, in the work of Moura *et al.* [17] the training and test data ratio was 80:20 whereas in the work of Arevalo *et al.* [2,3] these ratio was 60:40. In our work we have used k-fold cross validation scheme where the value of k was chosen as 5.

4   Conclusions and Future Work

Mammography based automated diagnostics of breast cancer will support the radiologists for double checking their observations. Numerous methods are proposed in literature for mammogram mass classification which mainly focus on separation on benign and malignant scenarios. In this paper we attempt to provide some experimental justification on the effect of mammogram image view for the performance of mammogram mass classification problem; experimental results show the effectiveness of CC view over MLO. We explored also the extreme learning machine as a classifier with five different kernels out of these five kernels, hard limiter perform best with an accuracy of 90.95% mass separation on CC view; the corresponding sensitivity and specificity found were 0.84 and 0.90 respectively.

In future, we plan to extend our experiments on other publicly available datasets to perform such experiments on effect of image view for mammogram mass separation. Tuning the extreme learning machine for better performance is also in our plan.

Acknowledgements. The first and second author of this paper are thankful to Erasmus Leader project funded by European Commission for their post-doctoral and doctoral research study at University of Évora, Portugal. The first author also acknowledges his employer Aliah University for granting study leave for post-doctoral research.

References

1. http://www.ntu.edu.sg/home/egbhuang/. Accessed 01 Mar 2017
2. Arevalo, J., González, F.A., Ramos-Pollán, R., Oliveira, J.L., Lopez, M.A.G.: Convolutional neural networks for mammography mass lesion classification. In: 2015 37th Annual International Conference of the IEEE Engineering in Medicine and Biology Society (EMBC), pp. 797–800. IEEE (2015)
3. Arevalo, J., González, F.A., Ramos-Pollán, R., Oliveira, J.L., Lopez, M.A.G.: Representation learning for mammography mass lesion classification with convolutional neural networks. Comput. Methods Programs Biomed. **127**, 248–257 (2016)

4. Belkasim, S.O., Shridhar, M., Ahmadi, M.: Pattern recognition with moment invariants: a comparative study and new results. Pattern Recognit. **24**(12), 1117–1138 (1991)
5. Constantinidis, A., Fairhurst, M.C., Rahman, A.F.R.: A new multi-expert decision combination algorithm and its application to the detection of circumscribed masses in digital mammograms. Pattern Recognit. **34**(8), 1527–1537 (2001)
6. Deans, S.: Applications of the Radon Transform, p. 2. Wiley, New York (1983)
7. Dhawan, A.P., Chitre, Y., Kaiser-Bonasso, C.: Analysis of mammographic micro-calcifications using gray-level image structure features. IEEE Trans. Med. Imaging **15**(3), 246–259 (1996)
8. Dua, S., Singh, H., Thompson, H.W.: Associative classification of mammograms using weighted rules. Expert. Syst. Appl. **36**(5), 9250–9259 (2009)
9. Eltoukhy, M.M., Faye, I., Samir, B.B.: A comparison of wavelet and curvelet for breast cancer diagnosis in digital mammogram. Comput. Biol. Med. **40**(4), 384–391 (2010)
10. Ferreira, C.B.R., Borges, D.L.: Analysis of mammogram classification using a wavelet transform decomposition. Pattern Recognit. Lett. **24**(7), 973–982 (2003)
11. Haralick, R.M., Shanmugam, K., et al.: Textural features for image classification. IEEE Trans. Syst. Man Cybern. **6**, 610–621 (1973)
12. Huang, G.B.: An insight into extreme learning machines: random neurons, random features and kernels. Cogn. Comput. **6**(3), 376–390 (2014)
13. Huang, G.B., Bai, Z., Kasun, L.L.C., Vong, C.M.: Local receptive fields based extreme learning machine. IEEE Comput. Intell. Mag. **10**(2), 18–29 (2015)
14. Huang, G.B., Zhou, H., Ding, X., Zhang, R.: Extreme learning machine for regression and multiclass classification. IEEE Trans. Syst. Man Cybern. Part B (Cybern.) **42**(2), 513–529 (2012)
15. Mallat, S.G.: A theory for multiresolution signal decomposition: the wavelet representation. IEEE Trans. Pattern Anal. Mach. Intell. **11**(7), 674–693 (1989)
16. Mazo, C., Alegre, E., Trujillo, M., González-Castro, V.: Tissues classification of the cardiovascular system using texture descriptors. In: Valdés Hernández, M., González-Castro, V. (eds.) MIUA 2017. CCIS, vol. 723, pp. 123–132. Springer, Cham (2017). https://doi.org/10.1007/978-3-319-60964-5_11
17. Moura, D.C., López, M.A.G.: An evaluation of image descriptors combined with clinical data for breast cancer diagnosis. Int. J. Comput. Assist. Radiol. Surg. **8**(4), 561–574 (2013)
18. Obaidullah, S.M., Ahmed, S., Goncalves, T., Rato, L.: RMID: a novel and efficient image descriptor for mammogram mass classification. In: 3rd Conference on Information Technology, Systems Research and Computational Physics (2018, accepted)
19. Obaidullah, S.M., Bose, A., Mukherjee, H., Santosh, K., Das, N., Roy, K.: Extreme learning machine for handwritten indic script identification in multiscript documents. J. Electron. Imaging **27**(5), 051214 (2018)
20. http://www.who.int/cancer/prevention/diagnosis-screening/breast-cancer/en/. Accessed 01 Mar 2018
21. O'Neil, A., Shepherd, M., Beveridge, E., Goatman, K.: A comparison of texture features versus deep learning for image classification in interstitial lung disease. In: Valdés Hernández, M., González-Castro, V. (eds.) MIUA 2017. CCIS, vol. 723, pp. 743–753. Springer, Cham (2017). https://doi.org/10.1007/978-3-319-60964-5_65
22. Pisano, E.D., et al.: Diagnostic accuracy of digital versus film mammography: exploratory analysis of selected population subgroups in DMIST. Radiology **246**(2), 376–383 (2008)

23. Ramos-Pollán, R., et al.: Discovering mammography-based machine learning classifiers for breast cancer diagnosis. J. Med. Syst. **36**(4), 2259–2269 (2012)
24. Rashed, E.A., Ismail, I.A., Zaki, S.I.: Multiresolution mammogram analysis in multilevel decomposition. Pattern Recognit. Lett. **28**(2), 286–292 (2007)
25. Sahiner, B., Chan, H.P., Petrick, N., Helvie, M.A., Hadjiiski, L.M.: Improvement of mammographic mass characterization using spiculation measures and morphological features. Med. Phys. **28**(7), 1455–1465 (2001)
26. Skaane, P., Hofvind, S., Skjennald, A.: Randomized trial of screen-film versus full-field digital mammography with soft-copy reading in population-based screening program: follow-up and final results of Oslo II study. Radiology **244**(3), 708–717 (2007)
27. Tang, J., Deng, C., Huang, G.B.: Extreme learning machine for multilayer perceptron. IEEE Trans. Neural Netw. Learn. Syst. **27**(4), 809–821 (2016)
28. Wang, D., Shi, L., Heng, P.A.: Automatic detection of breast cancers in mammograms using structured support vector machines. Neurocomputing **72**(13–15), 3296–3302 (2009)
29. Yu, S., Guan, L.: A CAD system for the automatic detection of clustered microcalcifications in digitized mammogram films. IEEE Trans. Med. Imaging **19**(2), 115–126 (2000)

Fast Object Detector Based on Convolutional Neural Networks

Karol Piaskowski[✉] and Dominik Belter

Institute of Control, Robotics and Information Engineering,
Poznan University of Technology, ul. Piotrowo 3A, Poznan, Poland
kar.piaskowski@gmail.com, dominik.belter@put.poznan.pl

Abstract. We propose a fast object detector, based on Convolutional
Neural Network (CNN). The object detector, which operates on RGB
images, is designed for a mobile robot equipped with a robotic manipu-
lator. The proposed detector is designed to quickly and accurately detect
objects which are common in small manufactories and workshops. We
propose a fully convolutional architecture of neural network which allows
the full GPU implementation. We provide results obtained on our custom dataset based on ImageNet and other common datasets, like COCO
or PascalVOC. We also compare the proposed method with other *state
of the art* object detectors.

Keywords: Objects detection · Computer vision ·
Deep neural networks

1 Introduction

Mobile robot assistants equipped with manipulators are designed to operate in
a real human environment. The intense interest is focused on industrial applications. The mobile robots may work in warehouses and stores to transport inven-
tory and place products on the shelves [2]. Robots can also work as a personal
assistants [8] in domestic applications or to help transport clinical supplies in
the hospital [9]. We are mainly interested in assistant robots which work in small
manufactures and help humans with repetitive manipulation tasks. In such scenario the robot can be used for machine tending, sorting, packaging with various
previously not defined objects or bringing required workshop tools on demand.
To operate in the unstructured environment and autonomously perform tasks
given by the human the robot has to detect and recognize manipulated objects
without any support.

The current state of the art object detection systems enable the robot to perform real-time object recognition with an RGB camera only. Advances in Convolutional Neural Networks bring the development of objects detection closer.
Currently, the neural networks can detect and recognize thousands of objects
categories and localize them on the image [11]. The progress is possible mainly

© Springer Nature Switzerland AG 2019
R. P. Barneva et al. (Eds.): CompIMAGE 2018, LNCS 10986, pp. 173–185, 2019.
https://doi.org/10.1007/978-3-030-20805-9_15

due to the capability of training neural detector using the entire image. In this case, the neural network implicitly uses contextual information about classes of objects.

In our application, we are interested in both accuracy and speed of detection. The robot moving freely in the environment should be capable of detecting objects needed to perform the task. Our robot is equipped with Kinect 2 RGB-D sensor which returns 30 frames per second. Similar framerate of the object detection and recognition is sufficient from the robot's perspective. The robot is mainly looking for static objects. The robot can also stop and pay more attention to interesting regions of the workspace if some object detections occur. On the other hand, the object classification is more crucial. False detection and classification may cause delays in the robot's performance or even may result in the failure of the mission.

In this paper, we review the recent development of object detection and classification methods and propose our improved general network architecture having in mind real-time objects detection for mobile manipulation.

1.1   Related Work

A good example of classical object detection algorithm is a work of Viola and Jones [14]. In this approach, the visual features (Haar features) are computed on the image. The computation of features is speeded-up by using an intermediate representation called integral image. Then AdaBoost is used to construct a classifier as a linear combination of simpler classifiers. The performance of the objects detection can be improved by using different features – Histograms of Oriented Gradient features [3]. In the deep learning, the convolutional neural network learns the most efficient representation features taking into account training data and outperforms other approaches in image classifications [6].

Object detection deals with searching instances of defined classes on the image. Object detector returns information about pixels which belong to specified object (in practice the position on the image and a bounding box). Object detection is closely related to image classification thus the most efficient approaches to object detection are also based on convolutional neural networks. The classification networks can be used to determine the category of the object inside single bounding box sliding across the image. The main disadvantage of this approach is related to the computational time. More sophisticated approaches generate candidate regions (Region of Interests) for the classifier [12]. However, the Region Proposal Network proposed in [12] still uses spatial sliding window thus the network utilizes only partial information about the image without contextual information about classes. The improved version called Region-based Fully Convolutional Network implements Region of Interest (RoI) detector using convolutional layer which improves the computational cost [1].

The new architecture YOLO proposed by Redmon et al. [10] solves this problem by defining the detection as a regression problem. The neural network directly generates bounding boxes, confidence for these boxes and class probabilities for each cell of the grid created on the image plane. After the improved training method, the YOLO neural network can detect 9000 object categories in real-time [11]. The similar approach to YOLO called Single Shot MultiBox Detector (SSD) is proposed by Liu et al. [7]. A single neural network predicts bounding box for all object categories for each cell of the grid with different scales. The predictor returns also the confidence of object category which allows filtering incorrect detections (bounding boxes). Similar MSC-MultiBox approach predicts object locations and confidences [13]. For improved performance, the network can provide region proposals which are later classified in the post-processing stage.

The important issue in robotics is the tradeoff between speed and accuracy of the detection. These practical aspects of convolutional object detectors are considered in [5].

2   Object Detection with CNN

2.1   Method Description

In this section, we describe two main modules of our method: the architecture of deep convolutional neural network and the data annotation algorithm. Our network takes the images of constant size $w = h = 448$ (it is not crucial to resize images to the same size, nevertheless we empirically tested it and found that it yields best results). The network is trained to convert input images into $S \times S \times C$ tensor of probabilities, where S stands for the size of input image downsized by the neural network and C is the number of classes in the dataset. The neural network predicts probability of presence of any part of object of class $k \in \{1 \ldots C\}$ in each cell c_{ijk} $(i, j \in \{1 \ldots S\})$. Unlike YOLO, our model is able to detect objects of multiple classes within a single cell.

The produced tensor can be perceived as C masks of probabilities - one mask for every class. The network should produce blob of pixels of coordinates $x_{min}\frac{S_t}{S_i}, y_{min}\frac{S_t}{S_i}, x_{max}\frac{S_t}{S_i}, y_{max}\frac{S_t}{S_i}$ for an object of a class k on the original image for which the bounding box coordinates are $x_{min}, y_{min}, x_{max}, y_{max}$, where S_t denotes the size of single output mask and S_i is the size of the original image. These coordinates are then rounded to their nearest integer values. In our experiments $S_i = 448$ and $S_t = 14$. Our neural network computes masks of objects presence, weighted by probabilities. The example masks weighted by probabilities are presented in Fig. 1b. To calculate bounding boxes for each blob of probabilities, a threshold T_p is applied (Fig. 1c). This threshold is applied to every pixel in the output tensor. It causes binarization of the output tensor. Then, the clustering algorithm is used independently for each mask. We used standard *findContours* and *boundingRect* algorithms available in the OpenCV library. Therefore, our clustering algorithm is able to differentiate objects instances belonging to common class only in cases, when their thresholded masks are separated.

To reduce the amount of false positive bounding boxes caused by finding contours and bounding box around too small probability masks (which actually doesn't point at real objects) we applied erosion on masks and rejected masks with the area less than threshold T_a. The process of masks generation is shown in Fig. 1. Note that only some of the mask were visualized due to clarity reasons.

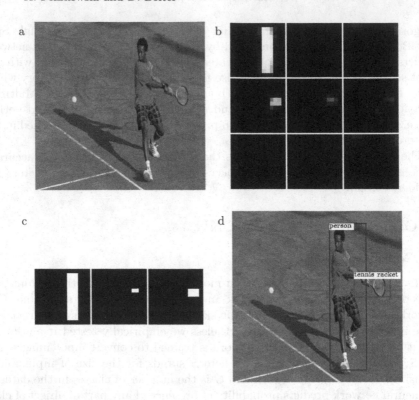

Fig. 1. Process of generating bounding boxes: original image (a), selected masks before thresholding (b), nonzero masks after thresholding (the second mask is rejected in later part of pipeline, because its area is too small), and predicted bounding boxes (d)

2.2 Neural Network Architecture

The architecture of our convolutional neural network is similar to YOLOv1 proposed in [10]. In contrast to YOLOv1, our network is fully convolutional, which allows the full GPU implementation. Our convolutional architecture accepts inputs of variable size, nevertheless we trained on images of fixed size (448 × 448 px).

The architecture of our network is presented in Fig. 2. Convolutional layers are based on the architecture proposed by Redmon et al. [10]. We interleaved convolutional layers with max-pooling layers. The convolutional layers are designed to learn features from the training dataset and extract features during inference. The size of the last layer is $S \times S \times C$ and is strictly related to the number of classes in the dataset. To avoid long training time, we used network pre-trained on ImageNet classification task.

Apart from last layer, we used Exponential Linear Unit (ELU) activation function, which is designed to reduce the problem of diminishing gradients in deep neural networks [20] (see Eq. 1). The ELU is also designed to avoid problems with zero gradients, known from Rectified Linear Units (ReLU). As a final

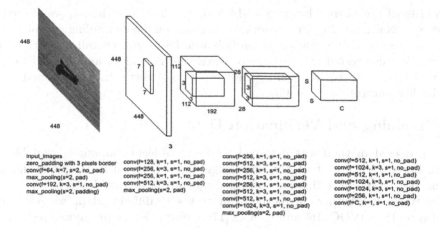

Fig. 2. The architecture of our neural network

activation function, we used standard sigmoid (see Eq. 2), due to its interpretability in terms of probability and ability to produce class independent probabilities:

$$f(z) = \begin{cases} z & \text{if } z \geq 0 \\ \alpha(e^z - 1) & \text{otherwise} \end{cases} \tag{1}$$

$$f(z) = \frac{1}{1 + e^{-z}} \tag{2}$$

where z is the weighted sum of inputs of neuron. The network produces a tensor of probabilities, therefore we trained it to minimize cross entropy loss function, averaged by cell numbers:

$$cost = -\frac{1}{S \cdot S \cdot C} \sum_i^S \sum_j^S \sum_k^C y_{ijk} \log \hat{y}_{ijk} \tag{3}$$

where y_{ijk} is the ground truth probability of cell c_{ijk} and $\hat{y}_{ijk}$ is the predicted probability of cell c_{ijk} belonging to class k. To reduce overfitting to the training set, we relied on intensive L2 regularization. Weights were initialized with popular Xavier initializer [21].

2.3 Training

The network is implemented in TensorFlow [18], popular deep learning network framework. We trained our models on ImageNet and PascalVOC datasets separately for 100 epochs and (due to its size) on COCO dataset for 20 epochs. We utilized Adam optimizer to update network weights [19]. It optimizes all of the weights independently and automatically reduces learning rate during training, therefore we didn't rely on implicit weight decay. During experiments, we tested two sizes of the output layer: $S = 14$ and $S = 28$. Nevertheless, we observed that $S = 28$ was too big for network relying only on downsampling convolutions and caused over-segmentation of probabilistic blobs and overall network overfitting. We also tested few variants of thresholds T_p and T_a and decided to use $T_p = 0.3$, $T_a = 4$, as they yielded best results. All networks were trained with initial learning rate $\eta = 0.00001$.

3   Training and Verification Data

The proposed method was designed to detect objects commonly available in workshops. To the best of our knowledge, there is no such dataset available. Thus, we relied on gathering custom detection data from ImageNet [15]. In order to check, whether our method can work with different data, we evaluated it also on PascalVOC [16] and COCO [17] datasets. Every image was resized to 448×448 px before training in order to preserve consistency of neural network architecture. We used networks pre-trained on classification task on ImageNet dataset, which is a standard preprocessing step in object detection.

3.1   Labels Preparation

Convolutional neural networks can't be used (without modifications) to generate outputs of variable lengths, like (in our case) lists of local bounding boxes $T = \{m_1, ..., m_C\}$. Therefore training labels have to be properly converted. The steps of applied data generation pipeline for single image $\mathbf{I}$ and corresponding bounding boxes for each class instances $b_1, ..., b_C$ are presented in Algorithm 1.

Algorithm 1. Prepare training data: $\mathbf{I}$, $b_1, ..., b_C \rightarrow T = \{m_1, ..., m_C\}$

Create tensor T of shape $H \times W \times C$ (where H, W denotes image height and width and C denotes number of classes in dataset) filled with zeros;
Group bounding boxes b_i on the image $\mathbf{I}$ by class identifiers c;
for $c \subseteq C$ **do**
  $\mid$ For each bounding box of class c (described by coordinates x, y, width w
  $\mid$ and height h), fill $T^{y...y+h, x...x+w, c}$ with ones;
end
return tensor T, which represents bounding boxes of objects on the image;

Description above suggests that ground truth labels for probability blobs are of rectangular shape. This may bias neural network toward generating outputs of rectangular shape as well. Nevertheless, we observed that the network actually tries to recreate the shape of the object (see Fig. 3d). We plan to examine it further in the future - we are going to create carefully designed dataset with pixelwise marked objects and check the improvement of the object detection quality. Due to the processing speed, the aforementioned transformation of annotations to tensor labels was performed offline, before actual training.

3.2   ImageNet Dataset

Apart from providing image classification data, ImageNet database contains also data for object detection. However, the number of annotated object classes, as well as training examples, is much smaller. We extracted images and annotated bounding boxes for the object of 12 classes: wrench, screwdriver, screw, scissors, nail, light bulb, hammer, button, driller, broom, bottle, axe. ImageNet images contain mostly object belonging to the same class. The number of examples per each class was unevenly distributed - to avoid bias, we artificially upsampled less numerous classes by adding small random variations in image brightness and contrast.

The total number of obtained images was 5160. It is difficult to train neural network on such small amount of data, therefore we relied on intensive data augmentation. Each image was randomly cropped, rotated, perturbed with noise. Apart from this, we randomly collected batches of 4 images of different classes and then stacked them on 2×2 grid to obtain the image which is two times larger. The purpose of this transformation was to reduce network bias towards detection of only one object class on images. We applied aforementioned augmentation pipeline in order to obtain a 10-fold increase of dataset size. The dataset was randomly split into train/test subsets in ratio 9:1, according to the initial number of images, resulting in obtaining 516 images in the test set.

3.3   PascalVOC Dataset

The PascalVOC dataset contains images belonging to 20 different classes of common objects, such as a car, person, dog, cat. The images were taken in everyday situations, therefore the presence of multiple classes of objects in one image is common. We used data from 2012 and 2007 for training and data from 2007 for testing (it is common to test object detectors on PascalVOC 2007 as it stands for standard benchmark). The dataset contains about 27 thousands of images.

3.4   COCO Dataset

COCO (Common Objects in Context) is a Microsoft's dataset, containing more than 100 thousands of images. The images contain objects of 80 different classes, highly varying in size, which makes COCO one of the most challenging datasets available. For training and validation, we chose 2017 version, which splits data into training (118k images), validation (5k) and test (41k) sets.

4   Results

4.1   Performance Measures

Before we describe the experiments in detail we introduce the metrics which are used to evaluate our method. For model performance evaluation, we measured precision, recall, average precision and mean framerate. To specify wheter predicted bounding box matches ground truth bounding box, we used method proposed in [4] - for any given class, we computed *intersection over union* (IoU):

$$IoU = \frac{area(B_p \cap B_{gt})}{area(B_p \cup B_{gt})} \tag{4}$$

where B_p is predicted bounding box and b_{gt} is ground truth bounding box. If IoU was higher than 0.5, we counted it as a hit. If there are more predicted bounding boxes for given ground truth bounding box, we reject them as false positives [4]. False negatives occurred, when our model didn't provide valid bounding boxes for ground truth bounding box. There were no true negatives. We sorted predicted bounding boxes by confidence scores, then computed measures:

Precision:

$$P = \frac{TP(c)}{TP(c) + FP(c)} \tag{5}$$

Recall:

$$R = \frac{TP(c)}{TP(c) + FP(c)} \tag{6}$$

and average precision (AP):

$$AP = \sum_1^k P(k)\Delta R(k) \tag{7}$$

where TP is the number of true positive detections, FP is the number of false positive detections, $P(k)$ denotes precision on set of boxes from 0 to k, c denotes class identifier, $\Delta R(k)$ is the delta of recall on set of boxes from 0 to k and k denotes index of predicted bounding box. We computed these measures for each class and a mean value for all classes (mAP).

4.2   Results on Custom ImageNet Dataset

We used our TensorFlow implementation of YOLO for comparison with our architecture on the custom dataset. We trained the YOLO on our dataset for 100 epochs (just like our model) to ensure the fair comparison. We tested different variants of YOLO with $B \in \{2,5\}$ and $S \in \{7,13\}$. We picked these values empirically as they yielded best results. Aside from standard YOLO, we tested its modified version, where the network was split at the end into two branches: bounding box regression layer and classification layer. Images were fed forward in two passes: first, where the regression layer generated bounding boxes, and the second when images were cropped to previously computed bounding boxes and forwarded through classification layer. The purpose of this modification was to increase classification accuracy (the original YOLO has troubles with correct classification despite correct bounding box generation) at the cost of speed of execution. We called it *two pass YOLO*. Results are presented in Table 1.

Table 1. Results on custom ImageNet dataset

Network	Mean precision	Mean recall	mAP	Mean FPS
2pass_YOLO_B2_S7	0.24	0.23	0.23	11.81
YOLO_B5_S13	0.014	0.013	0.013	26.82
Our model S_14	**0.36**	**0.36**	**0.35**	**44.08**

As can be seen, our model is about 1.5 times faster than YOLO (we tested both architectures on Geforce 1060 graphic card). Such small values in quality of YOLO can possibly be caused by the small size of our dataset and lack of proper diversity between examples (5160 images only).

Detailed results on our dataset are shown in Tables 2 and 3.

Table 2. Average precision per class on custom ImageNet dataset. Bold values represent the best result for the class.

Network	AP					
	Axe	Bottle	Broom	Button	Driller	Hammer
2pass_YOLO_B2_S7	**0.161**	0.226	0.296	0.000	0.207	**0.063**
YOLO_B5_S13	0.000	0.016	0.021	0.000	0.000	0.000
Our model S_14	0.103	**0.470**	**0.329**	**0.272**	**0.254**	0.048
	Light bulb	Nail	Scissors	Screw	Screwdriver	Wrench
2pass_YOLO_B2_S7	0.058	0.020	0.152	**0.136**	0.123	0.167
YOLO_B5_S13	0.000	0.021	0.054	0.020	0.000	0.000
Our model S_14	**0.242**	**0.164**	**0.263**	0.081	**0.135**	**0.425**

Table 3. Precision and recall per class on custom ImageNet data

Network	Precision/recall					
	Axe	Bottle	Broom	Button	Driller	Hammer
2pass_YOLO_B2_S7	0.161/0.160	0.244/0.226	0.296/0.296	0.000/0.000	0.207/0.206	0.062/0.062
YOLO_B5_S13	0.000/0.000	0.016/0.016	0.028/0.021	0.000/0.000	0.000/0.000	0.000/0.000
Our model S_14	0.107/0.107	0.475/0.476	0.333/0.333	0.331/0.277	0.254/0.254	0.048/0.048
	Light bulb	Nail	Scissors	Screw	Screwdriver	Wrench
2pass_YOLO_B2_S7	0.058/0.057	0.021/0.019	0.152/0.152	0.136/0.136	0.123/0.122	0.166/0.166
YOLO_B5_S13	0.000/0.000	0.022/0.022	0.044/0.054	0.038/0.02	0.000/0.000	0.000/0.000
Our model S_14	0.242/0.258	0.169/0.167	0.258/0.274	0.114/0.081	0.135/0.141	0.362/0.361

4.3 Results on PascalVOC and COCO Datasets

We can't directly compare our method using mAP metric on the PascalVOC and COCO datasets because our method provides a single bounding box for instances of objects grouped too tight. Then, our model is highly penalized for grouping mutual class objects together. The mAP value obtained on the

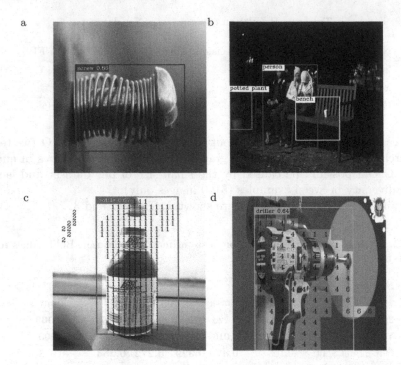

Fig. 3. Example detection results: correct object detection on COCO dataset (a), an example of incorrect clustering – grouping people into the same bounding box (b), correct *bottle* detection on an example image from ImageNet dataset – visible cells rejection (c), and correct rejection of class number 6 (bulb) and acceptance of class number 4 (driller); despite training on rectangular labels, the network actually tries to reproduce correct object shape with probability mask (d)

Fig. 4. Examples of detections on custom ImageNet dataset

Fig. 5. Comparison of our method and YOLO detections on custom ImageNet dataset: correct prediction of our network (a), YOLO - two false positives and one too small true positive detection of bottle, only bottle was detected (b), correct labelling, but false object separation, done by our method (c), incorrect labeling with YOLO method (d)

PascalVOC dataset is 0.39. On COCO dataset, the achieved mAP is 0.014. Additionally, we provide visual output from our detector (cf. Figs. 3, 4 and 5) to show the accuracy of the proposed method.

We also can't compare the speed of our network on PascalVOC and COCO datasets with respect to other object detectors due to the different GPU configurations. However, our network architecture is compact and can run efficiently on the robot with small computational resources (currently we use Geforce 1060 graphic card) in contrast to other CNN object detectors [1,7,10].

5   Conclusions and Future Work

We created a fast deep convolutional neural network, trained in an end-to-end manner, which is capable of detecting objects commonly available on workshops. We showed that our model can successfully operate in such environments, where the robot searches for manipulation objects. We also show that our architecture is faster than YOLO architecture, which is perceived as one of the fastest detectors available. Such great speed of detection has, however, its cost - we observed that due to its simplicity, our model cannot compete with bigger state of the art detectors on big datasets containing small, highly overlapping objects. Despite this fact, the proposed architecture can be implemented on mobile robots with limited computational resources.

The subject of our future work is to increase the quality of predictions made by our model. Our goal is to distinguish between instances of objects which overlap on the image. We are going to employ larger neural networks and use improved bounding box annotation algorithm, like the recurrent neural network. We would like also to test detectors other than YOLO on our hardware and compare their speed against our model. We are going to create also our own dataset, with richer information about objects than the dataset used in this paper. The images in the new dataset will be described not only by bounding boxes but also by information about depth and pose of the camera.

Acknowledgments. This work was supported by the NCBR Grant no. LIDER/33/ 0176/L-8/16/NCBR/2017.

References

1. Dai, J., Li, Y., He, K., Sun, J.: R-FCN: object detection via region-based fully convolutional networks. In: Lee, D.D., et al. (eds.) Conference on Neural Information Processing Systems (NIPS), Advances in Neural Information Processing Systems, vol. 29, pp. 379–387. Curran Associates (2016)
2. Correll, N., et al.: Analysis and observations from the first Amazon picking challenge. IEEE Trans. Autom. Sci. Eng. **15**(1), 172–188 (2018)
3. Dalal, N., Triggs, B.: Histograms of oriented gradients for human detection. In: IEEE Conference on Computer Vision and Pattern Recognition (CVPR), pp. 886–893 (2005)
4. Everingham, M., Gool, L.V., Williams, C.K.I., Winn, J., Zisserman, A.: The PASCAL visual object classes (VOC) challenge. Int. J. Comput. Vis. **88**(2), 303–338 (2010)
5. Huang, J., et al.: Speed/accuracy trade-offs for modern convolutional object detectors. In: IEEE Conference on Computer Vision and Pattern Recognition (CVPR), pp. 3296–3297 (2017)
6. Krizhevsky, A., Sutskever, I., Hinton, G. E.: ImageNet classification with deep convolutional neural networks. In: Proceedings of the International Conference on Neural Information Processing Systems, pp. 1097–1105 (2012)
7. Liu, W., et al.: SSD: single shot MultiBox detector. In: Leibe, B., Matas, J., Sebe, N., Welling, M. (eds.) ECCV 2016. LNCS, vol. 9905, pp. 21–37. Springer, Cham (2016). https://doi.org/10.1007/978-3-319-46448-0_2

8. Martiínez, E., del Pobil, A.P.: Object detection and recognition for assistive robots. IEEE Robot. Autom. Mag. **24**(3), 123–138 (2017)
9. Pineau, J., Montemerlo, M., Pollack, M., Thrun, S.: Towards robotic assistants in nursing homes: challenges and results. Robot. Auton. Syst. **42**(3), 271–281 (2002)
10. Redmon, J., Divvala, S., Girshick, R., Farhadi, A.: You only look once: unified, real-time object detection. In: IEEE Conference on Computer Vision and Pattern Recognition (CVPR), pp. 779–788 (2016)
11. Redmon, J., Farhadi, A.: YOLO9000: better, faster, stronger. In: IEEE Conference on Computer Vision and Pattern Recognition (CVPR), pp. 6517–6525 (2017)
12. Ren, S., He, K., Girshick, R., Sun, J.: Faster R-CNN: towards real-time object detection with region proposal networks. IEEE Trans. Pattern Anal. Mach. Intell. **39**(6), 1137–1149 (2017)
13. Szegedy, C., Reed, S., Erhan, D., Anguelov, D.: Scalable, high-quality object detection (2015). http://arxiv.org/abs/1412.1441
14. Viola, P., Jones, M.J.: Robust real-time face detection. Int. J. Comput. Vis. **57**(2), 137–154 (2004)
15. Russakovsky, O., et al.: ImageNet large scale visual recognition challenge. Int. J. Comput. Vis. **115**(3), 211–252 (2015)
16. Everingham, M., Van Gool, L., Williams, C.K.I., Winn, J., Zisserman, A.: The pascal visual object classes (VOC) challenge. Int. J. Comput. Vis. **88**, 303–338 (2010)
17. Lin, T.-Y., et al.: Microsoft COCO: common objects in context. In: Fleet, D., Pajdla, T., Schiele, B., Tuytelaars, T. (eds.) ECCV 2014. LNCS, vol. 8693, pp. 740–755. Springer, Cham (2014). https://doi.org/10.1007/978-3-319-10602-1_48
18. Abadi, M.: et al.: TensorFlow: Large-Scale Machine Learning on Heterogeneous Distributed Systems. http://download.tensorflow.org/paper/whitepaper2015.pdf
19. Kingma, D.P., Ba, J.: Adam: a method for stochastic optimization. In: Proceedings of the 3rd International Conference on Learning Representations (2015)
20. Clevert, D., Hochreiter, S., Unterthiner, T.: Fast and Accurate Deep Network Learning by Exponential Linear Units (ELUs). CoRR, abs/1511.07289 (2015)
21. Glorot, X., Bengio, Y.: Understanding the difficulty of training deep feedforward neural networks. In: Proceedings of the Thirteenth International Conference on Artificial Intelligence and Statistics, pp. 249–256 (2010)

Applying Computational Geometry to Designing an Occlusal Splint

Dariusz Pojda[⊠], Agnieszka Anna Tomaka, Leszek Luchowski,
Krzysztof Skabek, and Michał Tarnawski

Institute of Theoretical and Applied Informatics, Polish Academy of Sciences,
Baltycka 5, Gliwice, Poland
{darek.pojda,ines,leszek.luchowski,kskabek}@iitis.pl,
dr.tarnawski@gmail.com

Abstract. The occlusal splint is one of the methods of treatment of discrepancies between the centric relation and maximal intercuspation (CR/MI), and other temporomandibular joint (TMJ) disorders. It is also a method of reducing the effects of bruxism. Designing an occlusal splint for a given relation between the maxilla and the mandible involves: creating partial surfaces, integrating them, and producing the splint on a 3D printer. The paper presents and compares some techniques used to design splint surfaces under a required therapeutic maxilla-mandible relation.

Keywords: Computational geometry · Object modeling ·
Virtual impressions · Occlusal splint

1 Introduction

The occlusal splint is one of the methods of treatment of discrepancies between the centric relation and maximal intercuspation (CR/MI) [14], and other temporomandibular joint (TMJ) disorders [2]. It is also a method of reducing the effects of bruxism [3]. A comprehensive review of various types of occlusal splints was made by Alqutaibi and Aboalrejal [1].

An occlusal splint is a removable plastic overlay precisely fitted onto one dental arch. It has also been defined [1] as an artificial occlusal surface affecting the relationship of the mandible to the maxilla. For clarity, we shall assume throughout this paper that the splint is attached to the maxillary arch.

The traditional, non-computerized way of forming a splint [1] involves forming the inner and outer surface by a deep and a shallow impression of the upper and lower teeth, respectively, then instructing the patient to move his lower teeth against the splint with marking paper inserted, to guide the final cutting. The procedure is described in more detail in our earlier paper [11].

The use of computers to design intraoral appliances has been mentioned in literature; examples include surgical splints [4,7], occlusal splints [10], the Lingualcare Bracket System [12], orthognathic surgical wafers [16], and retainers [13]. However, few authors give any insight into the algorithms used beyond

© Springer Nature Switzerland AG 2019
R. P. Barneva et al. (Eds.): CompIMAGE 2018, LNCS 10986, pp. 186–200, 2019.
https://doi.org/10.1007/978-3-030-20805-9_16

a general reference to using CAD/CAM software. An exception is the work of Chen [4], who published all the algorithms used in their EasySplint software, and of Lauren and McIntyre [10], who described how they modify an occlusal surface to ensure the required guidance and pressure distribution.

Depending on the type of disorder, an occlusal splint reduces various symptoms [8], but it always changes the maxilla–mandible relation. Consequently, two principal groups of premises for the design of the splint are, on one hand, the anatomy of the patient and the current relation between his jaws at rest, and on the other - their desired mutual position, known as the *therapeutic relation*.

The shape of anatomical structures is contained in the models obtained from various types of medical imaging (Fig. 1), e.g. cone beam computed tomography CBCT and intraoral scanning or scanning of dental models or impressions [17].

Defining the therapeutic position is a strictly medical task, and as such it is out of scope of this paper. It will be performed by a medical specialist, e.g. by moving virtual models of teeth and of the TMJ in a 3D editor.

An occlusal splint has a tooth-borne (*inner*) and a working occlusal (*outer*) surface. The inner surface fits tightly onto the maxillary arch, while the outer one meets the mandibular arch allowing for a controlled amount of motion. The outer surface can be either a modified copy of the maxillary arch, or a modified negative of the mandibular one.

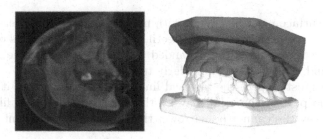

Fig. 1. 3D reconstructions from CBCT (left), 3D scans of dental models (right).

In our previous work [11], we proposed to form the outer surface of the splint as a shifted copy of the surface of the maxillary teeth. This produces a kind of extender, where the lower teeth meet the same shape which they met naturally, only shifted from the natural to therapeutic position.

In the present work, we implement and verify the idea by designing several techniques of forming the surfaces of the splint.

Moreover, where we previously delegate the graphical editing to Rapid Form (by *INUS* Technologies) a highly complex software package built for mechanical design - we now have a dedicated interactive and easy-to-use 3D editor *dpVision*, developed by our team [9,15].

2   Defining the Desired Shape of the Splint

We need to design three surfaces: the inner surface to match the upper teeth, the outer occlusal surface to interact with the lower teeth, and the lateral surface which completes the solid, closing it on the buccal (cheek) and lingual (tongue) side. The overall process of forming the splint can be described as follows:

- Segmenting the relevant surfaces from the patient's models:
  - determining the cutting line (Sect. 3.1),
  - determining the coronal surface (Sect. 3.1),
  - determining the occlusal surface,
- Positioning them in space in the required therapeutic relation;
- Forming the partial surfaces and connecting them so as to form a closed solid, while respecting the conditions related to applying/removing the splint, as well as the requirements of 3D printing:
  - dilating the coronal surface and reversing mesh face normals and performing impressions to create the inner surface of the splint (Sect. 3.2),
  - forming the outer occlusal surface (Sect. 4), which must not intersect the inner surface,
  - connecting working surfaces with a lateral surface (Sect. 4.4).

The following requirements apply:

- The final surface must be closed, with no open ends or self-intersections.
- The splint is to apply only to the teeth, not touching the gums or palate.
- The inner surface has to be expanded sufficiently to allow the splint to be inserted and removed perpendicularly to the occlusal plane.
- The mesh must respect the physical limitations of the printer it is intended for, e.g. no part of the solid may be thinner than the model filament, and holes and cavities cannot be narrower than the support filament.

3   The Proposed Design Techniques

Starting from virtual models the splint design methods use a number of geometric algorithms to assist the process. The present section describes the techniques for determining the cutoff line, dilating a 3D mesh and creating virtual imprints.

3.1   The Choice of the Cutting Line

The patient's models represents not only the teeth, but also parts of the gums and the palate. Moreover, usually the crowns of human teeth taper somewhat towards the collum (neck of the tooth), which is perceptibly narrower. A splint fully matching this shape would be impossible to apply or to remove (Fig. 2), unless made from an elastic material.

We need to find the approximate level where the teeth are widest and cut the model off there, removing the collum as well as gums and other tissues. The

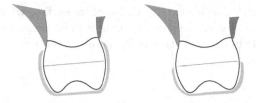

Fig. 2. Too deep and too close fitting occlusal splint (left) may lock on teeth.

remaining part is the surface that will support the splint. We shall refer to it as the *coronal surface*.

The cutting line can be determined fully manually by clicking successive points on the surface of teeth. This method gives the user the greatest freedom of choice. However, it requires the operator to show significant commitment and knowledge. A complete automation of the process is also possible, consisting of detecting specific shapes on the tooth surface, inflection points, or points of contact between the tooth and gum.

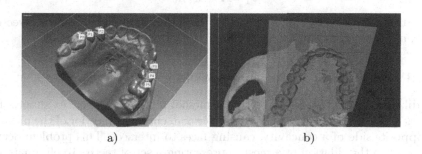

a)   b)

Fig. 3. The occlusion plane (a) and the cutting plane (b).

As the splint will be inserted more or less perpendicularly to the occlusal plane formed as the resultant of the chewing surfaces of most maxillary molars and premolars, the cutting plane may be set parallel to the occlusal plane. In our experiments, we opted for a plane positioned manually by an operator (Fig. 3). An advantage of using a cutting plane instead of an arbitrary line is that it allows us to clearly define a *coronal volume*.

3.2 Mesh Dilation

The inner surface has to be expanded sufficiently to allow the splint to be inserted and removed, and to accommodate some small variations in actual tooth shape due to natural growth/ageing, therapy, disease, or even plaque build-up and removal.

We shall call *mesh dilation* an expansion of its surface which preserves mesh topology while moving every vertex of the new mesh away from its original by a distance d (Fig. 4) in the direction of its normal vector $\mathbf{n_v}$:

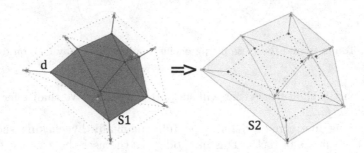

Fig. 4. 3D mesh dilation. Principle of operation.

$$\mathbf{v_1} = \mathbf{v} + d \cdot \mathbf{n_v} \tag{1}$$

where the normal vector of a vertex is the normalized sum of normal vectors $\mathbf{n_{f_1}} \ldots \mathbf{n_{f_n}}$ determined for all the faces $f_1 \ldots f_n$ this vertex belongs to.

3.3   Preparation of Virtual Impressions

The dilation method works correctly for meshes representing convex shapes. For meshes containing concavities, some vertices can enter the interior of the mesh on the opposite side of a concavity, causing faces to intersect. This problem occurs frequently in the dilation of a mesh representing a set of teeth. To eliminate the tapering left in the splint-supporting surface as well as the errors connected with dilation of non-convex areas of the mesh, we use a method for the creation of virtual impressions, which takes into account only the outer shape of the given mesh and also ensures that the tooth crossections do not decrease in the apical direction (Algorithm 1).

Let us imagine a flat plate made of a material that is both rigid and infinitely plastic. It is also capable of stably maintaining shape after deformation. Teeth biting into the plate leave an impression.

Let the dilated (and possibly self-intersecting) coronal surface be represented by a triangular mesh M (Fig. 5a). Let the plate be a planar rectangle parallel to the occlusal plane, tangent to M on the coronal side, and represented by another triangular mesh P. The occlusal plane was chosen as one of the planes forming the coordinate system. The density of the plate mesh is determined by the required accuracy of the resulting model.

The method consists in sending a line perpendicular to the plate through each plate vertex, and finding its nearest intersection with M, if any. The set of such intersection points produces a kind of impression shown in Fig. 5b.

Algorithm 1. Impression method.

Input: M – the mesh to be imprinted
Input: MAX_Z – constant that specifies the maximum depth of impression
Output: P – virtual impression

1 create a regular mesh P that lies on the plane XOY
2 position the model M relative to P
3 let $F[0 \ldots m]$ to be an array of faces in mesh M
4 let $V[0 \ldots n]$ to be an array of vertices in mesh P
5 let $D[0 \ldots n]$ to be a temporary distance array
6 **foreach** $d \in D$ **do**
7      $d \leftarrow MAX_Z$

8 **foreach** $f \in F$ **do**
9      $f' \leftarrow$ the perpendicular projection of a triangle f in a plane XOY
10   **for** $i \leftarrow 0$ *to* n **do**
11   **if** $V(i) \in f'$ **then**
12           $d \leftarrow$ distance from $V(i)$ to f
13           $D(i) \leftarrow \min\Big(D(i), d\Big)$

14 **for** $i \leftarrow 0$ *to* n **do**
15     $V(i).Z \leftarrow D(i)$

16 **return** P

The resulting mesh is regular, which greatly facilitates and accelerates further processing (Fig. 5c). It is also possible to set a required density of the mesh, which is needed for 3D printing. However, defining an excessively high mesh density results in a significant decrease in the speed of the algorithm.

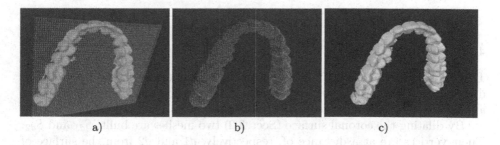

a)   b)   c)

Fig. 5. Impression method.

4 Forming the Splint Surfaces

Forming the inner surface is determined by the position of the coronal surface, the cutting plane and the required clearance. The occlusal part of the outer surface has to match the mandibular arch in the therapeutic position. The lateral part of the outer surface is only constrained to meet the two working surfaces (inner and occlusal), be watertight, 3D printable, and ensure the minimal splint thickness; no constraints determine its exact location. Consequently, it can be designed using various methods. In our previous publication, this stage of processing was limited to mesh dilation; in what follows, we add several other techniques, which the doctor may choose from based on clinical outcome.

4.1 The Patchwork Method

The *patchwork method* starts building the outer surface with a shifted copy of the coronal surface. To ensure that the outer surface does not intersect the inner one, some manually selected patches of it are slightly expanded. The resulting outer surface meets the condition for occlusal matching, as it is a copy of the coronal surface. A drawback of the method is that it requires a significant manual effort by a human operator (Fig. 6).

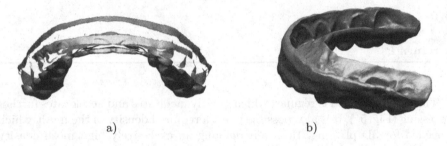

a)   b)

Fig. 6. Constructing the outer surface – patchwork method.

4.2 Dilation Method

The dilation method (Fig. 7) is based on the techniques mentioned previously: dilation and the forming of impressions. The method shown in Algorithm 2 allows the splint to be formed to a specified thickness.

By dilating the coronal surface (Sect. 3.2) two meshes are built: S_{d1} and S_{d2}. Their vertices are at a distance of, respectively, $d1$ and $d2$ from the surface of the model. The difference of these distances ($d2 - d1$) determines the nominal thickness of the splint. Virtual impressions (Sect. 3.3) are made of both S_{d1} and S_{d2}. The resulting surfaces S_{in} and S_{out} become, respectively, the inner and outer surface of the splint. The gap between the two surfaces on the apical side is then sealed with an additional surface such as a fragment of the cutoff plane.

The final splint has a uniform thickness over its entire surface. Whereas the inner surface of the splint is well adapted to the model of the patient's dental arch, the outer surface does not preserve the natural shape of the occlusion,

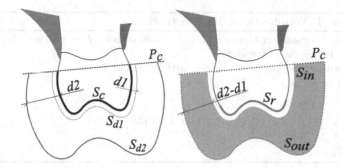

Fig. 7. Dilation method (general drawing). Left: crossections of the working meshes S_{d1} i S_{d2} obtained by dilating the coronal surface. Right: crossections of the impressions S_{in} and S_{out}.

leading to the splint slipping during chewing. This splint cannot be used therapeutically. However, the implementation of this method led to the creation of a set of programmatic tools used in other presented methods.

Algorithm 2. Dilation splint construction.

Input: S_c – coronal surface
Input: $d1$, $d2$ – required minimal distances of inner ($d1$) and outer ($d2$) surface of splint from teeth surface
Output: W – complete surface of the splint
1 **for** $n \in \{1, 2\}$ **do**
2 $\quad\lfloor$ dilate S_c by dn to get S_{dn}
3 create impression of S_{d1} to get S_{in}
4 create impression of S_{d2} to get S_{out}
5 connect S_{in} and S_{out} to get W
6 **return** W

4.3 Volumetric Method

The *volumetric method* creates the splint using a set of Boolean operators [6]: sum ($\cup^*$), intersection ($\cap^*$) and difference ($/^*$) applied to the transformed copies of the solids obtained by closing meshes with the cutting plane (Fig. 9).

The occlusal surface is determined by shifting the coronal solid V_c by $dr(3)$ to the therapeutic position $V(3)$ (Fig. 8a). Lateral parts of the splint are obtained by a Boolean sum of the copies of the solid based on the inner surface, shifted by given vectors $dr(1)$, $dr(2)$, $dr(4)$, $dr(5)$ (Figs. 9b and 8b). Finally, a Boolean difference of the summation solid and the inner surface solid V_{in} is determined (Figs. 9b and 8c). The process was described in Algorithm 3.

Algorithm 3. Volumetric splint construction.

Input: S_c – coronal surface, $dr[1\dots5]$ – shift vectors, P_c – cutting plane
Output: V_{out} – output volume.
1 close S_c with P_c to get V_c; close S_{in} with P_c to get V_{in}
2 **for** $i \leftarrow 1$ **to** 5 **do**
3 $\quad\lfloor\ V(i) \xleftarrow{dr(i)} V_c;$
4 $V_{out} \longleftarrow V(1) \cup^* V(2) \cup^* V(3) \cup^* V(4) \cup^* V(5);$
5 $V_{out} \longleftarrow V_{out}/{}^*V_{in};$
6 **return** V_{out}

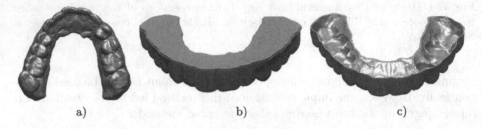

a)   b)   c)

Fig. 8. Enlarging the arch by translation of the impression solid.

4.4 Interpolation Method

The interpolation method consists in selecting the inner surface (Sect. 3.3) in its current position and occlusal surface moved to the therapeutic position, then including those fragments when shaping a watertight model (Fig. 10a).

The method requires the occlusal fragments of the coronal surface to be identified. For the purposes of this paper the segmentation was performed manually under a 3D editor. Segmentation can also be achieved automatically by detecting the faces of coronal mesh within given distance from lower teeth. A splint cannot be formed if the inner surface S_{in} intersects the occlusal surface in the therapeutic position S_t; in such case a different therapeutic position should be chosen.

As was mentioned above, the only assumption of the interpolation method is that the outer lateral surfaces of the splint should ensure the required thickness of the sides.

The implementation described in Algorithm 4 used the dilation technique to obtain an additional surface S_L (Fig. 10). The surface is then connected to the occlusal surface S_t and this entire construct is the basis for the impression S_{out} corresponding to the outer surface of the splint (Fig. 11).

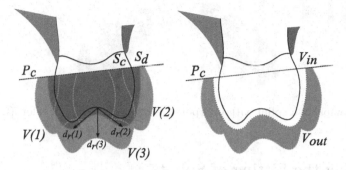

Fig. 9. Volumetric method: (a) crossections of the solids $V(1)$, $V(2)$ and $V(3)$ obtained by shifting the coronal solid, (b) crossections of the summation solid V_{out} and the inner solid V_{in}.

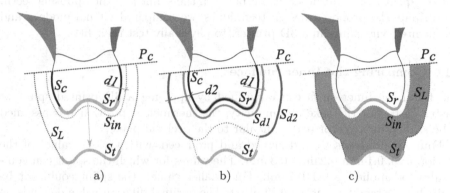

Fig. 10. Interpolation method. General drawing (a) and example of adapting the interpolation method (b, c). The lateral surfaces S_L of the splint were modeled by the dilation method. The occlusion surface S_r has been shifted to the therapeutic position S_t. Remaining fragments connecting S_L and S_t are formed by interpolation.

Algorithm 4. Adapting the interpolation method.

Input: S_c – coronal surface
Input: S_r – occlusal surface
Input: $d1$, $d2$ – expected minimal distances of inner ($d1$) and outer ($d2$) surface
         of splint from teeth surface
Output: W – complete surface of the splint

1 **for** $n \in \{1, 2\}$ **do**
2   dilate S_c by dn to get S_{dn}

3 create impression on S_{d1} to get inner surface S_{in}
4 move S_r to therapeutic position S_t
5 create impression on both S_{d2} and S_t to get outer surface S_{out}
6 connect S_{in} and S_{out} to get W
7 **return** W

Fig. 11. Example of a splint with interpolated fragments shown in color. (Color figure online)

5   Testing the Fitting of Splints

It is difficult to objectively evaluate the produced splint due to a lack of reference. It is essential to test two aspects: the possibility to apply the splint onto teeth, and the quality of occlusal matching between the splint and the opposing teeth. To evaluate the proposed design techniques, we compared virtual models, and also printed our splints in a 3D printer, to physically test their fit.

5.1   Comparing the Inner Surface

The fit of the inner surface was verified by applying a 3D printed splint to plaster casts. For the sake of simplicity, the therapeutic position was assumed to be shifted by a vector perpendicular to the occlusal plane.

Four 3D printouts were designed and produced, with various values of the dilation d: 0, 0.1 mm 0.2 mm, 0.3 mm. The values for which the splint can comfortably be applied is 0.1–0.2 mm. For smaller values, the splint could not be applied; for larger ones, it would fall off. The optimal dilation value depends on the 3D printer, and should be adjusted separately for each printer type.

The tests confirmed the importance of correctly chosen splint depth.

5.2   Testing the Outer Surface

Section 4 presents a number of techniques used to design the outer splint surface. This surface can also be tested on plaster models, by verifying if the outer occlusal surface intercuspates correctly with the opposing teeth, or if it will slide over their surface. Such verification, however, is not fully objective. Instead, we propose to compute the distance between the projected outer occlusal surface of the splint and the patient's coronal surface moved to the therapeutic position.

Traditional ways of mesh comparison calculate the distances in local areas from point p of the reference mesh to p' of the compared mesh [18]. One of the methods is Metro [5], which finds the maximum distance error (Hausdorff distance) between surfaces S and S'. In a similar way the average distance between S and S' can be formulated [5]:

$$E_m(S, S') = \frac{1}{|S|} \int\limits_S \min_{p' \in S'} \big(d(p, p')\big) ds \qquad (2)$$

Both of those distance measures assume disproportionately large values when one of the surfaces is not fully covered by the other. For our purposes, we chose to measure the difference between meshes as the weighted average of distances from the vertices of the occlusal surface to the outer surface of the splint. A normal vector n_p is calculated for each vertex p (Fig. 12) and next a projection p' of this vertex in the direction of n_p is created on S'. The distance d is measured between p and p'. To make the measurement representative of the whole surface, we weigh the error for each vertex p_i proportionally to the area A_i of its surrounding:

$$E_m(S, S') = \frac{1}{A_{sum}} \sum_{i=1}^{N} A_i d(p_i, p'_i) \tag{3}$$

where $A_i = \sum_{j=1}^{M_i} A_j$, $A_{sum} = \sum_{i=1}^{N} A_i$, M_i – the number of neighbour faces for p_i and A_j – the area of jth face. The distance error is calculated only for N vertices having projections on S'.

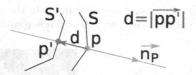

Fig. 12. The local distance d from surface S to S' at point p is equal to the length of the vector connecting point p and its projection p'.

The comparison was conducted for models obtained using the proposed methods of splint design.

The similarity between the outer surface of the splint and the occlusal surface of the maxillary teeth was verified (see Table 1). Predictably, the interpolation method, where the surface is directly copied, yielded a nearly perfect similarity ($d_{av} = 0.002$ mm). For the other methods, the distance distribution can be seen in Fig. 13. It should be noted that the interpolation method was the result of analyses and improvements after the implementation of the previous methods: patchwork, dilation and volumetric.

Table 1. Comparison of the splints - table of parameters.

	Patchwork	Dilation	Volumetric	Interpolation
d_av [mm]	0.040	0.199	0.049	0.002
std_dev	0.096	0.173	0.075	0.029

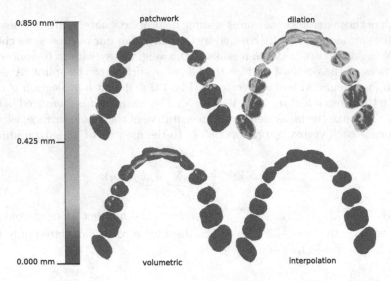

Fig. 13. Comparison of the splints. The colors indicate the calculated local distance error between the occlusal splint surface and the reference surface. (Color figure online)

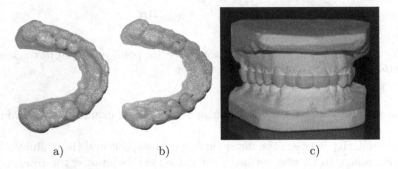

Fig. 14. Resulting splints: (a) dilation method, (b) volumetric method, (c) interpolation method - splint applied to model of teeth.

6   Conclusions

Algorithms have been proposed for computerized design of an occlusal splint. Computer graphics and vision techniques have been selected, such as morphological mesh processing, computational geometry, and Boolean operations on solids. These operations were adapted and critically compared. Necessary conditions and constraints have been identified for the manufacturing of occlusal splints. Important parameters have been identified, such as minimal thickness and minimal distance to the internal surface. Their values also depend on 3D printer parameters. Sample splints have been designed. Qualitative and quantitative methods have been proposed to evaluate them. The quality of their fit was verified by printing them in 3D and applying them to plaster models of teeth (Fig. 14a). Next, the splints can be submitted to clinical trials.

While designing the splints, a number of simplifying assumptions were made:

- undisturbed occlusion in the natural position, which can be transferred to the therapeutic position; only static occlusion was considered;
- known therapeutic position (leaving aside the issue of how it should be communicated by the doctor). We further assume that the position will only be shifted by a vector perpendicular to the occlusal plane.
- cutoff line in the form of a planar curve (intersection of cutoff plane with the virtual tooth model), potentially leaving overhangs and allowing the splint to reach the gums;

Despite these simplifications, the present work may be interesting for those who are looking forward to the automation of occlusal splint design.

References

1. Alqutaibi, A.Y., Aboalrejal, A.N.: Types of occlusal splint in management of temporomandibular disorders (TMD). J. Arthritis **4**, 2 (2015)
2. Ash, M., Ramfjord, S., Schmidseder, J.: Terapia przy użyciu szyn okluzyjnych. Urban i Partner - Wydawnictwo Medyczne, Wrocław (1999). in polish, ed. Teresa Maślanka
3. Baron, S.: Bruxism and occlusion. In: 137th ICM Seminar: Novel Methodology of Both Diagnosis and Therapy of Bruxism. Lecture notes of the ICB Seminar, pp. -. International Centre of Biocybernetics Polish Academy of Sciences, Warsaw, Poland, IBIB PAN (2015)
4. Chen, X., Li, X., Xu, L., Sun, Y., Politis, C., Egger, J.: Development of a computer-aided design software for dental splint in orthognathic surgery. Sci. Rep. **6**, 38867 (2016)
5. Cignoni, P., Rocchini, C., Scopigno, R.: Metro: measuring error on simplified surfaces. Comput. Graph. Forum **17**(2), 167–174 (1998)
6. Foley, J.D.: Introduction to Computer Graphics. Addison-Wesley, Boston (1994)
7. Gateno, J., Xia, J., Teichgraeber, J., Rosen, A., Hultgren, B., Vadnais, T.: The precision of computer-generated surgical splints. J. Oral Maxillofacial Surg. **61**(7), 814–817 (2003)
8. Graber, L.W., Vanarsdall, R.L., Vig, K.W.L.: Orthodontics - E-Book: Current Principles and Techniques. Elsevier Health Sciences, Amsterdam (2011)
9. Kowalski, P., Pojda, D.: Visualization of heterogenic images of 3D scene. In: Gruca, D.A., Czachórski, T., Kozielski, S. (eds.) Man-Machine Interactions 3. AISC, vol. 242, pp. 291–297. Springer, Cham (2014). https://doi.org/10.1007/978-3-319-02309-0_31
10. Lauren, M., McIntyre, F.: A new computer-assisted method for design and fabrication of occlusal splints. Am. J. Orthod. Dentofac. Orthop. **133**(4, Suppl.), S130–S135 (2008)
11. Luchowski, L., Tomaka, A.A., Skabek, K., Tarnawski, M., Kowalski, P.: Forming an occlusal splint to support the therapy of bruxism. In: Piętka, E., Badura, P., Kawa, J., Wieclawek, W. (eds.) Information Technologies in Medicine. AISC, vol. 472, pp. 267–273. Springer, Cham (2016). https://doi.org/10.1007/978-3-319-39904-1_24

12. Mujagic, M., Fauquet, C., Galletti, C., Palot, C., Wiechmann, D., Mah, J.: Digital design and manufacturing of the lingualcare bracket system. J. Clin. Orthod. **39**(6), 375–382 (2005)
13. Nasef, A., El-Beialy, A., Mostafa, Y.: Virtual techniques for designing and fabricating a retainer. Am. J. Orthod. Dentofac. Orthop. **146**(3), 394–398 (2014)
14. Palaskar, J.N., Murali, R., Bansal, S.: Centric relation definition: a historical and contemporary prosthodontic perspective. J. Indian Prosthodont. Soc. **13**(3), 149–154 (2013)
15. Pojda, D., Kowalski, P.: Assumptions for a software tool to support the diagnosis of the stomatognathic system: data gathering, visualizing compound models and their motion. In: 137th ICM Seminar: Novel Methodology of Both Diagnosis and Therapy of Bruxism. Lecture notes of the ICB Seminar. IBIB PAN, Warszawa (2015)
16. Shqaidef, A., Ayoub, A., Khambay, B.: How accurate are rapid prototyped (RP) final orthognathic surgical wafers? A pilot study. Br. J. Oral Maxillofac. Surg. **52**(7), 609–614 (2014)
17. Tomaka, A.A., Tarnawski, M.: Integration of multimodal image data for the purposes of supporting the diagnosis of the stomatognatic system. In: 137th ICM Seminar: Novel Methodology of Both Diagnosis and Therapy of Bruxism. Lecture notes of the ICB Seminar, pp. 68–75. International Centre of Biocybernetics Polish Academy of Sciences, Warsaw, Poland, IBIB PAN (2015)
18. Zhou, L., Pang, A.: Metrics and visualization tools for surface mesh comparison. In: Proceedings of SPIE 4302, Visual Data Exploration and Analysis VIII, 3 May 2001, pp. 99–111 (2001)

Author Index

Printed in the United States
By Bookmasters

Printed in the United States
By Bookmasters